Manual of Panic Focused Psychodynamic Psychotherapy – eXtended Range

Psychoanalytic Inquiry Book Series

Volume 36

PSYCHOANALYTIC INQUIRY BOOK SERIES

JOSEPH D. LICHTENBERG
Series Editors

Like its counterpart, *Psychoanalytic Inquiry: A Topical Journal for Mental Health Professionals*, the Psychoanalytic Inquiry Book Series presents a diversity of subjects within a diversity of approaches to those subjects. Under the editorship of Joseph Lichtenberg, in collaboration with Melvin Bornstein and the editorial board of *Psychoanalytic Inquiry*, the volumes in this series strike a balance among research, theory, and clinical application. We are honored to have published the works of various innovators in psychoanalysis, such as Frank Lachmann, James Fosshage, Robert Stolorow, Donna Orange, Louis Sander, Léon Wurmser, James Grotstein, Joseph Jones, Doris Brothers, Fredric Busch, and Joseph Lichtenberg.

The series includes books and monographs on mainline psychoanalytic topics, such as sexuality, narcissism, trauma, homosexuality, jealousy, envy, and varied aspects of analytic process and technique. In our efforts to broaden the field of analytic interest, the series has incorporated and embraced innovative discoveries in infant research, self psychology, intersubjectivity, motivational systems, affects as process, responses to cancer, borderline states, contextualism, postmodernism, attachment research and theory, medication, and mentalization. As further investigations in psychoanalysis come to fruition, we seek to present them in readable, easily comprehensible writing.

After 25 years, the core vision of this series remains the investigation, analysis, and discussion of developments on the cutting edge of the psychoanalytic field, inspired by a boundless spirit of inquiry.

PSYCHOANALYTIC INQUIRY BOOK SERIES

JOSEPH D. LICHTENBERG

Series Editors

Vol. 36
Manual of Panic Focused Psychodynamic Psychotherapy—eXtended Range
Fredric N. Busch, Barbara L. Milrod, Meriamne B. Singer, & Andrew C. Aronson

Vol. 35
World, Affectivity, Trauma: Heidegger and Post-Cartesian Psychoanalysis
Robert D. Stolorow

Vol. 34
Change in Psychoanalysis: An Analyst's Reflections on the Therapeutic Relationship
Chris Jaenicke

Vol. 33
Psychoanalysis and Motivational Systems: A New Look
Joseph D. Lichtenberg, Frank M. Lachmann, & James L. Fosshage

Vol. 32
Persons in Context: The Challenge of Individuality in Theory and Practice
Roger Frie & William J. Coburn (eds.)

Vol. 31
Toward an Emancipatory Psychoanalysis: Brandchaft's Intersubjective Vision
Bernard Brandchaft, Shelley Doctors, & Dorienne Sorter

Vol. 30
From Psychoanalytic Narrative to Empirical Single Case Research: Implications for Psychoanalytic Practice
Horst Kächele, Joseph Schachter, Helmut Thomä, & the Ulm Psychoanalytic Process Research Study Group

Vol. 29
Mentalization: Theoretical Considerations, Research Findings, and Clinical Implications
Fredric N. Busch (ed.)

Vol. 28
Transforming Narcissism: Reflections on Empathy, Humor, and Expectations
Frank M. Lachmann

Vol. 27
Toward a Psychology of Uncertainty: Trauma-Centered Psychoanalysis
Doris Brothers

Vol. 26
Living Systems, Evolving Consciousness, and the Emerging Person: A Selection of Papers From the Life Work of Louis Sander
Gherardo Amadei & Ilaria Bianchi (eds.)

Vol. 25
Sensuality and Sexuality Across the Divide of Shame
Joseph D. Lichtenberg

Vol. 24
Jealousy and Envy: New Views About Two Powerful Feelings
Léon Wurmser & Heidrun Jarass (eds.)

Vol. 23
Trauma and Human Existence: Autobiographical, Psychoanalytic, and Philosophical Reflections
Robert D. Stolorow

Vol. 22
Psychotherapy and Medication: The Challenge of Integration
Fredric N. Busch & Larry S. Sandberg

PSYCHOANALYTIC INQUIRY BOOK SERIES

JOSEPH D. LICHTENBERG
Series Editors

Vol. 21
Attachment and Sexuality
Diana Diamond, Sidney J. Blatt, & Joseph D. Lichtenberg (eds.)

Vol. 20
Craft and Spirit: A Guide to Exploratory Psychotherapies
Joseph D. Lichtenberg

Vol. 19
A Spirit of Inquiry: Communication in Psychoanalysis
Joseph D. Lichtenberg, Frank M. Lachmann, & James L. Fosshage

Vol. 18
Kohut, Loewald, and the Postmoderns: A Comparative Study of Self and Relationship
Judith Guss Teicholz

Vol. 17
Working Intersubjectively: Contextualism in Psychoanalytic Practice
Donna M. Orange, George E. Atwood, & Robert D. Stolorow

Vol. 16
The Clinical Exchange: Techniques Derived From Self and Motivational Systems
Joseph D. Lichtenberg, Frank M. Lachmann, & James L. Fosshage

Vol. 14
Affects as Process: An Inquiry Into the Centrality of Affect in Psychological Life
Joseph M. Jones

Vol. 13
Self and Motivational Systems: Toward a Theory of Psychoanalytic Technique
Joseph D. Lichtenberg, Frank M. Lachmann, & James L. Fosshage

Vol. 12
Contexts of Being: The Intersubjective Foundations of Psychological Life
Robert D. Stolorow & George E. Atwood

Vol. 10
Psychoanalysis and Motivation
Joseph D. Lichtenberg

Vol. 8
Psychoanalytic Treatment: An Intersubjective Approach
Robert D. Stolorow, Bernard Brandchaft, & George E. Atwood

Vol. 2
Psychoanalysis and Infant Research
Joseph D. Lichtenberg

Out-of-print titles in the PI series:

Vol. 15
Understanding Therapeutic Action: Psychodynamic Concepts of Cure
Lawrence E. Lifson (ed.)

Vol. 11
Cancer Stories: Creativity and Self-Repair
Esther Dreifuss-Kattan

Vol. 9
Female Homosexuality: Choice Without Volition
Elaine V. Siegel

Vol. 7
The Borderline Patient: Emerging Concepts in Diagnosis,
Psychodynamics, and Treatment, Vol. 2
James S. Grotstein, Marion F. Solomon, & Joan A. Lang (eds.)

Vol. 6
The Borderline Patient: Emerging Concepts in Diagnosis, Psychodynamics, and Treatment, Vol. 1
James S. Grotstein, Marion F. Solomon, & Joan A. Lang (eds.)

PSYCHOANALYTIC INQUIRY BOOK SERIES

JOSEPH D. LICHTENBERG

Series Editors

Vol. 5

Toward a Comprehensive Model for Schizophrenic Disorders: Psychoanalytic Essays in Memory of Ping-Nie Pao

David B. Feinsilver

Vol. 4

Structures of Subjectivity: Explorations in Psychoanalytic Phenomenology

George E. Atwood & Robert D. Stolorow

Vol. 3

Empathy, Volumes I & II

Joseph D. Lichtenberg, Melvin Bornstein, & Donald Silver (eds.)

Vol. 1

Reflections on Self Psychology Joseph

D. Lichtenberg & Samuel Kaplan (eds.)

Manual of Panic Focused Psychodynamic Psychotherapy – eXtended Range

Fredric N. Busch
Barbara L. Milrod
Meriamne B. Singer
Andrew C. Aronson

Routledge
Taylor & Francis Group
New York London

Routledge
Taylor & Francis Group
711 Third Avenue
New York, NY 10017

Routledge
Taylor & Francis Group
27 Church Road
Hove, East Sussex BN3 2FA

International Standard Book Number: 978-0-415-87159-4 (Hardback) 978-0-415-87160-0 (Paperback)

Library of Congress Cataloging-in-Publication Data

Manual of panic-focused psychodynamic psychotherapy, extended range /
Fredric N. Busch ... [et al.].
p. ; cm. -- (Psychoanalytic inquiry book series ; vol. 36)
Includes bibliographical references and index.
ISBN 978-0-415-87159-4 (hardback) -- ISBN 978-0-415-87160-0
(pbk)
1. Panic disorders--Treatment. 2. Psychodynamic psychotherapy. I. Busch, Fredric, 1958- II. Series: Psychoanalytic inquiry book series ; v. 36.
[DNLM: 1. Panic Disorder--therapy. 2. Psychotherapy--methods. W1 PS427F v.36 2012 / WM 172]

RC535.M36 2012
616.85'223--dc22 2011008395

Visit the Taylor & Francis Web site at
http://www.taylorandfrancis.com

and the Routledge Web site at
http://www.routledgementalhealth.com

Epigraph

...I found
myself in a dark wood, for the straight way was lost. Ah, how hard it was to tell what that wood was, wild, rugged, harsh; the very thought of it renews the fear! It is so bitter that death is hardly more so. But, to treat of the good that I found in it, I will tell of the other things I saw there.

I cannot rightly say how I entered it, I was so full of sleep at the moment I left the true way; but when I had reached the foot of a hill, there at the end of a valley that had pierced my heart with fear, I looked up and saw its shoulders already clad in the rays of the planet that leads men aright by every path. Then the fear was somewhat quieted that had continued in the lake of my heart through the night I had passed so piteously. And as he who with laboring breath has escaped from the deep to the shore turns to look back on the dangerous waters, so my mind which was still fleeing turned back to gaze upon the pass that never left anyone alive.

Dante Alighieri
The Inferno (Canto I)

Contents

Acknowledgments

The research that went into the creation of this book would not have been possible without generous grants from the National Institute of Mental Health (R01 MH70918-01A2) and a fund in the New York Community Trust, established by DeWitt Wallace.

We would like to thank Rolf Sandell, PhD, Pavel Snejnevski, MD, and Manfred Beutel, MD, for their contributions to the study of panic focused psychodynamic psychotherapy—extended range (PFPP-XR) at other sites. Additional thanks go to Marie Rudden for her work on reflective functioning and posttraumatic stress disorder.

About the authors

Fredric N. Busch, MD, is a clinical associate professor of psychiatry at Weill Cornell Medical College, and a faculty member at Columbia University Center for Psychoanalytic Training and Research. His writing and research have focused on the links between psychoanalysis and psychiatry, including psychodynamic approaches to specific disorders, psychoanalytic research, and psychoanalysis and medication. He has coauthored three books on the psychoanalytic approach to specific disorders: *Manual of Panic Focused Psychodynamic Psychotherapy* (APA, 1997), *Psychodynamic Treatment of Depression* (APA, 2004), and *Psychodynamic Approaches to the Adolescent With Panic Disorder* (Krieger, 2004). He is on the editorial board of *Psychoanalytic Inquiry* as well as also coauthor (with Larry Sandberg) of *Psychotherapy and Medication: The Challenge in Integration* (Analytic Press, 2007) and the editor of *Mentalization: Theoretical Considerations, Research Findings, and Clinical Implications* (Routledge, 2008).

Barbara L. Milrod, MD, is a professor of psychiatry at Weill Cornell Medical College, and a faculty member at New York Psychoanalytic Institute and the Columbia University Center for Psychoanalytic Training and Research. She has been the principal investigator of a number of National Institute of Mental Health (NIMH) and foundation-funded clinical research studies and has developed, tested, and demonstrated efficacy for the first manualized form of psychoanalytic psychotherapy for the *Diagnostic and Statistical Manual of Mental Disorders,* 4th edition (*DSM-IV*), concerning panic disorder with or without agoraphobia. Dr. Milrod is the recipient of the Heinz Hartmann Junior Award from the New York Psychoanalytic Institute for significant contribution to the field of psychoanalysis; the Norbert and Charlotte Rieger Award for Psychodynamic Psychotherapy from the American Academy of Child and Adolescent Psychiatry for a paper, "A Pilot Study of Psychodynamic Psychotherapy in 18- to 21-Year-Old Patients with Panic Disorder"; the Matthew Silvan Research/Clinical Scholar Award for distinguished research by the New York Psychoanalytic Institute; the Psychoanalytic Research Exceptional

Contribution Award given by the International Psychoanalytic Association at Berlin, Germany; the 1/09 APsaA Scientific Paper Prize awarded by the American Psychoanalytic Association for the best scientific paper in psychoanalysis for the year 2007; and the APsA Stuart Hauser Award for best poster of 2009 for poster "Symptom-Specific Reflective Function," presented at the APsA midwinter meetings in New York.

Meriamne B. Singer, MD, is an assistant clinical professor of psychiatry at Columbia College of Physicians and Surgeons; a faculty research associate at Weill Cornell Medical College; and a faculty member at Columbia University Center for Psychoanalytic Training and Research. She is involved in the development of and training in panic focused psychodynamic psychotherapy—eXtended range.

Andrew C. Aronson, MD, is an associate professor of psychiatry at Mount Sinai School of Medicine; the medical director of Ambulatory Psychiatry Services at Mount Sinai Medical Center; an adjunct research associate in psychiatry at Weill Cornell Medical College; and a member of New York Psychoanalytic Society and Institute, to which he is senior liaison within the Mount Sinai Department of Psychiatry. He has served as the curriculum and clinical director for psychodynamic psychotherapy training in the Mount Sinai Department of Psychiatry for over 10 years and as the director of Medical Student Mental Health for the Mount Sinai School of Medicine for over 20 years. He is the recipient of Teacher of the Residency and Educator of the Residency awards in psychiatry at Mount Sinai and the Excellence in Teaching award from the Institute of Medical Education, Mount Sinai School of Medicine. He is a coauthor of journal articles and publications concerning mood-, psychosis-, and anxiety-related disorders.

Chapter 1

The importance of a psychodynamic manual for panic and anxiety disorders

BACKGROUND

For decades, the field of psychoanalysis has struggled with whether the establishment of a scientific research base ought to become integral to the discipline (Busch & Milrod, 2010; Luyten, Blatt, & Corveleyn, 2006; Milrod & Busch, 2003a). For this reason among others, little scientifically credible, reliably reproducible outcome research has been conducted—with notable exceptions (Gerber et al., 2011)—that can inform mental health practitioners and the public about the utility of psychoanalytic treatments for specific psychiatric illnesses. Psychoanalytic treatments have been increasingly excluded from treatment guidelines of available psychiatric treatments (APA, 1998, 2000c) due to the field's relative lethargy in developing a viable research base, as other scientifically accepted psychiatric treatments have (Busch & Milrod, 2010; Milrod & Busch, 2003b). Fortunately, there has been an increasing recognition of the need to more systematically assess psychoanalytic treatments (Kernberg, 2006), and this is starting to be reflected in treatment guidelines. Panic focused psychodynamic psychotherapy (PFPP) is discussed in greater detail in the revised edition of the *Practice Guidelines for the Treatment of Patients With Panic Disorder* (APA, 2009), based on the study by Milrod, Leon, Busch, Rudden, Schwalberg, Clarkin, et al. (2007), which concludes that "these findings provide initial support for the use of PFPP as a treatment for panic disorder and suggest a need for further research in this area" (p.53). Since the publication of the *Guidelines*, further support of PFPP in patients with panic disorder and agoraphobia has been garnered (Subic-Wrana, Knebel, & Beutel, 2010). It is in this context that we have revised and expanded our *Manual of Panic Focused Psychodynamic Psychotherapy* for an extended range of anxiety disorders (panic focused psychodynamic psychotherapy—eXtended range [PFPP-XR]). Despite the broader articulation of the approaches we will describe in this manual compared with the last version (Milrod, Busch, Cooper, & Shapiro, 1997), we have already employed all of the interventions we shall outline here in our research studies to date in managing the multiple comorbidities with which these patients present.

For over a decade, our research group has been conducting clinical trials using our original treatment manual (Milrod et al., 1997). In the course of this work, we have trained a wide variety of psychotherapists to perform this intervention. Throughout our first study, all of our study therapists were psychiatrists and psychologists who were graduates of American Psychoanalytic Association–approved psychoanalytic training programs. As the scope of our research expanded, we have had experience training psychoanalytic candidates, psychoanalysts from Europe, experienced psychodynamic clinicians who have no affiliation with psychoanalysis, experienced interpersonal therapists, cognitive-behavioral therapists, and senior psychology graduate students who have not yet determined their primary clinical orientation. Most of our trainees have performed PFPP well.

In the course of disseminating this work to a wider variety of therapists, and with greater experience using PFPP clinically in an increasingly generalized patient population, we have begun to recognize areas that we did not adequately articulate or address in written form in our original psychotherapy treatment manual. We are grateful to Jacques Barber, PhD, our coprincipal investigator, professor of psychology in psychiatry at the University of Pennsylvania, in the two-site PFPP study (Milrod, B., Barber, J. P. (co-PIs), Dynamic therapy vs. CBT for Panic Disorder, NIMH 2-site R01 MH070918) for encouraging us to maintain a consistent focus on these clarifications. We believe this revised manual provides a more clearly articulated description of PFPP as it has been practiced in our successful efficacy studies.

Additionally, PFPP has appeared promising across diagnoses in clinical settings and case studies, although this has not been formally studied in a randomized controlled trial. In the context of increasing efforts in the mental health field to develop treatments that work transdiagnostically, we have worked to articulate how PFPP may be employed across anxiety disorders, with a particular focus on social anxiety disorder, generalized anxiety disorder, posttraumatic stress disorder, and cluster C personality disorders. In our work with PFPP, we have observed that there are certain common dynamics across the anxiety disorders and cluster C personality disorders. At the same time, we have also noticed that some traits and dynamics dominate certain specific diagnoses in contrast with others. For example, dynamics common to all of the anxiety and cluster C diagnoses discussed in this manual include the prevalence of conflicts around separation, anger, the development of autonomous functioning, and sexuality. They also include prominence of undoing and reaction formation as defenses. Across all of these diagnoses, anxiety and the ensuing disability serve to punish patients for competitive strivings they deem unacceptable. Individual differences between diagnoses include, among others, the magical assignment in agoraphobia of places that are "safe" and "not safe," in which physical reification in space comes to symbolize defended content as well as control of key attachment figures who are recruited as phobic companions. In social anxiety disorder, preoccupation with criticism of others and exhibitionistic conflicts seem to be particularly characteristic, and constant hypervigilance stemming from fears of conflicted feelings and wishes has a special significance in patients with generalized anxiety disorder.

All of these features that we describe as being more specific to certain diagnoses can also be present in patients with any of the other anxiety disorders. We highlight how PFPP-XR can elucidate dynamics common to these diagnoses, as well as accommodate differences among them, and how it thereby can be used to treat this wide spectrum of disorders.

Table 1.1 provides an overview of PFPP-XR theory and approaches to specific symptoms and disorders, described in depth in the chapters that follow. We believe this expanded range of PFPP (PFPP-XR) will broaden its value as a therapeutic tool and will aid in the study of the transdiagnostic utility of this focused psychodynamic approach.

WHY IS THIS BOOK IMPORTANT?

The past decades have seen substantial research progress in determining efficacious treatments for anxiety disorders. Cognitive Behavioral Therapy (CBT) has demonstrated efficacy for most anxiety disorders, with powerful effects on panic symptoms and agoraphobia (Barlow, Gorman, Shear, & Woods, 2000; Craske, Brown, & Barlow, 1991; Craske, DeCola, Sachs, & Pontillo, 2003), social phobia (Pontoski, Heimberg, Turk, & Coles, 2010), and generalized anxiety disorder (GAD; Huppert & Sanderson, 2010). In addition, a number of classes of medication have demonstrated efficacy (APA, 2009; Blanco, Schneier, Vesga-Lopez, & Liebowitz, 2010; Van Ameringen, Mancini, Patterson, Simpson, & Truong, 2010), although patients may struggle with side effects or risk of relapse when medication is discontinued (Bandelow & Baldwing, 2010). Not all anxiety patients (29–48%), however, respond to demonstrably efficacious treatment (Allen, McHugh, & Barlow, 2008; Barlow et al., 2000; Craske et al., 1991; Marks et al., 1993). A meaningful proportion of anxiety patients do not tolerate CBT and prematurely terminate their treatment, never receiving the "dose" of psychotherapy demonstrated to be helpful (Barlow et al., 2000; Chambless & Peterman, 2004; Marks et al., 1993). Several negative CBT studies also exist (Arntz, 2002; Beck, Stanley, Baldwin, Deagle, & Averill, 1994; Bouchard, Gauthier, Laberge, French, Pelletier, & Godbout, 1996; Chambless & Peterman, 2004). Not all negative studies arise from high placebo response (Black, Wesner, Bowers, & Gabel, 1993; Hofmann & Smits, 2008). A proportion of panic disorder (PD) patients

Table 1.1 Relationship between psychodynamic theory and interventions for anxiety/panic spectrum patients

Panic and anxiety disorder symptoms	*Psychodynamic theory in PFPP-XR*	*PFPP-XR treatment strategies*
(Seemingly) out-of-the-blue panic attacks	Panic attacks arise from specific unconscious conflicts/fantasies. Panic attacks carry symbolic meaning. As patients grasp this meaning, panic symptoms diminish.	Focus on the emotional significance of panic: Identify and interpret psychological meaning of symptoms. Explore and interpret emotional significance of triggers. Help patients to understand their internal emotional states. This raises ability to mentalize about symptoms with increased reflective functioning.
Agoraphobia	Agoraphobia is an unconscious way of controlling central attachment figures while retaining a nonthreatening, childlike stance that serves to deny aggression.	Explore management of rage at attachment figures. Interpret need to avoid aggression, with anger expressed as dependent and controlling anxious neediness. Openly discuss, normalize, and detoxify rage. Focus on how agoraphobia and dependence on phobic companions maintains childlike stance.
Separation anxiety	Fears of separation necessarily emerge in the transference, making termination a key time to address this problem.	Explore the transference relationship, an emotionally vibrant paradigm for understanding and altering separation fears. The emotional significance of termination is a key topic to address in the final third of treatment.
Anxiety about establishing appropriate adult autonomy	Conflicts and fears about autonomy common in panic disorder, social anxiety disorder, and generalized anxiety disorder patients emerge in transference. Assertiveness and competitiveness are confused with destructive anger, creating conflict.	PFPP-XR focus on the patient's passivity highlights conflicts about autonomy. Focus on detoxifying and understanding anger makes desire for independence less threatening.
Social phobia	Conflicted wishes to exhibit oneself and outshine others are laden with guilt and self-punishment; competitive wishes are associated with unacceptable aggression. Underlying feelings of inadequacy can trigger compensatory grandiose fantasies that often lead to disappointment.	Explore feelings of inadequacy, conflicted aggression, and guilt-ridden and highly defended exhibitionistic and grandiose fantasies. Help patients identify these dynamics as they emerge in their overly critical evaluation of themselves and others. This raises reflective function.

Generalized anxiety disorder	Inability to relax and need to maintain constant vigilance related to fears of usually unconscious conflicted feelings and wishes becoming out of control.	Focus on terror of internal urges, including aggressive and sexual, which are actively connected with symptoms and persistence of anxiety. Underpinnings of hypervigilant state are identified.
Posttraumatic stress disorder	Overwhelming trauma causes dissociation and unconscious repetition of trauma. Rage at perpetrators of trauma may lead to identification with the aggressor, which in turn perpetuates guilt.	Focus on understanding the meaning and impact of dissociation; explore conflicted feelings that fuel dissociation brought on by trauma. Diminish patients' impulse to punish themselves by identifying sources of guilt, including identification with the aggressor. Focus on the unacceptable state of helplessness in trauma that leads to reenactments.
Cluster C personality disorders	Chronic passivity, avoidance, and dependence are hallmarks of severe inhibition of autonomy and the experience of aggression	PFPP-XR focus on conflicted aggression detoxifies it, leading to improved autonomous function, greater ability to assert oneself, less conflict about taking action, and less need for others to care for patient. PFPP-XR focus on passivity and dependence through articulation of the transference, facilitating more adult behavior.
Comorbid major depression (when present)	Conflicted aggression leads to guilt and negative self-evaluation, depressive symptoms, and somatic panic and anxiety symptoms.	PFPP-XR focus on conflicted aggression detoxifies it, leading to improved autonomous function, greater ability in assertion. This mitigates guilt and, with improvement in autonomy, negative views of self improve.

who meet criteria for "response" in carefully conducted clinical trials continue to meet diagnostic criteria for PD after completion of their treatment (Barlow et al., 2000; Craske et al., 2003; Shear & Maser, 1994) and continue to experience high levels of distress even after adequate treatment dosages. Similar findings have emerged from social phobia and GAD studies (Huppert & Sanderson, 2010; Pontoski et al., 2010). What are we to do for these patients? It has been essential to develop and test alternative psychotherapies that can effectively treat patients with anxiety disorders.

No single treatment, however excellent, can be expected to benefit all patients with any psychiatric disorder, and anxiety disorders are no exception. Given the high ongoing cost and disability associated with untreated and partially treated anxiety disorders (Katon, 1996; Kessler, Berglund, Demler, Jin, Merikangas, & Walters, 2005), there is a compelling need for psychotherapists in the community to learn additional efficacious psychotherapies for patients with anxiety disorders. Among this group is the relatively large number of psychodynamic therapists in the community who may want to learn a brief psychodynamic approach for anxiety disorders that has been shown to help these patients. This focused psychodynamic approach differs from more traditional generalized psychoanalytic psychotherapies that are practiced by many psychoanalytic clinicians.

Panic focused psychodynamic psychotherapy—eXtended range (PFPP-XR) is an operationalized form of psychoanalytic psychotherapy for anxiety disorders. Its importance lies in the fact that it is the very first psychoanalytically based psychotherapy to have demonstrated efficacy as a sole treatment modality for a *Diagnostic and Statistical Manual of Mental Disorders*, 4th edition (*DSM-IV*; APA, 1994) Axis I anxiety disorder (panic disorder with or without agoraphobia, ± Ag). This book is designed to capture the range of psychodynamic interventions that we have used in our PFPP studies among our very diverse patient population who nonetheless met *DSM-IV* criteria for primary panic disorder.

Anxiety disorders remain a serious, chronic public health problem (Cougle, Keough, Riccardi, & Sachs-Ericsson, 2009; Kessler et al., 2005). The lifetime prevalence of PD, SAD, and GAD in the National Comorbidity Survey-Replication (NCS-R) was 22.5% (Kessler et al., 2005), compared with 16.6% for major depression and 0.5% for schizophrenia (Wu et al., 2005). In the NCS-R, suicide attempt rates were 14.3% for SAD, 17.3% for PD ± Ag, and 16.4% for GAD (Cougle, Keough, Riccardi, & Sachs-Ericsson, 2009). These figures provide a window on the magnitude of the problem of anxiety.

The need to better develop additional nonpharmacological treatments for anxiety patients is rooted in the need to provide care for an understudied yet large group: those who refuse to take medication or are exquisitely sensitive to side effects (Donald Klein, personal communication, 2004; Hofmann et al., 1998). Panic disorder patients, and patients with other anxiety disorders, often prefer psychotherapy treatments to medication. In the Cross National

Collaborative Panic Study (1992), PD patients favored psychotherapy over medication. In Hofmann et al.'s study, 34% of patients presenting with PD to two sites in the multicenter panic disorder study refused to undergo randomization because they were unwilling to take medication. By contrast, only 3% refused randomization because they might get placebo, and less than 1% refused psychotherapy. Many anxiety disorder patients are women of child-bearing age, with attendant concerns about psychopharmacological interventions, making alternative psychotherapies for anxiety important. Furthermore, the most commonly prescribed class of medications for anxiety disorders, the selective serotonin reuptake inhibitors (SSRIs), have been implicated in elevated suicide risk among adolescents and young adults, resulting in a "black box" warning mandated by the U.S. Food and Drug Administration (FDA; Leon, 2007). While the utility of SSRIs in adolescents evokes mixed reactions (Sarles, 2004), this latter development makes it imperative to disseminate specific, potentially efficacious psychotherapies for patients with anxiety disorders. It is a major advance that panic patients now have more than one option for effective psychotherapy.

Psychodynamic psychotherapy and CBT provide different approaches to psychotherapy. CBT is highly structured, assigns homework, and induces exposure to patients' worst fears and physical anxieties. In contrast, psychodynamic psychotherapy is far less structured, has no homework, and never emphasizes exposure, attending instead to understanding psychological significance of anxiety symptoms and phobic avoidance and to articulation of the relationship the patient develops with the therapist (the transference). The radical differences between these therapies may mean that they will appeal to and effectively treat different groups of patients with anxiety. From a research perspective, differences may reflect epiphenomena of the anxiety syndrome that can illuminate aspects of underlying pathology.

Critics argue that all psychotherapies are much alike, since all make use of underlying "common factors," presumed to account for much of the outcome variance (Frank, 1971). In contrast to researchers who study depression, most CBT researchers in anxiety disorders believe that patients' outcome is not due to nonspecific factors alone but rather to specific components of treatment such as interoceptive exposure (Chambless & Ollendick, 2001). PFPP's and CBT's strikingly divergent strategies to psychotherapy provide very different ways of approaching anxiety and panic. Having these different treatments available leads to improved patient care and satisfaction.

THE UTILITY AND LIMITATIONS OF PSYCHOTHERAPY TREATMENT MANUALS

All contemporary scientifically credible psychotherapy outcome research leans heavily on specifically articulated guidelines that clearly describe methods of performing the treatments, or so-called psychotherapy treatment manuals. Psychotherapy treatment manuals are essential tools that make outcome research in nonpharmacological treatment strategies possible. Treatment manuals have the additional value of helping experienced clinicians to become acquainted with the nuts and bolts of psychotherapeutic methods that have been demonstrated to make patients better. This in turn can widen clinicians' expertise in treatment delivery to a greater range of patients.

Psychotherapy treatment manuals, however, are insufficient tools to enable clinicians to master the performance of any psychotherapy (Sholomskas, Syracuse-Siewart, Rounsaville, Ball, Nuro, & Carroll, 2005). One cannot learn psychotherapy from a book alone. In clinical trials, all psychotherapy manuals are supplemented with specific therapist training courses (Kocsis et al., 2010). This manual is intended to be used by clinicians who are trained in the use of psychodynamic psychotherapy and in the diagnosis of anxiety disorders. For clinicians with other areas of expertise or those in training, we recommend supervision by a therapist who is dynamically trained. This supervision should highlight identification of dynamics and conflicts and management of transference and countertransference reactions.

PFPP has been taught to experienced psychotherapists in a 12-hour course. In clinical studies, study therapists commonly have ongoing supervision in their treatment modalities (Barlow et al., 2000). Furthermore, in clinical trials, adherence to the treatment guidelines is carefully monitored with treatment-specific adherence scales to demonstrate that clinicians are performing the treatment adequately and accurately. Treatment-specific adherence measures are the most parsimonious distillation of any testable psychotherapy; they are its essence. These scales, for both PFPP and other tested psychotherapies, are specific research tools, and most tested psychotherapies have their own treatment-specific adherence scales.

Finally, while psychotherapy treatment manuals can be helpful in shaping clinical approaches for a wide range of patients, as any experienced clinician knows, they also have limitations. Clinical situations arise, even under the fairly well-controlled circumstances of research studies, in which manuals must be discarded in favor of sound medical and clinical judgment. For anxiety patients, these situations can emerge surrounding medical comorbidities, in which apparent panic symptoms may mimic or mask medical illness, and in patients who present with a range of emerging comorbidities, particularly in the bipolar spectrum.

Although we do not discuss the use of medication in our patients, we recognize that medication is often employed in patients with anxiety disorders and has demonstrated efficacy. However, medication often has ongoing and troubling side effects, and a psychopharmacological treatment does not typically address the dynamics we describe here. In our efficacy trial

(Milrod, Leon, Busch, et al., 2007), patients who presented on a stable dose of medication (15% of our *N*) and who still met study entrance criteria for primary *DSM-IV* panic disorder were accepted and medications were held constant. The other 85% of subjects were not on medication. Response rates did not differ between these two groups. Medication is certainly essential in some patients who are having difficulty functioning or who present significant suicide risks, and it can be helpful for others. It is clear, however, that many patients can be effectively treated with psychodynamic psychotherapy alone. This book does not attempt to educate clinicians about these clinical decisions.

We have expanded this manual to other anxiety disorders, and we often discuss approaches to anxiety in these patients. In these instances, we are referring to high levels of anxiety that accompany *DSM-IV* anxiety disorders rather than to anxiety that would be considered within normal range. Although we believe that these approaches are of value in treating symptoms of comorbid depression in patients with anxiety disorders (Busch, Rudden, & Shapiro, 2004; Rudden et al., 2003, see Table 1.1), we do not focus on treatment of these symptoms in this manual.

These constraints notwithstanding, our initial manual has been useful to students of psychotherapy, clinicians conducting treatments, and researchers. We believe that our expanded manual will further enhance its effectiveness in reaching its goals.

Chapter 2

Vignette, part I

The following case vignette describes the initial presentation of a patient who was treated with Panic Focused Psychodynamic Psychotherapy—eXtended Range, along with the therapist's preliminary thoughts about the origins of the patient's symptoms. We will return to this case in Chapter 4 to provide clinical illustrations of the development of a psychodynamic formulation, and in extended form in Chapter 18 to demonstrate the treatment of a patient with PFPP-XR.

Mr. A was late for work. He had to hurry, as he had an important presentation that morning. He barely had time to wolf down a piece of toast and half a glass of orange juice. His 3-year-old daughter let out a bloodcurdling scream when he chose her shoes for her and tried to help her put them on. Exasperated, he went to finish dressing for his meeting, and he let his wife contend with the shoe debacle. As he looked in the mirror when putting on his tie, he saw his complexion was wan. He suddenly began to feel queasy and as though he were being strangled, so he loosened his tie and ran out the door, saying a hurried good-bye to his family. He told himself that the fresh air would clear his mind. He felt slightly better as he got into the car. For a few minutes he allowed himself the pleasure of listening to his favorite samba music, until he reminded himself he had better prepare mentally for his meeting.

Sitting at a red light in a silent car, he was suddenly very worried. Had he cut off the driver behind him? Would he feel weak in the meeting because he had not had enough breakfast? He did not have his usual glass of milk or any other protein. Mr. A worried about things like protein all the time. Did he leave without kissing everyone in his family? Was his daughter mad at him? He was upset that he was still mad at her. Would they give him the account? If not, would he be able to pay for the new school he and his wife wanted to send their daughter to in the fall? His heart began to race and pound, he began to sweat and feel shaky and dizzy, and his lips and extremities went numb. His vision became blurry, and he worried that he would lose his eyesight. He sensed he was not getting enough air, and suddenly he felt as though he was going to die—not sometime far off in the future, but right here and now at this red light. He had been through this many times before, so he had to pull over until he could regain his composure enough to drive the rest of the way to work.

Mr. A was a 42-year-old married Latino business consultant with two daughters, ages 3 and 6. He said at intake that he was seeking treatment primarily for his panic attacks, although it later emerged that he wanted treatment to help him control his temper, to raise his self-esteem, and to earn more money. Of note, he made the decision to seek treatment after he became so enraged at his daughter that he grabbed a doll from her hands.

Mr. A described having grown up in a sunny part of the United States, in a close-knit Latino family, with four younger siblings. He spoke about a "fun and fairly uneventful" early childhood, with particularly fond memories of playing in the water. His parents had been raised Catholic but were themselves "nonpracticing." He described his mother as the strong one who ran the family. She was diagnosed with a rare malignancy when the patient was 9 and died after several "disfiguring" surgeries when the patient was 12½. He said that after she died, his father, although sweet and affectionate, did not run the household well and was demoted repeatedly at work, forcing the family to move into ever smaller homes.

From the outset of his treatment, Mr. A was playful and engaged. At times he appeared tentative and plagued by self-doubt, squirming and looking to the therapist for guidance, while at other times he seemed confident and forthright. He was personable and funny, highly motivated, and able to use his intelligence and insight to make good use of his treatment.

The therapist wanted to understand from the outset as much as she could about the thoughts, feelings, and fantasies that underlay Mr. A's panic. Once she knew more about the triggers for Mr. A's anxiety and panic attacks, she and Mr. A would be able to explore their meaning. She began by investigating the circumstances that provoked his panic attacks. He described long-standing panic and constant, general anxiety that worsened when his first daughter was born and grew even more severe when she began to walk and talk. Episodes occurred when he left home for a variety of places, when he went to meetings and felt he had to perform, and when he was asked to do things that took him away from things he "really wanted to be doing" (water sports, music, and building models, among other things). He got anxious when his mind wandered freely, as it did when he was driving. His first panic attack took place when he was in his early 20s, when he was working in a small office with an older male colleague and felt cramped. He could not remember the details of that episode. He thought at the time that the panic had been precipitated by something "in the water."

As the therapist listened to the circumstances that made Mr. A anxious, she heard several themes. She wondered silently whether the episodes might have been related to Mr. A's feelings about separation (they came on when he was leaving home and worsened when his daughter was growing more independent) or to a fear of his inadequacy (they came on when he felt he had to perform). She wondered whether the attacks were connected to Mr. A's discomfort with generally letting himself feel his feelings, as his anxiety and panic worsened when his mind was free to wander and abated when he could be distracted by details or chores. She wondered more specifically what role Mr. A's anger played in his attacks, as his grabbing his daughter's doll and the ensuing terrible panic attack was the ultimate impetus for Mr. A's seeking treatment, and attacks were often prompted by his having to do things he did not want to do. These various factors—separation, performance, and anger—appeared to be involved in the panic attack he described. She believed the meaning of all of these details would become clearer in the course of treatment. In an effort to see what was most important to Mr. A, she listened as he spoke freely. As noted already, Mr. A's case is continued in Chapter 18.

Part I

Theoretical background

Chapter 3

Basic psychodynamic concepts

Knowledge of central psychodynamic concepts is essential to an understanding of the psychodynamic theory of anxiety disorders and to performing Panic Focused Psychodynamic Psychotherapy—eXtended Range (PFPP-XR). These concepts constitute the building blocks of theoretical and clinical understanding of patients' symptoms, fantasies, and conflicts and provide the basis for psychodynamic psychotherapeutic interventions. There is considerable overlap among many of these concepts, and they are not meant to be rigid categories. For example, although *resistance* and *transference* describe different aspects of the psychodynamic clinical process, transference can be employed in the service of resistance. These concepts, which will be referred to throughout the explication of theory and practice of PFPP-XR, will be roughly divided into intrapsychic factors and clinical manifestations.

INTRAPSYCHIC FACTORS

The unconscious

From a psychodynamic perspective, psychic content is either readily available to consciousness or it exists in a more inaccessible realm described as "the unconscious" (Freud, 1893–1895). Specific wishes, feelings, and fantasies (Shapiro, 1992) are maintained in an unconscious state, or *repressed*, because they are experienced as painful, frightening, or unacceptable. This is referred to as the *dynamic unconscious*, which implies that psychic contents that are unconscious remain in this state for a dynamic reason, because of the emotional danger they represent. Individuals typically respond to the emergence into consciousness of these unconscious wishes, fantasies, or feelings as potentially threatening to their safety or well-being, or as morally unacceptable. Conflict between wishes and fantasies and internalized prohibitions about them is referred to as *intrapsychic conflict*, a central psychoanalytic principle. The mind in a state of well-being is a mind in conflict; this is the normal state of affairs. When internal wishes, such as needs or desires, or external factors, in the form of situations or relationships, can be adaptively accommodated or gratified, well-being can be preserved. However, when there is significant conflict about specific feelings and fantasies, or frustration of wishes by external factors, emotionally engendered symptoms can be triggered. Throughout this book we will describe intrapsychic conflicts that trigger panic attacks, agoraphobia, and other anxiety symptoms and manifestations.

For example, patients with panic attacks and severe anxiety are often entirely unaware of angry feelings toward people to whom they feel closely attached. These feelings and the associated fantasies remain unconscious, and any emerging awareness of either triggers anxiety and a host of avoidant mental responses, the purpose of which is to prevent any further awareness, enactment, or expression of the unacceptable wishes. These individuals commonly maintain the fantasy that the expression of any anger would endanger and disrupt the relationship, which is felt to be essential for security and safety (Busch, Cooper, Klerman, Shapiro, & Shear, 1991; Shear, Cooper, Klerman, Busch, & Shapiro, 1993). A central component of psychoanalytic treatment, and of PFPP-XR, is helping patients to gain access to aspects of their unconscious mental lives that otherwise persist and persistently trigger maladaptive patterns and symptoms. Symptoms diminish as wishes, fantasies, and conflicts become conscious, are better understood and verbalized, and thereby are rendered less threatening. *Unconscious fantasies* (Shapiro, 1992), that often relate to developmental experiences and contain wishes that are a source of conflict, can be an important determining factor in panic and anxiety symptoms. In the following case, symptoms symbolically represent an unconscious fantasy of the patient's identification with her brother.

Case example

Ms. B, a 22-year-old woman, presented with panic disorder and long-standing depression while taking a year off between college and graduate school. She was able to articulate very little about the content of her panic episodes, other than to say that they made her feel "a peculiar sense that the world is going dark." In the course of psychotherapy she became curious about her past, about which she at first remembered very little. She recalled a home environment in which her father was viewed as "the genius" and her mother as an "emotional dingbat." She saw her older brother as more interesting and intelligent than she was and felt she, like her mother, was devalued and ignored in family conversations. She denied being aware of any anger at how she felt treated. Ms. B realized, in the course of exploring her relationships, that she was attracted to men who treated her like her brother did, in a disdainful or dismissive manner.

> Ms. B developed an intensification of panic and depression after being accepted to a prestigious graduate school. At the same time she experienced an increased concern for her brother, who had recently lost his job. In therapy she "suddenly" recalled that her brother had suffered from a serious, chronic, and disfiguring medical problem throughout their childhood that had required multiple medical interventions, which she had previously "forgotten." On her way to the session following this "realization," she had the onset of such severe panic that she became paralyzed and unable to move on the street. Her father had to come from another state to pick her up and take her to the therapist's office. She became angry at her father "because now the fact that I needed him to come and get me will make him think that he has license to treat me like I'm a pathetic, sick child." The therapist pointed out to Ms. B that she had just been discussing "another sick, pathetic child in the last session." She said, "Oh, right. So you mean to tell me that you think this stuff about me forgetting that my brother was sick is somehow connected to my panic?"
>
> Further exploration confirmed that Ms. B had been living with the unconscious fantasy that if she were ill or impaired she would become closer to her brother, toward whom she had intensely ambivalent feelings. Additionally, if she were incompetent, this would help prevent aggressive and competitive wishes toward her brother from emerging. Her acceptance to a prestigious graduate school disrupted this fantasy in many ways, as it threatened this pathetic image of herself. The severe panic episode after her acceptance and the session in which the memory emerged represented an unconscious attempt to maintain this fantasy. She felt guilty about her success, with the unconscious fantasy that this would somehow damage her brother; the panic episode in this way also functioned to punish her for her success. Her panic symptoms resolved after she consciously was able to understand how she maintained the magical identification with her brother, in part through her panic, and was able to recognize and more carefully evaluate her guilt about her acceptance to graduate school.

Defense mechanisms

Unacceptable or frightening unconscious fantasies and feelings are screened from consciousness by psychological processes called defense mechanisms (Freud, 1911) that operate outside of conscious awareness. An example of a defense mechanism is *denial*, a process in which the individual disavows the presence of a compelling, uncomfortable feeling or fantasy. An example of the use of denial is panic and anxiety disorder patients' lack of awareness of angry feelings and fantasies. For example, patients may deny angry feelings at someone even though they have just expressed them or do not acknowledge being angry at someone even though anger would be appropriate in the situation in which they find themselves.

In addition to denial, other defense mechanisms found prominently among patients with panic attacks and anxiety disorders in studies and clinical observations include *reaction formation* and *undoing* (Busch, Shear, Cooper, Shapiro, & Leon, 1995), both similarly used in management of overwhelming ambivalence and separation fears. The process of reaction formation involves the apparent conversion of feelings into their opposite, such as anger into excessive caring or loving feelings into spiteful ones (as is often observed among amorous children and adolescents). Patients may demonstrate an effort to help others with whom they would be expected to be angry, making an affiliative effort rather than risking disruption of the relationship. In the process of undoing, an individual symbolically makes amends for the internal experience or outward expression of a conflicted wish or fantasy, usually an angry one. One example of this process involves patients "taking back" angry comments they have made about another person, thereby reassuring themselves that the terror they experience that such a comment might endanger the relationship no longer exists. For example, a patient might say, "I hate him, but I really love him." Patients are typically unaware of this, but their curiosity can be engaged when it is identified by the therapist.

Somatization is a ubiquitous defense in panic and anxiety disorders, as unacceptable feelings and fantasies are avoided unconsciously through a focus on bodily concerns and are experienced as bodily events rather than as emotional ones. Sometimes physical symptoms symbolize an unconscious fantasy. In the previous example, the paralysis that Ms. B experienced on the street represented her fantasy that she had become ill like her brother. It also served to punish her for being successful in a way she feared or wished her brother could not be. In PFPP-XR, the therapist seeks to identify the presence and meanings of defenses and shares these with the patient, with the goal of exploring underlying conflicted feelings and fantasies that trigger symptoms and of resolving the conflicts in a more adaptive way.

The following case illustrates the unconscious use of defense mechanisms in an attempt to manage frightening angry feelings and fantasies.

Case example

Ms. C, a 31-year-old health-care provider, had the onset of panic attacks a few days after observing a patient's sudden death. She said that she found this death to be "unfair," because the patient was young and had been improving. Ms. C had the thought, "God, you can't do this to her," and then had her first panic attack, accompanied by fears of her own death and of the deaths of others close to her. With exploration, Ms. C described having struggled with feelings of unfairness throughout her life, generated at first by the behavior of her temperamental father toward her, her siblings, and her mother, and the jealousy she routinely had of a younger sister whom she viewed as more socially adept and attractive than she. These frustrated feelings about her life had intensified in the months prior to panic onset: She felt underpaid and overworked in her job and angry with her "cold and callous" boyfriend. Ms. C had difficulty acknowledging her angry feelings. In an example of the defense mechanism of undoing, she kept taking back comments about being angry. For instance, she described holding grudges but then said, "I'm not a vindictive person." She reported having fantasies of her boyfriend being injured but then emphasized, "But I would never hope he died."

Employing reaction formation, she viewed herself as "the helping kind," always wanting to help others. The adaptive choice of being a health-care provider in part permitted her to expiate her guilt over some of her more chronic feelings of disappointment and envy but also fueled underlying resentment. She viewed herself and her colleagues as "overworked and underpaid." Exploring with Ms. C how she felt she had to "take back" her anger (through denial, undoing, and reaction formation) and providing the opportunity for her to express her vengeful fantasies safely allowed her to recognize her anger as an acceptable and expectable emotion. These explorations helped her to understand aspects of her early life and current circumstances that evoked such rage and helped to relieve her anxiety.

Compromise formation

A *compromise formation* (Freud, 1893–1895) is an unconscious aspect of mental life that symbolically represents a compromise between an unacceptable wish and the defense against that wish. Symptoms, dreams, fantasies, and aspects of personality can be understood as compromise formations. Panic attacks and other anxiety symptoms often represent a compromise between unacceptable or frightening aggressive fantasies, conflicted dependency wishes, and self-punishment for these fantasies. The aggressive wishes emerge in patients' coercive efforts to control others the patient feels are necessary for his or her safety but toward whom he or she has ambivalent feelings (like Ms. B and her father). Unacknowledged and unacceptable dependency wishes can be expressed in this way, as the patient's wishes for attention and comfort are communicated indirectly through help-seeking for fantasized physical problems. The patient's terror and disability function as self-punishment for these forbidden wishes. The following case example illustrates panic attacks in which the underlying compromise formations can be easily apprehended.

Case example

Ms. D was driving from one city to another to attend a party for her 21st birthday when she experienced her first panic attack. The attack was so severe that she had to pull off the road and call her mother in the city to which she was driving and ask her to come and pick her up on the highway. It took her mother several hours to find another person to drive with her who could also drive Ms. D's car back, and in the meantime Ms. D's party had to be canceled. At the moment she experienced the attack, Ms. D had found herself thinking that her 21st birthday was very important to her: It symbolized her "total independence" from her family and a new ability "to get rid of them." In unraveling the onset of her illness later in psychotherapy, it became clear that, in her fantasy, turning 21 and being "independent" represented the emotional equivalent of killing off her parents and siblings, all of whom enraged her. The fantasy was appealing but also was a source of terror, as she felt guilty and frightened about these wishes. The conflict was so severe that it triggered her first panic attack. The panic attack represented both the *wish* to be rid of her family (feeling unable to drive suddenly, she could not possibly reach her family) and the *defense* against this wish—a sudden-onset, severe illness that made "independence" from her family (and her birthday celebration/fantasized independence) impossible and effectively immobilized her in her escape/fantasy plan.

Additionally, the panic represented a punishment for her unacceptable wishes: now she could not be free of her family. Her symptoms also effectively expressed aggression by punishing her mother, who had to spend hours canceling everything she had been planning to do to take care of Ms. D.

Representation of self and others

In the course of development, individuals form internalized (inner mental) representations of themselves and of others with whom they have significant relationships (Klein, 1948). From a psychoanalytic perspective, the nature and development of these representations play an important role in the emergence of psychic symptoms. These internalized models of developmentally central relationships continue to exert compelling unconscious influence and shape the way people see relationships, what they anticipate from others, and how they behave toward others. Clinical and research evidence suggests that patients who are vulnerable to severe anxiety and panic attacks have particular patterns of internalized representations, including expectations of control, overprotection, and rejection (Arrindell, Emmelkamp, Monsma, & Brilman, 1983; Parker, 1979; Silove, 1986). Clinically, they frequently describe caregivers who were frightening, temperamental, and judgmental. Based on these representations, they often anticipate that their relationships will be easily disrupted and that a range of feelings and experiences, particularly surrounding separation and anger, are unsafe.

The following case demonstrates the powerful influence of unconscious internal representations on anxiety onset and persistence.

Case example

Ms. E, a 56-year-old woman with a long-standing history of panic disorder and social anxiety disorder, sought treatment for panic attacks particularly triggered by the idea of returning to work after not working for many years and entered the PFPP study. Although she had been laid off from one job, she had been mostly successful in the financial industry. She reported being fearful of interactions with male superiors on her return, with concerns about "looking stupid" and being criticized or fired. At first Ms. E insisted that her anxiety was completely understandable as a reaction to her situation and that her fears were realistic. She gradually began to accept the point the therapist emphasized: that the intensity and focus of her fear of men in the workplace was not entirely realistic, particularly given her prior success at work. It emerged that Ms. E had had a series of experiences with frightening and temperamental men in her life, beginning with her father. Discussion of her father's intrusive behavior and criticisms of her, particularly when he was intoxicated, suggested that her history with him contributed to her expectation that bosses or older men would inevitably be erratic and critical and that they would see her as inadequate and reject her. Her father's behavior included verbal attacks on her mother for being incompetent and needy and either ignoring the patient or criticizing her for trying desperately to make emotional contact with him.

This compelling, unpleasant history contributed to her being prone to feeling abused by men. This included her husband, as she tended to feel unsafe responding when he attacked and rejected her, and to some extent she felt such treatment was expected in a marriage. Her husband criticized her for complaining that he spent too much time at work, and after particularly intense fights he left home, sometimes for days at a time. Ms. E did not confront him about his whereabouts at such times for fear that he would abandon her permanently. An understanding of these relationships and of her internalized representations and expectations of self and others helped her to more accurately identify why she felt so terrified about returning to work.

Mentalization

Mentalization refers to the capacity to conceive of behavior in terms of mental states in oneself and others (Busch, 2008; Fonagy & Target, 1997). For patients with anxiety disorders, the absence of knowledge about internal, emotional contributors to anxiety symptoms can be viewed as a focal impairment in mentalization. Patients often defensively deny these emotional contributors and report "not knowing" in an unconscious effort to avoid frightening feelings and fantasies that underlie symptoms. Thus, panic and anxiety symptoms can feel as if they present "out of the blue." PFPP-XR treatment in part helps patients to develop the capacity to mentalize about their anxiety symptoms, fostering greater understanding about the relationship among anxiety symptoms, unconscious emotional conflicts, and how they are triggered by the external stressors in which patients find themselves. *Reflective function* (Fonagy, 2008) refers to a measurement of the capacity for mentalization. A measure of Panic Specific Reflective Functioning (PSRF) has been developed by Rudden, Milrod, Target, Ackerman, and Graf (2006) for the purpose of assessing this capacity. Patients with panic disorder experienced improvements in PSRF after PFPP.

Case example

The previously given case of Ms. B illustrates an improvement in mentalization with regard to panic symptoms. Ms. B had difficulty describing her anxiety, and she was unable to identify psychological or environmental contributors to her feelings. In the course of her treatment with PFPP, Ms. B gained a clearer understanding of the developmental experiences that contributed to her vulnerability to panic onset, including her father and brother's criticism of her and the way her brother's chronic illness made her feel guilty about being angry at him for being so mean. She recognized her guilt about her own health and successes. She also became aware of her wishes to be close to her brother, and her guilt about secretly wanting to outdo him, contributed to her overwhelming anxiety. Her improved ability to mentalize helped reduce her anxiety and permitted her to stop focusing on worries about her body.

CLINICAL MANIFESTATIONS

Symptoms

According to psychoanalytic theory, symptoms derive in part from the threatened emergence into consciousness of frightening or unacceptable unconscious feelings and fantasies (Freud, 1926). The conflicted unconscious content triggers anxiety and guilt and the operation of defense mechanisms. Symptoms emerge as compromise formations representing both the expression of a forbidden wish and the defense against that wish. Thus, symptoms are viewed as carrying important meanings, and symbolize central conflicted fantasies and feelings. In anxiety disorders, for example, physical symptoms can represent conflicted feelings and fantasies, a defense against these fantasies in their somatic symbolic disguise, and punishment for unacceptable wishes. Physical symptoms can be associated with unconscious identifications with significant others, as in the case of Ms. B and her sick brother, or in patients who develop specific panic or acute anxiety symptoms after the death of a close attachment figure.

As with dreams, symptoms can be understood in terms of *primary process*, manifestations, a developmentally earlier form of mental functioning described by Freud (1900) connected with immediate satisfaction of drives and wishes, and marked by an absence of logic and linearity of time. This is contrasted with *secondary process*, which is associated with conscious or preconscious mental activity as well as postponement of wish gratification in the service of reality. Secondary process thinking is characterized by logic, a linear timeline, and causal reasoning. Primary process mechanisms through which symptom formation can occur include *displacement*, in which a previously insignificant idea becomes invested with meanings and feelings associated with another, more emotionally significant one, and *condensation*, a process in which several meanings become associated with a specific idea or set of symptoms (Freud, 1900). Additionally, symptoms can encapsulate contributions from specific self and object representations. Perceptions of the self as incompetent and others as rejecting and critical can heighten conflicts surrounding independence, and anxiety symptoms can include a view of the self as helpless. The following case demonstrates how the therapist works with the patient to untangle meanings behind symptoms.

Case example

Ms. F, a 45-year-old woman, described panic and anxiety symptoms that occurred primarily at work, which included chest pain, other physical symptoms, fears of falling down because she had "nothing to hold onto," and an experience of depersonalization, "not being sure who I am." She found her job dehumanizing and believed that the bosses disregarded the needs of their employees, viewing them as automatons. She was angry at the rigidity of the rules at work, such as the dress code. She experienced her own boss as intrusive, critical, and demanding. This situation created significant anxiety all the time.

Ms. F's boss repeatedly questioned her about the status of projects, suggesting that Ms. F's pace was inadequate. She viewed her boss as rigid and incompetent and believed it was unfair that she should have to answer to him. On the other hand, she worried that if she registered any of her complaints, she would be "being a bitch" and thought this could result in retaliation, including threats to her job.

In therapy, Ms. F described growing up in a critical and demanding family and agreed with the therapist that this likely related to her anxiety. She was the youngest child, and when she was a young adolescent she was the only one still spending significant time with her mother, whose increasingly severe alcohol use led to her being drunk during the day on a regular basis. During these periods her mother was verbally abusive, calling Ms. F fat and stupid. Ms. F worried that if she fought with her mother it would trigger a more vicious assault. She was also fearful that her mother would get injured from being intoxicated and found herself spending more time at home to protect her.

In an example of condensation, several underlying emotional factors were found to contribute to her onset of severe anxiety and panic attacks. These included intense fears of expressing her anger at her boss, potentially disrupting their relationship, which were found to mirror her early struggles with her mother. Ms. F's panic symptoms of feeling there was "nothing to hold onto" and not being sure who she was related to the lack of support and recognition of her as an individual person by her mother. These various intrapsychic dangers were displaced onto bodily concerns. Recognition of how these various factors became represented as panic and anxiety symptoms aided in the resolution of Ms. F's symptoms.

Resistance

Resistance refers to the patient's often unconscious efforts to oppose the therapeutic effects of the treatment to avoid the emergence of threatening or frightening unconscious material or upsetting feelings, or to maintain an unconscious attachment to aspects of the symptoms. This phenomenon may take several forms, including more overt behaviors such as forgetting or coming late to appointments on a regular basis, or expressly refusing to discuss a topic. Resistance may emerge in more subtle forms, such as changing the subject from an uncomfortable topic or becoming silent. The concept of resistance may appear counterintuitive at first, as it is assumed that patients wish to take whatever steps are necessary to improve their condition. Efforts to rationally instruct or exhort patients to follow up on a given topic often fail, as these exhortations do not address underlying reasons for resistance.

In psychoanalytic treatments, resistance is seen as a valuable therapeutic tool. An increase in the patient's resistance is viewed as an important indicator that the treatment is approaching threatening or conflicted unconscious fantasies. The therapist can demonstrate to the patient the resistant behavior and suggest that the patient is avoiding something that appears to be important. Resistance presents opportunities to address the emergence of conflicts in the relationship with the therapist (see "Transference").

Examples of resistance are found throughout the cases described in this chapter. Ms. E became angry with the therapist after the third session of PFPP, when the therapist informed her of his upcoming vacation schedule. It emerged that Ms. E had imagined that the 24 sessions of PFPP allotted to her in the research study needed to take place within 12 consecutive weeks, even though this was not part of the protocol and no one had told her this. She initially expressed frustration that the therapist had not mentioned his vacation plans sooner, but then focused on feeling humiliated and stupid that she had made changes to her own plans to accommodate something that was not necessary. The therapist seized this opportunity to explore how easily Ms. E seemed to feel humiliated, how she automatically directed her anger toward the therapist at herself by calling herself stupid, and how she unconsciously had imagined herself in a position of being poorly treated. Ms. E demonstrated resistance to this transference interpretation by reversing course, saying that this was "no biggie" and that she really did not have strong feelings about it. The therapist noted to the patient her tendency to minimize painful feelings. In a subsequent session the therapist and Ms. E further explored the anxious pressure she felt to accommodate others, followed by anger, humiliation, and self-criticism about being overly yielding.

Regression

Regression refers to a shift in thinking, adaptation, emotional and mood states, and often behavior to an earlier developmental phase (Arlow, 1963; Freud, 1917). Regression can extend to thought processes (including a shift to primary process thinking), representations of oneself and others, and fantasies. Intrapsychic conflicts can trigger regression, which can occur generally, across many areas of functioning, or in more isolated ways. Stressors that activate underlying emotional fault lines, such as moves toward independence or coping with losses, can contribute to regression. Panic and other anxiety disorders frequently involve a shift to a regressed state in the expression of needy, helpless behavior. The patient's shift to a focus on the body rather than feelings is also characteristic of earlier developmental phases.

In the case of Ms. B, the patient's panic and paralysis is a form of regression: rather than being able to think verbally, in a more adult and organized manner, and to tolerate her guilty feelings about her acceptance to graduate school, she experienced her emotions literally in her body in nonverbal form. Her identification with her ill brother was physically enacted when she was in this state. With her paralysis, panic attack, and confusion, she regressed to a childlike, helpless stance in which she needed to be cared for by others. Ms. B's regression could be understood in part as a guilty and anxious reaction to competitive and aggressive wishes associated with her success in being accepted to graduate school and as a response to a threat she experienced from the acceptance's implied acknowledgment of her increased autonomy and independence.

Transference

Patterns of perceptions of significant primary attachments that develop in early life emerge in all relationships, including with the therapist. This psychological phenomenon, known as *transference* (Freud, 1905), is a cornerstone of psychodynamic theory and therapy. Awareness and focus on the transference can prove helpful to therapists and patients in articulating underlying, organizing fantasies that surround the therapeutic relationship, regardless of the type of treatment in which the patient is engaged or the therapeutic orientation of the therapist. From a psychodynamic perspective, the transference situation has far-reaching effects and necessarily influences therapeutic outcome. The transference provides both a directness and immediacy in illustrating and understanding emotional conflicts as they come to life in the relationship between patient and therapist. It also provides conditions for the emergence and exploration of unacceptable unconscious wishes, fantasies, and feelings. Transference phenomena include both affectionate and angry feelings and fantasies, which may be experienced safely by the patient or alternatively may be a source of conflict.

Affectionate feelings toward the therapist, either deriving from developmental expectations or realistically related to the therapist's role in helping the patient, can contribute to what is called the *therapeutic alliance* (Crits-Christoph & Connolly Gibbons, 2003; Zetzel, 1956). The therapeutic alliance constitutes the sense that the patient and therapist are working collaboratively on similar goals and that the approaches they are employing are helping to achieve these goals. In psychodynamic psychotherapy, disruptions of the therapeutic alliance can be important indicators of resistance and are opportunities to address transference fantasies.

As transference develops in the course of PFPP-XR, patients often experience feelings and conflicts with the therapist that are central to anxiety. For instance, angry feelings typically develop toward the therapist in the setting of separations or termination, along with fears about losing or disrupting the relationship with the therapist. Separations and termination of the treatment provide important opportunities for patients to better articulate, understand, and manage their conflicts about anger and autonomy in the setting of the transference.

The next case example illustrates the centrality of transference phenomena in a nonpsychodynamic, psychopharmacological treatment. A psychopharmacologist who specializes in the treatment of panic disorder reported this case.

Case example

Ms. G, a patient with panic disorder who had been receiving treatment from the psychopharmacologist for years, had been taking very high doses of benzodiazepines.

She and her physician had been engaged in a very slow and gradual taper of the drug because her panic attacks had remitted. She was in the middle of this taper, continuing on a substantially high dose of benzodiazepines, and had been tolerating the taper well. The pharmacologist lowered her dose again by a "microscopic decrement" before leaving for a vacation. Ms. G had "the worst panic attack in my life," for which, years later, she still had "not forgiven" him.

Benzodiazepine taper is well known to be difficult in this patient population because withdrawal syndromes and rebound anxiety are common. Thus, benzodiazepine taper is best accomplished over a period of months. Nonetheless, in the Cross National Collaborative Panic Study (1992) discontinuation phase, most of the patients who received alprazolam experienced their most severe withdrawal syndromes and rebound anxiety at the very end of the drug discontinuation phase or during the first week in which they were medication free (Pecknold, Swinson, Kuch, & Lewis, 1988). Ms. G was in neither situation. However, this patient was experiencing another equally common panic and anxiety-related phenomenon: anxiety when separated from important attachment figures in her life—in this case, her psychopharmacologist. Even in the context of a pharmacological treatment, an awareness and some degree of focus on the transference can be valuable.

Countertransference

Therapists develop reactions to patients based on their own internalized representations of themselves and others, phenomena referred to as *countertransference* (Gabbard, 1995). Although countertransference can interfere with treatment, the therapist's awareness of the feelings the patient inspires in her can be an important clinical tool, as these feelings may provide clues about the patient. The therapist needs to remain aware of her reactions toward the patient that may be expressed directly or indirectly, such as feeling frustrated or angry, which, if not acknowledged may disrupt the therapy. For example, a therapist may be drawn into a patient's sense of emergency or experience guilt about termination in connection with a patient's difficulty with separation.

Case example

After Ms. E minimized her reaction to learning about the therapist's vacation schedule, the therapist became aware of urges to argue with Ms. E to get her to recognize the similarity of the transference situation to the conflicts she experienced with job-seeking and with the other men in her life, in which she also routinely felt angry, humiliated, and anxious. The therapist's further efforts in this direction were met with increased resistance from Ms. E, who said that the therapist was making a big deal of nothing. The therapist recognized that his urge to argue with this patient was unusual for him. This recognition helped him to become aware of the degree to which Ms. E resisted awareness of some of her feelings. The therapist was able to stop pursuing this topic with her at that moment and allow Ms. E to more safely explore the intense threats of humiliation she experienced and what contributed to them before directly addressing her discomfort about discussing their relationship.

Chapter 4

The psychodynamic formulation

In this section we address general principles of the psychodynamic formulation. We then describe specific modifications of the general formulation needed to create a psychodynamic formulation in panic focused psychodynamic psychotherapy—eXtended range (PFPP-XR). Finally, we delineate components of the psychodynamic formulation in PFPP-XR, including aspects we have come to understand more fully from our work over the past decade. Excerpts from the case of Mr. A. (Chapter 2) are used to illustrate elements of the formulation; a more complete presentation of the development of a psychodynamic formulation for Mr. A is presented in Chapter 18.

GENERAL PRINCIPLES

What is a psychodynamic formulation?

A psychodynamic formulation is an integrated understanding of the patient's inner mental life, with a focus on its unconscious aspects (Perry, Cooper, & Michels, 1987). The formulation serves as a tool the therapist employs to understand how patients came to feel and behave as they do and how their symptoms developed, and it reflects hypotheses about how their past affects their current life. Factors identified in developing the psychodynamic formulation are central in understanding the patient's current overall psychology, conflicts, and symptoms and are important in guiding treatment interventions. The traits and internal experiences we seek to understand in current life include but are not limited to the following:

- The meaning of symptoms in patients' lives now
- How they see and feel about themselves, others, and themselves *in relation* to others

- Predominant affects and modes of expressing them
- Style of coping and adapting, including prominent defense mechanisms
- How they relate and form attachments to others, choices of love objects and how these relationships unfold
- Needs and how they get them met
- Sexual needs, fantasies, and ways of relating sexually
- Career choices and modes of pursuing desired paths
- Talents, strengths, interests
- Core conflicts and problems in all areas of life, including feelings and fantasies, relationships, work, and recreational outlets

Where do we look for answers to these questions?

The answers come from the stories patients tell and the manner in which they tell them. There is much to learn from the order in which patients relate the events of their lives. Some of the specific information that is kept in mind as we try to understand patients' narratives and associations include their experience of the following:

- Symptoms
- Past environmental factors: family circumstances and history, including those preceding birth
- Salient relationships (with mother, father, siblings, grandparents, caretakers, other significant people in their lives, from earliest days)
- Important relationships among prominent people in patients' lives; how they react to these relationships
- History of relationships: choices, course, quality of connections, joys and strengths, problems, identifications
- Culture
- Dominant experiences of school and work endeavors
- Fantasies, either conscious as related by patients or unconscious, emerging from flow of their associations and what they clearly omit reporting
- Transferences to the therapist, which serve as a window on salient past relationships, modes of relating in the present, and unconscious memories and fantasies
- Dominant affects, both past and emerging in treatment, including fears and phobias
- Defenses and resistances
- Sexual fantasies, desires, choices
- Significant memories
- Dreams

- Patterns of any kind in patients' narratives
- Countertransference reactions the therapist notes within him or herself.

The psychodynamic formulation is "dynamic" in more than one way: It is psychodynamic (concerned with inner mental life), and it evolves in the course of psychotherapy, deepening with each new expansion of the therapist's and patient's understanding.

What is the value of a psychodynamic formulation?

The material that emerges in the course of giving and gathering historical material and the mutual experience of the patient and therapist observing their relationship is vast. The formulation provides a way of organizing the developmental factors and intrapsychic conflicts that contribute to the patient's emotional state, behavior, and symptoms. The synthesis of this material, as the therapist steadily develops a psychodynamic formulation, enables the therapist to organize his thinking and becomes central in communicating his understanding to the patient.

Sharing a psychodynamic formulation with a patient can have many beneficial effects. By offering possible emotionally salient understandings of the underpinnings of the patient's symptoms, the therapist can give the patient a greater sense of connection and control over warded off ideas, fantasies, and affects that engender symptoms. A growing experience of inner coherence and consistency, garnered in the process of therapy, in turn generates increased comfort and less resistance to further exploration.

Another advantage of sharing the psychodynamic formulation is that patients rapidly develop a greater sense that events in their lives (internal states as well as external circumstances) are often choices they make, rather than a fate that simply befalls them. This understanding is what imparts a sense of personal agency and an ability to bring a new perspective to bear so that patients feel empowered to make new and better choices, and arrive at better resolutions of conflicts, with greater fulfillment of needs and desires, less pain, and fewer symptoms.

An important function of the psychodynamic formulation is to aid the therapist in making connections among its core components, which in turn helps patients to integrate the most salient aspects of their inner lives. We illustrate one example of such connections by examining how resistances and transferences can be linked as part of the development of a formulation.

Resistance (see Chapter 3) is the opposition—conscious, unconscious, or both—to the deepening of the dynamic/therapeutic process. It can, for example, be manifested by patients' withholding their physical presence in treatment (lateness, absence) or stonewalling the process of giving information or associating freely. Resistance can also take the form of attempts, often unconscious, to avoid recognition of the meaning of their own associations or the therapist's interventions.

Resistance is maintained in an effort to avoid unwanted mental contents and their intrapsychic significance. It usually occurs in the service of warding off feelings, memories, fantasies, and impulses, the awareness of which might trigger negative self-views or unbearable affects (shame, fear, rage, guilt). Examples of fantasies that trigger resistance include: "I will not be lovable if my rage is discovered"; "My mother died because my anger killed her"; or "I will die or he'll kill me if he sees how competitive I am" (see the treatment of Mr. A, Chapter 18).

As resistance is triggered by pervasive fantasies, it will invariably arise in the transference. When it does, it is of value to link a particular resistance to the underlying fantasies in the transference to identify the transference fantasy and its profound impact on patients' behavior with the therapist. For example, the therapist might say, "I think you became quiet suddenly and felt guilty because you have difficulty tolerating your angry feelings and may be worried how I would react to them." Parallel resistances can also be traced in relationships outside of the treatment (e.g., becoming quiet and self critical rather than acknowledging anger at a spouse). As the connection between the resistance (silent withdrawal) and the transference fantasy (the therapist will reject me for my anger) is identified, patients gain increased understanding of how their minds function.

The integrative function of the dynamic formulation is crucial in psychodynamic psychotherapy. It is of added importance in PFPP-XR, as one of the main problems with panic and anxiety is that patients' defensive styles create significant compartmentalization and disconnection between various aspects of their emotional lives, specifically with regard to their anxiety symptoms.

MODIFICATIONS OF THE PSYCHODYNAMIC FORMULATION IN PFPP-XR

Rather than addressing more globally how persons came to feel and behave as they do, the question that the PFPP-XR psychodynamic formulation aims to answer is, "What psychological factors cause this patient to have such severe anxiety?"

The principles used in constructing a psychodynamic formulation in open-ended, nonsymptom-focused psychodynamic psychotherapy apply in PFPP-XR. The main differences in PFPP-XR include the focal goal of the formulation, and the means of acquiring the information. The therapist's goal is to develop a formulation that highlights patients' anxiety and symptoms of panic and avoidance to understand their emotional meaning. The spectrum of anxiety symptoms is the lens through which the therapist can organize the dynamic formulation in PFPP-XR.

Panic attacks and anxiety symptoms occur in response to thoughts, feelings, and imagined dangers that are often largely outside of patients' awareness. The "realm" outside of conscious awareness is full of wishes, fears, feelings, identifications, fantasies, and memories that often stem from aspects of early life and that exert a powerful influence on current thoughts, feelings, and behavior.

There are psychologically understandable reasons that patients' thoughts and feelings are warded off from conscious awareness. These reasons are almost always related to wishes, feelings, and fantasies that are in some way unacceptable, frightening, or difficult for patients to tolerate. Emotional reasons for patients' being unaware of specific determinants of their anxiety are central, and also shed light on the meaning of the symptoms. Symptoms do not come "out of the blue," as patients frequently express them. This view represents an unconscious defensive disavowal of overwhelming emotionally distressing triggers.

Because this treatment focuses primarily on psychodynamics underlying anxiety and anxiety-engendered physical symptoms, and because of the time limitation of PFPP-XR, the therapist explores developmental factors, intrapsychic conflicts, relationship patterns, and defenses as they relate to anxiety symptoms and panic attacks, to elaborate the formulation. In phase I, as an initial dynamic formulation is determined, we look for the following:

- Triggers of the first panic attack or anxiety symptoms and their emotional significance to patients
- Triggers for subsequent panic attacks, avoidance, and anxiety and their meanings to patients
- Specific symptoms during panic attacks and anxiety and associations to those symptoms
- Conflicts that emerge in relationships, work, recreation, and life goals, particularly as they relate to panic, avoidance, and anxiety
- Factors in past and present relationships that contribute to conflicts, panic, and anxiety vulnerability
- Pivotal intrapsychic conflicts generating and perpetuating panic and anxiety
- Current developmental tasks, with special attention to conflicts around separation, conflicted anger, sexuality, and the guilty need for self-punishment
- Apparent compromise formations (especially those that appear to be essential to patients' panic and anxiety) and patients' feelings about them
- Issues of self-esteem and self-image
- Early transferences and response to starting treatment

- Defenses
- Multiple functions served by panic attacks, avoidance, and anxiety
- Patients' responses to interpretations
- Countertransference experiences

As we "build" the formulation in a clear and stepwise fashion, we expand our sources of information in phase II to include the following:

- Newly emerging transference/countertransference paradigms, memories, associations, life changes, and defenses
- Patients' specific responses to therapeutic interventions
- New information about panic and anxiety triggers that inevitably emerge in this form of treatment
- Change in symptomatology as panic and anxiety improve and new conflicts emerge—this bolsters understanding of the original anxiety symptoms
- Hypotheses about what was being defended against earlier in light of new material
- New information about what functions panic attacks and anxiety symptoms serve

Finally, as we enter phase III, we look particularly for new material, transferences, and countertransference emerging in the context of separation/termination that can enrich the therapist's understanding of the patient's dynamics.

Panic and anxiety are not inevitable. There are new ways patients can begin to understand their heretofore inaccessible mental life such that they can find new solutions to old and enduring emotional conflicts that can eradicate anxiety and permit greater joy and success. The tools used in PFPP-XR can be given to patients in such a way that they can use them in an ongoing manner after treatment is finished to promote better emotional self-awareness. This improved reflective function in turn can help in identification of progressively better solutions to emotionally challenging situations, including those involved in close relationships, permitting greater freedom from anxiety and minimizing vulnerability to anxiety and panic.

A PSYCHODYNAMIC FORMULATION FOR PANIC AND ANXIETY DISORDERS

Busch, Cooper, Klerman, Shapiro, and Shear (1991) and Shear, Cooper, Klerman, Busch, and Shapiro (1993) suggested a psychodynamic formulation for panic disorder based on neurophysiological vulnerabilities, temperamental characteristics, and childhood experiences. These factors lead vulnerable individuals to be easily frightened by separation or loss and to develop a sense of fearful dependency on caregivers, who are experienced as unreliable or rejecting. Autonomy represents an additional danger in the symbolic loss of the caregiver. In this context, individuals develop a fear that angry feelings or their expression will disrupt the needed tie to the caregiver, and feelings of guilt ensue from fears of damaging the caregiver as a result of rageful fantasies. Children attempt to cope with these conflicts through the unconscious triggering of defense mechanisms aimed at denying or disguising angry and dependent feelings and fantasies, including denial, reaction formation, undoing, and somatization (see Chapter 10). However, these defense mechanisms are ineffective at preventing anxiety and guilt, as the underlying conflicts persist unconsciously or subconsciously. In addition, individuals do not develop a normative ability to mentalize, as the capacity to know the minds of themselves and others is interrupted by defensive avoidance of feelings and fantasies. In adulthood, when threats to attachment trigger regression, the conflicts, guilt, anxiety, and somatic symptoms can be become intolerable and overwhelming, and can be expressed as panic or other anxiety disorders. Anxiety and panic can also function as a self-punishment for unacceptable feelings or fantasies. In addition to struggles surrounding attachment and anger, Milrod (1995) noted that in some panic patients, the panic episodes can have a frightening and arousing inherent excitement, often closely tied to sadomasochistic sexual conflicts and characterological traits.

Our clinical experience in the treatment of comorbidities in our panic disorder studies, and the work of other psychoanalytic theorists and clinicians (see Chapters 12–16), indicate that conflicted dependent and angry wishes, separation and autonomy fears, guilt, and the defensive avoidance of intrapsychic states are significant factors in a variety of anxiety disorders. Thus, addressing these dynamics has transdiagnostic utility in relief of these symptoms.

CORE CONFLICTS IN PANIC AND OTHER ANXIETY DISORDERS

As per the above formulation, various common conflicts underlie panic attacks and anxiety, typically involving an ambivalent relationship to the developmental tasks of separation, and the challenges of becoming autonomous, as well as core difficulties experiencing anger in the context of attachments. Identifying these conflicts is an important aspect of developing a formulation for specific patients. A core fantasy that many patients with anxiety disorders share is that they are personally inadequate, incapable, incapacitated, and in dire need of another person for survival. For people with agoraphobia, this need becomes reified in the person of the phobic companion. These fantasies are pervasive and can become overwhelming, rendering patients' actual areas of competence psychologically irrelevant. Fears of being unable to function heighten the imagined dangers of loss and being alone. This sense of personal incompetence frequently arises from patients' experience of parents as being absent, neglectful, or incompetent, or of a traumatic relationship or loss that left them feeling overwhelmed.

Patients' view of themselves as passive, childlike, and helpless can accompany the sense that panic attacks and anxiety symptoms come "out of the blue" and befall them, like many other events in their life. Patients often have the fantasy that by being weak and helpless they will obtain needed care from adults, relieving the dangers of loneliness and inadequacy. The type of dependency that panic and anxiety engenders prevents a deeper kind of mutual intimacy or trust from developing with attachment figures, and in this way the compromise offered is limiting. Severe anxiety can function to prevent patients from engaging in a fuller, more adult way, especially as people with anxiety can view the need to function maturely as a threat to relationships.

Despite the experience of panic attacks or other anxiety symptoms per se as out of control anxiety, they can also be an unconscious (and maladaptive) way of maintaining control over other frightening feelings by focusing on anxiety and bodily fears. Patients with panic attacks and other anxiety symptoms are often afraid of being overwhelmed by intense emotions, including anger and aggression, as well as by needy, loving, and sexual wishes. In addition to experiencing emotions as being potentially threatening or destabilizing, patients frequently convey the belief that their feelings are messy or unacceptable, causing them to feel weak and guilty. They may anticipate that a feared or desired parent, or significant others in their lives, will reject or avoid them because of their feelings. Alternatively patients may believe that parents (or significant others) cannot tolerate their feelings, as in the case of patients whose mothers were depressed or highly anxious. The aversion to strong emotions may be intensified by past trauma. Ultimately, patients insulate themselves and others from the full range of their emotions by denying them and expressing them through panic attacks and anxiety. This tendency adds to feelings of isolation, intensifying separation fears.

For patients with anxiety, the experience of anger is frequently associated with fantasies that they will destroy others or that others will abandon or destroy them. Strength, competence, and sexuality can become conflated with ideas of destructive aggression. Patients defend against the dangers of being aggressive by repeatedly placing themselves in a weakened, deprived, and emotionally disempowered state of severe anxiety. This childlike state can be reassuring on one level but is also terrifying, as it fuels fears of incompetence, inadequacy, dysfunction, and failure. This self-disempowerment also serves to punish patients for angry and destructive impulses. Guilt and an associated unconscious desire for or expectation of punishment are important dynamics underlying anxiety. The symptoms of anxiety can also function to punish patients. To complicate matters, anxiety can also serve as a disguised form of aggression, a coercive effort to get significant others to respond, and to punish them for not responding sooner. Thus, panic and anxiety can function as a compromise between an aggressive wish (to hurt the other), a fear (of harming the other and thus losing him, leading to being abandoned and alone), a self-punishment (by undercutting competence), and a fulfillment of the regressively expressed wish to obtain care. This conflicting set of at least partially unconscious determinants of anxiety is an example of a compromise formation (see Chapter 3).

As a consequence of the fantasy that patients' rage might destroy important others and of reliance on crippling anxiety in part to prevent fulfillment of competitive or aggressive strivings, patients experience terror that they will never get what they feel they most need or want. For many of these patients, the fantasy of persistent deprivation is in part warranted, as patients have organized a life that ensures their own deprivation as self-punishment.

Case example

As described in more detail in Chapter 18, an emblematic moment in Mr. A's history occurred when he was a boy and refused to accede to his mother's telling him to do his homework because he was busy swimming. His mother responded that she wished she had a different son. When his mother, who was ill from cancer, died shortly after this altercation, her loss triggered terrible guilt for Mr. A and a fear that his anger had somehow killed her. From this and other experiences in his life, Mr. A became fearful that expressing his anger could damage others or lead them to disappear, reject, or abandon him. Mr. A became broadly inhibited about expressing his feelings and being assertive with others and could not permit himself the luxury of asking for help when he needed it. This further increased his anger and his fear of expressing it, intensifying his anxiety at times to panic levels.

MULTIPLE FUNCTIONS OF PANIC AND ANXIETY

One way to see the task of building a dynamic formulation is through the lens of the multiple functions that anxiety serves for given patients. Severe anxiety can serve the following emotional purposes:

- It can be a way of *experiencing and communicating feelings*. Often the feelings communicated ("Help! I need you! I'm lonely. I'm scared. I can't do this by myself. I'm bad") are those patients cannot acknowledge or express more directly. Panic attacks and anxiety symptoms can substitute for other potentially destabilizing feelings such as anger and sexual excitement (which the frenzy of a panic attack can sometimes simulate). Anxiety can express anger unconsciously through a demand for others' attention.

- It can serve as a defense and can *keep a range of emotions out of conscious awareness*. Feelings and fantasies can be experienced somatically and symbolically. Despite how excruciating panic attacks and anxiety can be, they may be less disorganizing than confronting what feels like a terrifying abyss of patients' inner mental worlds.
- It can represent *a memory or may reenact old relationships*. It may represent an identification with a love object in the past or present, thereby keeping the loved one close in fantasy. This identification can also defend against feelings of greater competence than the sick or absent loved one, which can trigger overwhelming guilt about competitive fantasies. While identification through panic attacks can represent a form of mourning, it can interfere with mourning as well (Klass et al., 2009), as feelings of loss are expressed unconsciously and are essentially avoided and not addressed.
- It can *provide a way of relating and expressing attachment* and can be a compromise that permits at least partial fulfillment of dependent wishes and needs while protecting against their imagined dangers by expressing these wishes somatically rather than with a direct acknowledgment.
- It can function as *guilty self-punishment*.

Case example

Mr. A's symptoms demonstrated several of these functions in elucidating the unconscious determinants of his panic attacks and anxiety. It was with his panic attacks that he unconsciously expressed frustration and anger with others for not being more responsive, feelings that triggered guilt and terror when he experienced them consciously. Thus, his panic attacks served to defend against an acknowledgment of his longings for and anger at others by disguising these feelings and fantasies as bodily symptoms. Mr. A's panic attacks represented a way of reenacting his relationship with his mother, whose loss he had not fully acknowledged, by repeatedly revisiting the longings, anger, guilt, and struggles he had felt when she was ill and dying. These attacks were a means through which he could obtain attention by seeking help. Finally, the panic attacks appeased his guilt by punishing him for what felt like unacceptable anger at his mother and subsequent anger he experienced toward others whom he felt were unresponsive or rejecting. His panic furthermore served to weaken him and quell his terror about his power to destroy.

THERAPEUTIC APPROACHES TO DEVELOPING A PANIC AND ANXIETY FORMULATION

From the first moment of PFPP-XR, the therapist's goal is to listen for evidence of conflicts and fantasies, as they connect to the central emotional symptoms of panic and anxiety, and to bring to light ways patients demonstrate feelings of which they may be unaware. In this context, the therapist keeps in mind the previously noted question: "What makes this patient anxious?" The personal, psychological meanings of events, feelings, and triggers associated with anxiety onset are specifically articulated. The therapist identifies ways anxiety makes psychological sense in the context of patients' intrapsychic life. Specific events and feelings leading to the first panic attack or first episode of anxiety and subsequent anxiety events are explored in detail. Circumstances of each anxiety event and the meaning to patients of the apparent precipitants are carefully explored.

A view of oneself as passive is prevalent in patients with anxiety disorders. When patients perceive themselves in this way, the PFPP-XR therapist helps them reevaluate why they might cling to this view. The therapist pays close attention to ways patients may play a passive role in the treatment and draws their attention to their passive stance as a choice over more assertive and adaptive attitudes and behaviors. Together, patient and therapist explore how these interactions mirror those in other areas of life. The understanding of these transferences fosters an affectively charged understanding of unconscious wishes, fears, fantasies, and modes of relating.

Unlike more open-ended psychodynamic psychotherapies, where possibilities for diverse transference explorations are wider, the PFPP-XR therapist pursues aspects of the transference that are most central to the understanding of panic and anxiety. Often, these aspects of the transference are germane to more global conflicts in patients' lives that predispose to anxiety (such as patterns of choices that make patients feel disempowered). Core transferences usually involve fantasies related to the previously described dynamics, such as fears that the therapist will be angry or indifferent to patients, will find them unlovable and will reject them, and will not be able to tolerate their intense feelings and fantasies. Patients may anticipate feeling worthless, unlovable, and humiliated as they enter therapy and may be wary about discussing these feelings. Patients may imagine that they and the therapist will battle for control and that one might destroy the other, often accompanied by sadomasochistic undertones. The therapist identifies ways patients perceive the therapist, verbally acknowledges them, guides patients to associate, and connects these experiences to patients' experiences of early relationships.

As these relationships are clarified, the therapist must show patients how the underlying transference fantasies are ultimately connected with anxiety and panic. The therapist employs patients' growing awareness of transferences and improving self-observation and reflective function to shed light on other relationship patterns and how those might contribute to maintenance of anxiety and panic and vice versa. The therapist must keep in mind details of past sessions to be able to deepen patients' understanding of these transferences and their ramifications incrementally (so interpretations are digestible and not overwhelming), so that progress covers sufficient ground to provide rapid, sustained relief.

Articulation of the transference is of value in understanding the emotional distortions brought to bear on relationships that form part of the meaning of anxiety. To make these interpretations useful, it often requires an effort to show patients that the relationship between them and the therapist is important and that some aspects of the feelings they bring into therapy about the therapist stem from earlier, formative relationships. Many anxiety patients can initially be skeptical about these ideas, defended as they are from noticing and identifying some of their emotional reactions. To address this skepticism, PFPP-XR therapists demonstrate to patients ways the same patterns are evident in other situations and relationships outside of the treatment. The therapist also explores with patients how fears of acknowledging their fantasies and emotions can lead them to resist the idea that they have feelings about the therapist. Emotionally conflicted aspects of the therapeutic relationship are brought to patients' attention at times that they will further patients' understanding of their dynamics or when these dynamisms threaten to interfere with the progress of the treatment. The therapist also pays attention to his own emotional responses to the patient, his countertransference, and uses these to shed light on his understanding of the patient.

Case example

The therapist noted a pattern with Mr. A in which he alternately was compliant with her wishes and then struggled with what he viewed as the "rules" of treatment. For instance, Mr. A at one point asked the therapist what he should talk about (highlighting his discomfort in taking charge) and at another time debated her unwillingness to answer a question directly. It emerged that he engaged in similar power struggles with others in his life, including his wife. The therapist was able to articulate Mr. A's view that he felt he needed to be compliant to be loved, which left him feeling resentful. Alternatively, he could assert his wishes, risking retaliation or abandonment. This conflict left him feeling alone, resentful, and unlovable. Articulation of this struggle within the transference provided a clarity and emotional immediacy for Mr. A that helped him to integrate these disparate views. In addition, it provided the opportunity to more directly confront his fears in treatment by speaking about his dependent and angry fantasies to the therapist.

Chapter 5

The role of development in the pathogenesis of panic and anxiety disorders

The notion of psychological development is anchored in the concept of a normative progressive arc originating in the capabilities of early childhood. Development encompasses a multidimensional trajectory of psychological changes occasioned by maturational milestones, normally culminating in the capacity for independent, autonomous functioning in an adult role. Rather than a uniform change, functional capacities (e.g., sexuality, management of aggression, self- and object representations) develop at varying rates in a given individual (Freud, 1963). Optimally, adult functioning encompasses a relatively stable sense of self, a capacity for self-definition and intimacy, and an ability to manage a wide range of affective states and frustrations. The concept of such a developmental thrust toward mature psychological capacities is central to understanding the organization of psychological vulnerabilities and intrapsychic conflict generally and to the formation and emergence of anxiety symptoms specifically.

Clinically, the concept of progressive development posits a maturational pressure toward higher levels of functioning, with disruptions in development creating vulnerability to psychopathology. Patients often seek treatment for panic and anxiety disorders in relation to experiences that actually or symbolically represent developmental challenges, which the patient has been unable to negotiate owing to ego weaknesses or unresolved emotional conflicts. Intrapsychic conflict about developmental progression can trigger a regression to an earlier developmental phase. Therapeutic considerations focus on the circumstances and timing of the presentation for treatment, the role and nature of the psychological factors that may impede higher functioning, and the defenses employed to mitigate such pressures.

From a psychodynamic perspective, panic and anxiety symptoms never occur "out of the blue." The timing and life context of their presentation frequently involve developmental challenges and offer essential clues as to the nature of the evolution, meaning, and conflicts central to the anxiety symptoms. Such developmental tasks include strivings toward independence, intimacy, and role-related success, such as are necessary to proceed with school, college, marriage, pregnancy, parenting, and career success, to name a few normative developmental changes. Effective anxiety treatment should define and address ego weaknesses and conflicts that disrupt or inhibit these developmental tasks.

DEVELOPMENTAL VULNERABILITIES, CONFLICT, AND REGRESSION

Developmental vulnerability, intrapsychic conflict, and regression are all crucial elements to consider in the evaluation of the onset and persistence of panic and anxiety disorders (Arlow, 1963). We posit that patients with panic and anxiety disorders struggle with particular developmental issues from early in their lives. They often feel unsafe or unable to manage on their own and believe an attachment figure is required for security. In the context of this fearful dependency, the normative developmental pressure that they experience toward autonomy and independence carries with it the threat of loss of needed attachment figures and frames the challenges that attend such autonomy, such as competition, rivalry, and guilt. Developmental achievements such as assertion, success at work, sexual pleasure, and formation and maintenance of intimate relationships often feel like dangerous acts of aggression and evoke fantasies that one has defeated and often destroyed a rival. Particular stressors, including traumatic events that threaten attachment, can also exacerbate this fear of loss.

People who ultimately develop panic and anxiety disorders maintain a central, organizing fantasy of being more immature and less competent than they are in reality. Actual or perceived separations become highly threatening for such individuals, triggering anxiety symptoms amid feelings of intense helplessness and dependency. Accompanying their regressive fantasies of being incapable, anxiety patients demonstrate an intolerance of affect and an inability to self-soothe. They often have a propensity toward primary process and magical thinking. Patients' shift to a focus on their body rather than on their feelings is also characteristic of earlier developmental modes of processing emotions.

Alternatively, patients may generally view themselves as capable and competent, but may develop a sense of inadequacy and fear of autonomy in the context of a regression triggered by intrapsychic conflict. These patients often link being assertive and competent with anger and aggression and unconsciously fear that any autonomy they develop may destroy their attachment figures. Seeing themselves as helpless and incapable, hallmark features of panic and anxiety disorders, can help to defend against these images of themselves. A sense of weakness and inadequacy fuels the same feelings of incapacity and rage that initially give rise to the anxiety.

PANIC AND ANXIETY TREATMENT AND THE DEVELOPMENTAL PERSPECTIVE

In PFPP-XR, the process by which such vulnerabilities and conflicts are defined, understood, and addressed involves the complex task of integrating clinical material from several related domains. As symptoms and behaviors of distress, avoidance, helplessness, and dependency recur during the course of treatment, it becomes possible to directly examine these experiences and related fantasies with a sharply clarified understanding of fears of more adult functioning. The developmental history and the context of presentation are informative in this regard. The brief treatment frame of panic focused psychodynamic psychotherapy—eXtended range (PFPP-XR), with explicit focus on treatment termination, facilitates the emergence of issues surrounding separation and autonomy. As such, these conflicts become directly accessible to intervention, particularly within the transference, which may contribute to the large, measurable therapeutic effects in PFPP-XR.

An understanding of regression is an essential aspect of the treatment frame in PFPP-XR. For example, when a young adult at the threshold of independent living begins to experience panic attacks, the therapist should investigate the nature of his fears of being alone, feelings of incapacity, and fears of losing family support through greater independence. In addition, the therapist pursues an understanding of the nature of the impediments to more progressive and adaptive functioning. From the dual perspectives of conflict and development, the onset of panic and anxiety disorders can be considered to be a potentially defensive effort to avoid the challenges of more independent functioning.

PFPP-XR works by identifying and addressing problematic perceptions, conflicts, and defenses that operate in the context of developmental challenges. Clarifying these specific developmental challenges can be enormously helpful to patients in gaining an understanding that their panic attacks and anxiety do not occur "out of the blue" and therefore are potentially understandable and hence manageable. Elucidating ego weaknesses allows the therapist to confront fantasies that intensify fears of separation and progressive autonomy. Thus, therapists can address patients' fantasies of incapability, which persist despite their ability to function effectively in many areas of life. The therapist can demonstrate how primary process thinking and somatization, aspects of a regressive mode, can lead patients to view threats as coming from their bodies rather than arising out of their mental lives. Identification of unconscious fears and fantasies about autonomy, such as loss of important attachments or fantasies of damaging significant others through developmentally normative wishes for greater independence can detoxify these threats, reducing the pressure toward regression.

Case example

A married woman in her mid-30s, Ms. H, presented for treatment with increasingly frequent panic attacks in the weeks following the birth of her second child. She described the onset of panic during her first semester of college. She had matriculated at a school sufficiently far from her home to require several hours' air travel. Her first panic attack occurred while starting her initial trip home. Over the ensuing years, her symptoms became increasingly generalized.

Ms. H was the only child of parents who divorced when she was 5. During their tumultuous marriage, Ms. H had been witness to her mother being physically abused by her alcoholic father. Despite her father's abusiveness, after the divorce and his departure, Ms. H idealized him and yearned for his further involvement in her life, a wish that was only irregularly gratified. In this disappointment, she felt rejected, failed, and "forsaken." She idealized her mother as well, whom she described as tremendously deserving of respect and admiration. A working-class laborer, Ms. H's mother struggled relentlessly to advance the social station of her daughter and successfully negotiated her acceptance to a private school attended mainly by children of affluence. In her devotion, according to Ms. H, her mother prioritized little else in her life, and Ms. H felt her mother neglected herself and her appearance and grew to look haggard and unkempt, especially in contrast to the affluent parents of Ms. H's friends. In her single-minded and self-sacrificing devotion to her daughter, Ms. H's mother likely contributed to her own early and sudden death from heart disease 10 years before Ms. H came for treatment. In the setting of the affluent private school and in her friendships with children of intact families, Ms. H felt deep gratitude for her mother's devotion, but also an intense, guilty shame about her mother's impoverished appearance and of her own provenance.

Ms. H remarked, "My mother was a sweet, gorgeous woman, my best friend, my idol. We were super close. Since her death, I have always chased after the feeling that I had with her. I am constantly looking for that feeling—of someone loving you that much—that way of being safe."

In the safety of the treatment it became possible to clarify and define how Ms. H struggled with intense feelings of guilt and fear in her conscious ambition to become a successful and independent adult woman, mother, and wife. To succeed was to satisfy her mother's wishes for her, even as it involved forsaking her identification with her mother and some loss of the fantasy of closeness to her. Success and independence had become linked to an experience of loss, separation, and guilt. Independence represented an abandonment of her mother in fantasy and a reckoning with what she construed were the inevitable dangers of adult womanhood and wifedom—as exemplified by the physical abuse and abandonment suffered by Ms. H's mother. The onset of her panic attacks was understood in the therapy to have occurred at her crossing the threshold into young adulthood: of success and movement away from the complicated, guilty relationship with her mother.

At the time of her presentation to the study, these conflicts were vividly revived on the occasion of becoming a "mother times two," an achievement her sad mother had never accomplished. To Ms. H, one meaning her panic attacks carried was that of a restoration of her identification with her damaged mother. In psychotherapy, Ms. H was able to more fully understand her childhood memories of "not wanting to grow up," sucking her thumb and using "baby words" until she was 6, resisting independence upon each new threshold. She gained convincing perspective on how over time, and particularly after the birth of her second child, she had become inattentive about her physical health, in this way assuming aspects of her mother's pitiful self-neglect. She said she had come to feel like and thought that she looked like her mother. Clarification of these themes, recognized with increasing definition and perspective, afforded the development of a newfound and exciting sense of recourse from feeling forsaken, guilty, helpless, and panic-stricken. Ms. H was able to newly contemplate how the dangers she anticipated attending adult independence—guilt in forsaking, fear of being forsaken, the specter of harmful intimacy with a man—were a carryover from her childhood perspective and experiences. Ms. H was able to recognize the presence of these themes in her panic experiences.

In association with her understanding of these factors, her panic remitted. Ms. H became less vulnerable to guilt and fear in her independent activities and aspirations and was better able to affirm her substantial capacities. She began to proudly describe how she had become able to approach familiar experiences of anxiety with a newly confident sense of capacity, thinking of these experiences as opportunities both to learn and to further affirm a sense of herself as a capable adult woman and mother. She took newfound pride in her role as mother, feeling more comfortable as a peer with other mothers, even assuming a leadership role in her children's school. She was able to undertake an active approach to improving her physical health status as well, no longer bound in identification with her debilitated mother. She recognized that she could have matriculated to a college closer to home but had not, owing to her strivings for independence. She was able to newly take comfort in appreciating how her independent strivings were consonant with those that her mother had cherished for her.

Termination revived the familiar anxiety that had attended so much of her autonomy and progress heretofore, although this time it became possible to contemplate anxiety in this context more comfortably. She observed how "this is a strange process.... The feelings in ending are the same as those that were part of the original problem." In her concluding sessions Ms. H was able to newly tolerate sadness in ending the relationship with her therapist, and she was able to recognize and reflect on the associated sad memories of movement away from her mother with less guilt, a sense of prideful accomplishment, and much less fear or need to undermine her achievements. Ms. H achieved panic remission, and as of her last contact, 6 years post-treatment, she remained in remission.

Part II

Treatment

Chapter 6

The framework of panic focused psychodynamic psychotherapy—eXtended range

This chapter provides an overview of the concepts of the *treatment frame* as well as core principles of how to conduct psychodynamic psychotherapy. These include the following:

- Letting the patient guide the content of the sessions
- Following the patient's associations and affects
- Not being directive or giving advice

Panic Focused Psychodynamic Psychotherapy—eXtended Range (PFPP-XR) includes a modification of these basic psychodynamic techniques, as the therapist guides patients in identifying how emotionally laden ideas, conflicts, and affects relate to a growing dynamic understanding specifically of their anxiety disorder.

Another crucial modification of the framework of psychodynamic psychotherapy in PFPP-XR is its time-limited format. PFPP has been tested as a 24-session, twice-weekly treatment for patients with primary *DSM-IV* panic disorder (Milrod, 2007). The preset termination and brief nature of the treatment make it essential to explore the patient's reaction to termination for at least the final eight sessions. The time limitation and the emotional intensity this engenders can permit therapists and patients to identify and articulate reactions to separation more rapidly than they might otherwise in more open-ended treatments. This may be an advantage in treating people for whom a heightened and complicated response to separation is such a pivotal part of their vulnerability to panic and anxiety.

GENERAL FRAMEWORK OF TREATMENT IN PSYCHODYNAMIC PSYCHOTHERAPY

The framework of psychodynamic psychotherapy consists of a set of concepts, techniques, and agreed upon practical arrangements that constitute the therapeutic situation in which transference, resistance, and related conflicts can be recognized, clarified, and understood by both participants. Basic components of this treatment framework include the following:

- Management of confidentiality and disclosure
- The format of meetings
- Session schedule, frequency and length
- The overall duration of treatment
- Orientation to dynamic unconscious phenomena
- Consistency
- Flexibility
- Technical neutrality and the nonjudgmental attitude of the therapist
- Therapist activity and related interventions

The psychodynamic clinician anticipates that patients inevitably bring highly patterned expectations and reactions to various aspects of the treatment situation related to their preexisting fantasies, conflicts, and sometimes barely recognized emotional states. Examined within a suitably established framework, these reactions provide vital information about key conflicts. Such reactions are often manifestations of transference and resistance that occur in the treatment relationship itself and are thereby particularly accessible for therapeutic work in an emotionally convincing manner. Correspondingly, departures by the therapist from the established parameters previously listed can be examined independently by the therapist as possible enactments of countertransference or as other responses to patients' transferences.

In the clinical practice of psychodynamic therapy, organizing principles can be described, although there are few, if any, rules. Employing these principles, witting and unwitting departures and mistakes are inevitable. The rationale for thinking closely about the treatment framework is to minimize unwitting and recurrent mistakes, such as problematic enactments with the patient, which then render complex clinical phenomena more difficult to understand.

Willingness on the therapist's part to work flexibly with the patient's behavior in the service of furthering the understanding of anxiety and its meanings may contribute to both therapeutic efficacy and retention in psychodynamic treatment, as has been observed in PFPP (Milrod, Leon, Busch, Rudden, Schwalberg, Clarkin, et al., 2007). For example, the therapist may initially note but not comment on recurrent lateness or missed sessions. Over time the therapist identifies such behavior as a form of resistance and works with patients to understand the feelings and fantasies they may be attempting to manage or defend against through these actions.

In the section that follows, definitions and rationales for the basic components of a treatment framework are provided. Modification of certain aspects of the therapeutic frame of open-ended psychodynamic psychotherapy for PFPP-XR is then discussed.

SPECIFIC COMPONENTS OF THE FRAMEWORK OF TREATMENT IN PSYCHODYNAMIC PSYCHOTHERAPY

Confidentiality and disclosure

Effective psychodynamic psychotherapy involves facilitated disclosure of the most intimate aspects of the patient's inner life. Establishing conditions in which confidentiality is assured and understood by both participants is an essential aspect of the treatment frame. The confidentiality of communications between patient and therapist is afforded the highest levels of regulatory and legal protection. To the extent that patients express specific concerns, setting an effective treatment frame obliges that practical protections of confidentiality be explained in a factual, straightforward manner. Similarly, potential reasons for communication and disclosure to third parties should also be defined at the outset of treatment.

After practical assurances have been provided, patients are advised to verbalize their thoughts with a minimum of self-censorship. Communications initiated by the patient outside of scheduled sessions (e.g., telephone or e-mail correspondence received between regularly scheduled sessions) should be brought back to scheduled sessions for further discussion. Impediments to disclosure, both conscious and unconscious, are inevitable and understood to comprise a form of resistance to experiencing painful or frightening ideas, affects, and their associated fantasies. Working with such resistance is one of the core aspects of this treatment (see Chapter 3). However, until realistic concerns regarding confidentiality are addressed, it is not possible to identify the more central underlying conflicts relevant to self-disclosure and anxiety.

Recurring questions and concerns regarding confidentiality, once the principles have been clearly articulated and established, should be approached as an expression of resistance and deserve exploration. Typically, the expression of such concerns suggests that material of particular significance is emerging. For instance, a patient may suddenly exclaim, "You can't tell anyone about this, right?" before discussing a particularly difficult topic. Persistent concerns may also stem from patients' difficulties with trusting others, which can then be further articulated.

Although clinicians who have not had the experience of videotaping their patients might imagine that videotaping sessions, as has been conducted in the PFPP studies, would aggravate resistance and confidentiality concerns, this has not been found to adversely affect the process of treatment (Busch et al., 2001). This finding may indicate that once confidentiality is adequately articulated (patients sign informed consent for videotaping in our studies), the treatment framework provides a powerful basis for self-disclosure.

Consistency

As much as possible, changes and variations in setting, schedule, and therapist behavior should be minimized to facilitate recognition of resistance, transference, and conflict. Although inevitable, variations from the established framework can become powerful distractions, which can accentuate resistance and disrupt the therapeutic process. The therapist also demonstrates consistency in his efforts to understand the patient. Patients typically experience consistency in practical arrangements and in the behavior of the therapist as reassuring. For such reasons, consistency may have particular significance for patients with severe anxiety disorders, for whom conflicts involving dependency and separation play a central role (Busch et al., 1991; Shear et al., 1993).

Flexibility

Although consistency is important, overly strict or rigid management of treatment parameters can itself become a powerful distraction, accentuating the challenge of engaging or retaining the patient in treatment. Requests for changes in schedule, communication outside of sessions, and other departures from the established treatment framework are best approached, at least initially, with a focus on understanding the motives that underlie such behaviors, rather than with prohibitions, or setting limits without an attempt to understand the meaning of what patients are doing.

Limiting therapist self-disclosure

Beyond professional qualifications, the therapist should reveal little personal information. Curiosity about the therapist offers a robust opportunity to understand important transference material and should be approached therapeutically. Rather than provide direct answers to personal questions, such as would be appropriate in social situations, the therapist helps patients understand the greater value to their understanding of themselves by exploring the meaning and context of this curiosity. Self-reflection of this sort is a skill patients gradually learn in treatment. Limiting self-disclosure is essential because of the therapeutic complication of premature closure that comes with specific knowledge about the therapist. Apart from direct verbal communication of personal information, office décor, family pictures, personal memorabilia, and effects are all sources of information that assume exceptional significance to patients in psychodynamic work. In fact, such specifics are important to all patients in all clinical settings, but it is in psychodynamic treatment that patients have the opportunity to explore these meanings. Substantial information about the therapist is also freely available on the Internet. Optimal technique does not oblige a cloistered existence for the therapist, although it does involve mindful regard of opportunities lost or gained in communicating personal information and of the powerful potential distraction afforded by offhand factual answers to seemingly unobtrusive personal questions. While the therapist's reactions to patients are generally not communicated, some schools of psychoanalytic thought have argued for such revelation in specific situations. Discussion of this topic is beyond the scope of this book, although therapist self-disclosure would be more difficult to employ effectively in a short-term anxiety focused treatment than in longer, or more open-ended psychotherapy.

Technical neutrality

Therapeutic interventions primarily aligned with adaptive and integrative functions of the patient's ego, neither proscribing nor promoting motives, are described as *technically neutral.* This therapeutic stance aids in the emergence and comprehension of subjective experiences including motives, behaviors, perceptions, fantasies, wishes, and fears. Technical neutrality does not imply indifference to patients' suffering and does not in any way preclude an attitude of interpersonal warmth and deeply held concern for the patient, essential attributes of the therapeutic stance.

Case example

Ms. I, a 51-year-old woman with severe, chronic anxiety that interfered with sleep and kept her nervous all the time, particularly at work, presented during an episode of heightened anxiety in which she experienced recurrent choking sensations. These sensations were so severe that she could not sleep and had to cut back at work. Although the depth of her fears seemed irrational to her, she earnestly believed she was dying from throat cancer. She ate only oatmeal for fear of making her throat worse. She had undergone extensive medical workups and was informed by several doctors that her symptoms were "emotional" and that she needed psychiatric help.

In psychotherapy, it emerged that her heightened anxiety and fears of choking had begun soon after her sister, Laura, 2 years her senior, had physically attacked her and tried to strangle her, an experience that Ms. I found almost impossible to integrate. To illustrate the extreme state of confusion she experienced about this, although she refused ever to enter Laura's house again (appropriately), fearing Laura's erratic, homicidal behavior, she continued to nurture fantasies of wanting to "be closer" to her and to "normalize relations." Focus in therapy on Ms. I's lifelong denial of her sister's and her other siblings' hostility toward her and one another and her habit of pretending that "I'm from a normal, happy family," which could not have been further from the truth, was accompanied by anxiety remission. After several months in therapy in which Ms. I and her therapist explored her relationship with all of her siblings, Laura was diagnosed with recurrent colon cancer, needed chemotherapy, and asked Ms. I to accompany her.

Ms. I warily agreed, yet almost immediately she was beset by anxiety, agitation, and coughing. She had a feeling that Laura's needs were unbearable and overwhelming, particularly because Laura had taken to calling her at all hours of the day and night with endless complaints and intrigues involving their other siblings and unassuagable worries she did not want to know about. The therapist noted that Ms. I had been feeling well until she agreed to accompany Laura to her chemotherapy, yet since then she was plagued by feelings of guilt about not wanting to go, "when I ought to," and also with a deep anxiety accompanied by overwhelming anger. Ms. I had the clear sense that she was still too angry at Laura to see her, much less to care for her.

The therapist maintained neutrality in this situation, which meant that she did not take "sides" with either the guilty, self-punitive aspect of Ms. I's feelings that led her to agree to help Laura nor with the enraged, vengeful aspect to her feelings. Instead, the therapist highlighted Ms. I's conflict to her, linked the conflict to her recrudescence of anxiety, and continued to help Ms. I to explore reasons that Laura's request felt so overwhelming at this moment. This exploration ultimately permitted Ms. I to make a more rational, less conflicted choice about how she wanted to pursue her relationship with her sister.

Therapist activity

Verbalization by the therapist is the essential therapeutic intervention in psychodynamic psychotherapy (see Chapter 7 for further discussion of the terms and concepts describing classifications of interventions). An explicit goal of psychodynamic treatment is to help patients acknowledge, tolerate, and integrate previously avoided aspects of their experiences. In psychodynamic psychotherapy, particularly time-limited psychotherapy, the therapist is mindful from moment to moment of the need to calibrate the level of activity and the type of verbal intervention that will best address the current mental state of the patient. We now discuss some guidelines for helping to determine an appropriate activity level.

Supportive and clarifying comments typically precede interpretive comments. As increasingly difficult, painful, and frightening material is approached, as it inevitably will be in any effective treatment, a greater level of activity by the therapist is typically required to manage resistance and to facilitate further verbalization. However, overactivity on the part of the therapist with advice, direction, counsel, or reassurance, however well intentioned, may interfere with progress as it can disrupt patients' free associative process and the emergence of threatening material. Overuse of silence may also preclude the progress of treatment.

As with all psychiatric treatments, verbal interventions can have both intended effects (furthering understanding and exploration and symptom relief) and side effects (increased resistance or worsening symptoms). The therapist should be alert to how patients respond to the intervention (facilitation or resistance, fluctuation in symptoms) and adjust her subsequent comments accordingly. In the context of treatment that has been sufficiently explained to patients, uncertainty, perplexity, and confusion may be a defensive expression of anxiety or anger that would be better approached by trying to further articulate the experience rather than by emergently trying to bring relief.

As much as possible, the therapist should allow each treatment session to proceed according to patients' agenda of concerns and according to their increasing capacity to think about their experience. Achieving this goal obliges the therapist to actively facilitate verbalization by patients while scrupulously avoiding the imposition of extraneous structure or organization on patients' communications. However, in PFPP-XR, a therapeutic focus will always include linking ongoing emotional material back to symptoms of anxiety. Facilitating progressive exploration of patients' reactions to emerging material is a basic component of managing the treatment framework and is fundamental to the process of psychotherapy. Even as parameters and principles are established and maintained, each treatment unfolds in a unique sequence and pattern, according to highly individualized factors. These factors constitute component considerations of the psychodynamic formulation, which is further discussed in Chapter 4.

THE SPECIFIC FRAMEWORK OF PFPP-XR

PFPP-XR is an empirically supported psychodynamic psychotherapy, distinguished from other forms of psychodynamic psychotherapy by symptom focus, defined duration, and a set of modified techniques that inevitably follow from the introduction of these parameters. The short-term nature of this treatment, which has been tested in a 24-session, twice-weekly format, has significant impact on the psychotherapy. The intensity of a brief treatment allows for the emergence of feelings and conflicts in a more rapid way than would be the case in an open-ended treatment. Although in some instances anxiety inducing, the pressure of the time limitation in PFPP may permit patients to more rapidly develop the capacity for reflection about their anxiety symptoms. The activity of the therapist may be a particularly good match for passive, needy patients, such as those with severe anxiety. The time limitation and the ensuing emotional intensity facilitate and oblige therapists and patients to identify and manage reactions to separation more rapidly than they might otherwise in more open-ended treatments. This may be an advantage in treating people for whom responses to separation are such a pivotal part of their vulnerability to anxiety.

Therapists can anticipate feeling pressured to get a complete enough picture of patients' dynamics. The time limitation introduces the need for listening on the part of the therapist that requires an active search for opportunities to rapidly enhance patients' understanding of core psychodynamics of panic. The therapist tries to strike a balance at every turn between exploring material and making observations and interpretations that are adequately accurate to be useful.

OVERVIEW OF TREATMENT

PFPP-XR can be divided into roughly three phases of treatment. Although these phases can be divided to some extent into early, middle, and later periods, the focus may vary significantly for different patients. For example, transference may emerge as a prominent focus early in the treatment of some patients (commonly those with Cluster B pathology and agoraphobia), and concerns and anticipation of termination may need to be addressed quite early with others.

In the first phase (see Table 6.1), interventions are aimed at exploring and relieving anxiety, panic attacks, and phobic avoidance. The therapist focuses on the circumstances preceding anxiety and panic onset, thoughts and feelings during anxious episodes, and the meanings of anxiety symptoms. As this exploration proceeds, the therapist is able to formulate psychologically meaningful issues involved in the genesis of patients' anxiety, panic, and avoidance. This includes conflicts about separation, anger, and sexuality as well as feelings of guilt, as described in Chapter 9.

In the second phase of treatment (Table 6.2), the therapist explores the mental configurations that elicit patients' anxiety symptoms in greater

Table 6.1 Phase I: Treatment of acute anxiety and panic: Anxiety symptoms carry psychological meanings and PRPP-XR works to uncover unconscious meanings to achieve relief.

Phase of treatment	*Therapist Focus*	*Expected Responses*
Initial evaluation and early treatment	Exploration of circumstances and feelings surrounding anxiety onset Exploration of personal meanings of anxiety symptoms Exploration of feelings and content of anxiety episodes Common psychodynamic meanings, including: separation and autonomy, anger recognition, management and coping, sexual excitement, and guilty self-punishment	Panic and anxiety relief Reduced agoraphobia and avoidance

Table 6.2 Phase II: Treatment of anxiety and panic vulnerability: To lessen vulnerability to anxiety and panic, core unconscious conflicts must be understood and altered.

Phase of treatment	*Therapist Focus*	*Expected Responses*
Treatment of anxiety and panic vulnerability	Addressing conflicts intrapsychically, interpersonally, and in the transference	Improved relationships Less conflicted and anxious experience of separation, anger, sexuality and the need to punish oneself with anxiety (guilt)
	Working through—demonstration that the same conflict emerges in many settings	Reduced anxiety recurrence

Table 6.3 Phase III: Termination: Termination permits reexperiencing of conflicts directly with the therapist so that underlying feelings are articulated, understood and rendered less frightening.

Phase of treatment	*Therapist Focus*	*Expected Responses*
Termination	Reexperiencing central separation and anger themes in the transference with termination	Possible temporary recrudescence of symptoms as feelings are experienced in therapy New ability to manage separations, autonomy, anger, and guilt

Note: Patient reaction to termination should be addressed for minimally the final third (1 month) of treatment.

depth and the dynamic underpinnings of them, including developmental factors. As patients' unconscious conflicts emerge in therapy, dynamic connections are actively sought with the emotional configurations that occur during anxiety events. During this phase, the intensification of the transference allows for increasing work on patterns in relationships as they can be seen emerging in the relationship with the therapist. The goal of this phase of psychotherapy is to reduce vulnerability to anxiety through increased acknowledgment and understanding of intrapsychic states (improved reflective function) along with increased tolerance of affects and fantasies. Such internal shifts also lead to changes in problematic aspects of interpersonal relationships.

The third phase of treatment (Table 6.3), termination, permits reexperiencing of conflicts surrounding anger, autonomy, and separation directly with the therapist so that underlying feelings and fantasies are further articulated, understood, and rendered less frightening. A new ability to manage separation, autonomy, anger, and guilt will aid patients in managing intrapsychic and interpersonal conflict independent of the therapist after the therapy ends. Patient reaction to termination must be addressed minimally for the final third (4 weeks) of treatment.

Chapter 7

Some techniques of psychodynamic psychotherapy as they apply to panic and anxiety disorders

WORKING WITH DREAMS AND OTHER FANTASY MATERIAL

In his early work, Freud (1900) referred to dreams as the "royal road to ... the unconscious" (p. 608). Although the centrality of the use of dreams in psychoanalytic treatment as the most unalloyed expression of patients' central unconscious fantasies is currently debated, dreams continue to be one of a number of valuable sources of information about patients' unconscious fantasy life. Reasons for dreams' centrality revolve around their use of *primary process* (i.e., irrational, nonverbal) thinking and their symbolic, affectively charged, sensual nature. Symptoms, such as the physical symptoms of panic attacks and anxiety, involve the use of the same primary process and immature and symbolic aspects of the mind (see Chapter 3); hence, unraveling underlying meanings related to these symptoms can be seen as equally central in psychodynamic psychotherapy as the understanding of dreams.

For patients with panic disorder and other anxiety disorders, who often have a propensity to somatize and disavow their emotional states and impulses, dreams can take on a central significance in the therapeutic unraveling of the meaning of symptoms. A description of the techniques of dream analysis is beyond the scope of this volume, but a case example is presented in which a dream is instrumental in revealing important core fantasies about a patient's anxiety symptoms and intrapsychic life.

Case example

Ms. J, a 14-year-old eighth grader who presented with the acute onset of severe panic disorder with agoraphobia that did not permit her to be alone even for a few minutes, had been troubled by a recurrent dream that she brought to the attention of the therapist during the second week of her twice-weekly psychodynamic psychotherapy. In the dream, she saw herself climbing up an endless ladder that seemed to be precariously placed over a cliff or abyss. Her mother was above her on the ladder, and Ms. J was aware of her mother's skirt brushing her face in an irritating way. She couldn't see much because of the skirt and was terrified.

She associated to the dream over several sessions, at a time when she again had the dream. She said that before she had gotten ill with panic, her mother had frequently made her feel confined or squelched because of her mother's unreasonable anxieties about the dangers of the city. In particular, her mother seemed to object to Ms. J's attending coed parties, with what Ms. J felt were just excuses about transportation.

THERAPIST: Why do you think they're just excuses?

PATIENT: Because, she never does that when I have to travel around the city with my girlfriends. It's ridiculous. She's constantly lecturing me that I'm going to get pregnant! I don't even have a boyfriend, but she's been saying this to me since I was 12.

THERAPIST: How come?

PATIENT: I dunno. I guess since I got my period. It's totally retarded; she treats me like I'm from her stupid culture where girls get pregnant when they're my age. But I'm not from her culture; I'm from here! She just doesn't get it.

THERAPIST: You talk as though there's something about her culture that you object to. [*Mother was a Latin American immigrant*]

PATIENT: I dunno, it's okay. Just there are some stupid things about it, like this thing with women. They lose their brains around men. It's disgusting! I'm American. I could never be like that.

THERAPIST: In the dream, you're stuck on this scary ladder, following your mother. Have you ever had the thought that there's something about your mother's behavior with men that upsets you?

PATIENT: No, I don't think so. [*Here, the patient became thoughtful and was preoccupied throughout the rest of the session*]

In the next session, Ms. J again seemed preoccupied and talked about being angry with her mother. Toward the end of the session, she made a slip about her half-sister's age that embarrassed her. With exploration, it emerged that the embarrassing thing about the slip was that it belied her knowledge that her parents had been having an affair while her father had been married to his first wife and that she owed her own existence to her mother's not having used adequate contraception during this relationship.

This case highlights an example of how a central unconscious fantasy (in this example, the unconscious, conflictual identification with mother's sexual mores as she enacted them in the events leading up to this patient's conception) can be contained within a dream and how the careful exploration of the dream can provide the patient with an opportunity to learn more about her unconscious conflicts and fantasies.

CLARIFICATION AND CONFRONTATION

Clarification and confrontation represent techniques in which the therapist brings feelings, thoughts, and behavior to the attention of the patient. According to Greenson (1967), confrontation involves making psychic phenomena evident to the patient's conscious ego, and clarification aims at placing psychic phenomena in sharp focus. Many authors feel that confrontation and clarification cannot be sharply differentiated. Clarification enlists the observing ego of the patient to gain distance and a degree of objectivity toward the experiencing self. Clarification lays the groundwork for interpretation. An example of this technique is the therapist pointing out that the patient always talks about terminating the treatment before the therapist's vacations. Another example would be the therapist clarifying to the patient that he is no longer a helpless child and that therefore his helpless, powerless image of himself is a distortion of reality in accordance with long-standing childhood feelings and fantasies. According to Bibring (1954):

> Clarification ... does ... not refer to unconscious (repressed or otherwise warded off) material but to conscious and/or preconscious processes, of which the patient is not sufficiently aware, which escape his attention but which he recognizes more or less readily when they are clearly presented to him.... Clarification in therapy aims at those vague and obscure factors (frequently below the level of verbalization) which are relevant from the viewpoint of treatment; it refers to those techniques and therapeutic processes which assist the patient to reach a higher degree of self-awareness, clarity and differentiation of self-observation which makes adequate verbalization possible. (p. 755)

Clarification is a necessary tool in the psychotherapeutic approach to patients' gaining a more objective view of themselves and also can be essential in understanding their childhood history.

For patients with anxiety disorders, these techniques are often extremely useful in psychotherapeutic work around the anxiety or phobic symptoms per se. Panic and anxiety patients often experience normal physical variations in their body (e.g., feeling hot, cold, or hungry) as being signs of underlying illness or disease. Their fantasy that they are sick and desperately in need of help becomes easily confused with reality. Clarifications about emotional states being the source of physical sensations, given the somatic focus of defenses, are almost universally essential in the treatment of anxiety patients.

Case example

Mr. K, a 19-year-old male college student with panic disorder and obsessive-compulsive disorder, frequently complained to his therapist about believing himself to be ill because of myriad tiny physical sensations. His complaints were often about how hot, cold, or hungry he was or how well he remembered barely studied course material. He often became frightened about intermittent abdominal pain, which seemed to be associated with irregular bowel habits. Mr. K construed ghastly interpretations of the most minimal alterations in his body and believed himself at one and the same time to have lead poisoning, Lyme disease, and AIDS. Internists had assured him that he was in robust physical health. The following dialogue comes from the fourth month of treatment.

PATIENT: I know you probably think I'm crazy, but last night I was thinking that I'm sure that there's lead in the water in my apartment. It's possible, you know. All the problems in my life could be due to lead poisoning.

THERAPIST: Of course it's possible that there's lead in the water, but the fact is that you do seem to prefer to assign frightening interpretations to your physical sensations rather than to think about how anxious you've been since exams began.

PATIENT: I know I do that. But the point is I could be sick too. I could be in treatment for years for my emotions when really it's lead poisoning. I know my doctor said I'm fine, but it's hard to believe.

THERAPIST: Reality doesn't carry as much weight for you as your scary fantasies do. Also, you know that you always feel frightened about trusting people. You feel that about your internist, and also about me, here. But the truth is that when you get particularly anxious, your assumption is that the feelings you're having are physical.

PATIENT: Yeah. I wonder why I do that. Actually, if I spent any time thinking about how much work I have left to do in the next 3 days, I'd completely lose it. I'm really in danger of getting Fs this time.

Successful clarifications aid in further exploration of the patient's fantasies. They help the patient to feel less threatened by terrifying misperceptions, thereby facilitating further, more detailed exploration. In Mr. K's case, it was only after the therapist pointed out his fear of trusting people in charge, and his need to see his problems as being "physical," that the patient was able to begin to explore his sense of physical vulnerability that had arisen following a childhood sexual seduction.

SIGNIFICANT INTERPRETATIONS

Interpretations involve the therapist's defining dynamic patterns in the patient's mental life. They may come in several forms, including identifying the patient's use of defenses (defense interpretations), aspects of intrapsychic conflicts (dynamic interpretations), the link between present and past experiences (genetic interpretations), and the relationship with the therapist (transference interpretations). Interpretations appear to be significant when changes in symptoms, behavior, or therapeutic process are noted subsequently. However, it is not always clear to which portion of the interpretation the patient is responding and what precisely the patient has heard the therapist say. It is a common experience for most therapists to have patients' paraphrased repetitions of what they believe the therapist has said to differ in many ways from what the therapist believes he has said. These differences can often be accounted for by the intense transferential and countertransferential overlay that develops between therapist and patient in the psychotherapeutic setting. This process has been elaborated upon extensively in many formats and goes beyond the scope of this manual (see Jacobs, 1986).

Changes occurring as a result of significant interpretations do not necessarily occur immediately subsequent to the interpretation. This makes the assessment of the utility of any given interpretation complicated. A period in which the interpretation is stated in different contexts and ways is often necessary (the process of *working through*). Much important interpretive work often precedes significant interpretations, making them possible. When a "significant interpretation" is successful, it brings about a process of recapturing of early memories, affects, or fantasies relevant to the childhood experiences that are operative in the patient's current situation and connects the transference with developmental conflicts. Changes can be seen following the interpretation in the elaborated material that the patient brings to treatment, in the flow of the associations which the patient reports, and in the severity or content of symptoms.

Case example

A young woman, Ms. L, experienced panic attacks when enraged with her boyfriend, with thoughts that she needed his help and that he was not helping her because he was mean and did not care. This interplay had been explored over a series of sessions. The patient's panic attacks had grown more frequent and disturbing since entering treatment one month previously. (An exacerbation of symptoms sometimes occurs in the early course of treatment and does not necessarily indicate that the treatment is failing. Instead, it may indicate that the therapeutic relationship is intensifying and that the patient's conflicts that gave rise to anxiety are emerging in the therapeutic relationship.)

THERAPIST: So what occurs to you about how much worse your panic attacks have become since you started coming to see me last month?

PATIENT: I don't know. This is the worst I've ever been in my life. Doesn't say too much about the treatment, huh? [*laughing*]

THERAPIST: You know, I think that's a very important point. I think you feel like I don't care about you and like I don't want to or can't help you, just like you've been telling me you feel about your fiancé. I think you've been feeling as furious at me as you have at him. It's very uncomfortable for you, having such mixed feelings about me. That's why your panic attacks are so bad now.

PATIENT: [*laughing*] It's you! You're my problem! I guess this is really interesting. I don't know what to think about this.

It was only when the therapist made the interpretation to the patient that her panic attacks were worse since entering treatment because she was enraged at the therapist and felt that the therapist "didn't care and was not helping," that the patient seemed to gain insight into an important dynamic underpinning to her panic. Her panic attacks disappeared subsequent to this session. The patient began to produce a flood of childhood memories over the several sessions following the one described, of panic attacks in childhood, in which she had felt alone and terrified, in particular when she was alone with her older sister, who physically beat her when their parents were out.

Patients may find one interpretation to be particularly important and may return to it over and over in different settings, as Ms. L did subsequently with the therapist's interpretation about getting worse in treatment because she felt neglected by her therapist.

WORKING WITH TRANSFERENCE

In the course of Panic Focused Psychodynamic Psychotherapy—eXtended Range (PFPP-XR), the anxiety patient's conflicts in relationships become increasingly focused on the person of the therapist, allowing for more direct exploration. In this context, unconscious fantasies that underlie panic attacks and specific symptoms of anxiety emerge. The transference (Freud, 1905) is a powerful tool that permits the patient to reexperience affective states and fantasied aspects of relationships within the confines of the therapeutic dyad and to explore conflicts within the safe framework of psychotherapy. Careful focus on the transference is a central therapeutic element of psychodynamic psychotherapy, and proper work in this arena can aid in reduction of the vulnerability to the recurrence of anxiety and panic episodes. The occurrence of anxiety, limited symptom attacks, or full-blown panic attacks in the psychotherapeutic setting can sometimes help to identify highly specific triggers of panic otherwise inaccessible.

Care must be taken not to unnecessarily influence the nature of the transference with issues brought into the treatment by the therapist, as the transference provides a powerful window into the patient's unconscious fantasy life. For this reason, the therapist remains as professional and nonjudgmental as possible. Even if patients' fears and phobic concerns sound extremely unrealistic, they should be treated as real concerns, because the fantasies that underlie the fears are based on some core of historical reality that should be understood and not merely dismissed. Many highly anxious patients attempt to actively engage their therapists in the decision-making difficulties with which they struggle, trying to avoid the anxiety that attends active decision making. Giving advice is a pitfall that should be avoided. Disruption in the exploration of the transference is an important reason a psychodynamic psychotherapy should not be combined with exposure-based therapy. The goal of this form of psychotherapy is to help patients to make their own decisions, to take a more active role in their lives, and to understand why they are so frightened of taking charge, *not* to take over the executive functions of decision making.

Patients have real reactions to therapists as real people. However, even "real" reactions are influenced by underlying unconscious fantasies, which are important for the patient to explore and understand. The therapist should stay alert to the patient's feelings and fantasies about the treatment and the therapist as they arise.

It largely depends on the nature of patients' comfort in describing their reactions to the treatment situation and the therapist as to how rapidly and directly transference can be addressed. If the topic is skirted by the therapist for too long or if patients' cues are missed, it may reinforce anxious patients' fears that their negative feelings about the therapist are intolerable for the therapist, and hence off-limits, just as they often experienced their parents' reactions to these feelings. Therefore, when transference analogies can be made, they should be. On the other hand, early, aggressive focus by the therapist on the transference can be experienced as an attack or intrusion and is often met with denial and anger if too vigorously pursued. If patients become angry or anxious when their feelings about the therapist are touched upon, this phenomenon should be pointed out to them before further transference observations are made. This can often lead to valuable insights about their discomfort or resistance to examining the transference and will necessarily be connected to their problems with other significant relationships in their life.

Some panic and anxiety patients manage intense feelings about the therapist by never mentioning them or by not permitting themselves to acknowledge or experience them at all, in a similar way as other intense feelings are managed. These patients may experience intense transferences that, if avoided throughout the course of the treatment, can interfere with the reduction of anxiety and panic vulnerability. Interpretations can be pursued with a focus on extratherapeutic relationships, even if the displacement from the transference easily can be observed, until such time that patients can more readily discuss feelings about the therapist. Another approach in this type of situation is to focus on patients' reticence: for example, "One thing we know is that you don't wish to admit to any feelings about me at all."

Case example

Ms. M, a 24-year-old woman with panic disorder, frequently came to sessions feeling upset and hurt by one of a series of girlfriends whom she wanted to impress. Ms. M could cite many instances in these relationships in which she felt she had been slighted. In her fantasy, this was often on purpose. In psychotherapy, there was evidence that Ms. M frequently felt slighted by her therapist as well. Issues about the timing of sessions and the fact that her therapist had once been 5 minutes late for a meeting reinforced this fantasy. She did not openly express her feelings of hurt but instead kept them to herself and dropped inadvertent comments to her therapist about her therapist's "busyness" and how she thought that she was in the way. She denied feeling hurt by the therapist when the therapist directly pointed out her side comments to her on several occasions, and each time it was mentioned she seemed quite irritated that the therapist had brought it up. The following dialogue comes from the end of the third month of psychotherapy.

PATIENT: This really has nothing to do with you; it's just me, the way I talk.

THERAPIST: You seem set against our even thinking about why you've been telling me that you feel like your problems are in my way.

PATIENT: Well, it's just my stuff. It's irrational I guess. Anyway, it's embarrassing.

THERAPIST: How come?

PATIENT: [*crying*] I just feel so beholden to you and kind of dependent on you. I told myself that I'd never let myself get like that. How could I mean anything to you in the way our relationship means so much to me? Sometimes I feel that I just live from session to session, but at the end of our 50 minutes you just leave and go live your life, and I'm left hanging on.

THERAPIST: Why do you think it's been so hard to talk about this? I know that you think it's important.

PATIENT: I just feel I'll lose you altogether if I don't keep some of this to myself.

Chapter 8

Initial evaluation and early sessions

INITIAL EVALUATION

The initial evaluation of the patient with an anxiety disorder includes an assessment of specific anxiety symptoms. Although this period roughly corresponds to phase I of treatment, investigation of these factors, such as the circumstances of specific anxiety episodes, can occur at any point in panic focused psychodynamic psychotherapy—eXtended range (PFPP-XR). The psychodynamically oriented clinician explores patients' characters (e.g., features of their personalities that have evolved in response to ongoing unconscious fantasies that shape the way they respond to intercurrent stressors), developmental history, level of functioning, and perception of significant relationships. Patients' ability to express themselves in words is assessed to determine the types of interventions that will be of value early on in psychotherapy, as the therapist begins to link symptoms to psychological factors. In the evaluation, attention should be paid to topics that are uncomfortable or trigger patients' defenses. Throughout the initial evaluation, as throughout PFPP-XR, the therapist maintains the focus on anxiety symptoms and associated dynamics.

The following guidelines cover areas that we have found to be important in anxiety assessment. However, these guidelines should not be adhered to rigidly:

1. Assessment of anxiety symptoms and panic attacks:
   a. Symptoms as per the *Diagnostic and Statistical Manual of Mental Disorders*, fourth edition (*DSM-IV-Rev.*; APA, 2000a)
   b. Situations preceding anxiety onset: circumstances, feelings, stressors (losses, changes in location, alteration in level of responsibilities, relationships with significant others)
   c. Prior anxiety or panic episodes with associated symptoms, thoughts, feelings, circumstances of onset

2. Developmental history:
   a. Perception of parents and family life, with attention focused on the way anger, anxiety, physical illness, and other emotional topics were managed in the family; history of early losses and separations and how the family and patient were affected
   b. Childhood anxiety symptoms: school phobias, shyness, fears, and worries
   c. Adolescence: Dependence/autonomy conflicts, relationships, struggles around control, anxiety management; the way anger, separation, and sexuality were handled
   d. Adult relationships: The types and quality of relationships patients conduct with significant others, including the nature of the conflicts, levels of responsibility with which the patient is comfortable, and degree of assertiveness versus passivity
3. Assessment of the patient's ease of adaptation to a psychodynamic approach: This includes the ability to think psychologically, to describe relations to others, to make dynamic connections, to put feelings into words, and to maintain curiosity about one's motivation and role in one's difficulties. This assessment has no bearing on how well the patient will do in dynamic therapy; the development of these capacities is part of the work of PFPP-XR. Rather, this will help the therapist evaluate in what form he will introduce the link between intrapsychic factors and symptoms.

The patient's motivation to work in psychotherapy and to take the process seriously can have an important impact on outcome (Malan, 1979). Motivation is often very high for anxiety patients when they begin a new treatment, as they experience such a significant degree of distress about their symptoms. As patients can have a rapid relief of symptoms, the therapist may need to communicate the value of exploring psychological vulnerabilities to anxiety recurrence. The therapist should actively verbally note dynamic themes that emerge during the assessment to the patient as a part of the evaluation process to begin identifying the psychological meanings of the anxiety.

Case example

Mr. N sought treatment for his crippling panic disorder only when the severity of his panic attacks, agoraphobia, and obsessional ruminations had become so compelling that he had to drop out of college. At the time of his first session with the therapist, he was preoccupied with the fantasy that he had acquired AIDS during a social encounter with a homosexual male friend, during which they had watched pornographic movies together.

Although he was aware as he entered the office that the concern about AIDS was probably unrealistic, he was initially not able to expand further about the reasons for his anxiety.

THERAPIST: From what you've described just now in your history, it sounds like you're frequently this anxious but that your specific concerns change.

PATIENT: Well, that's true. But now, I think that the other things I've worried about in the past were silly compared with this. [*Pause*] You know what, though? I always think that no matter what I'm worried about.

THERAPIST: It sounds like you think there's a pattern to your anxious concerns.

PATIENT: If you had said that to me yesterday, I wouldn't have agreed. But now that you say that, I think I'm starting to think that it's true. The bottom line is I always think I'm going nuts.

THERAPIST: Do you have any idea why you tend to think these things?

PATIENT: No. Well, yes, actually. I think my parents are crazy and that they've messed me up somehow.

THERAPIST: That sounds like quite a disturbing thought.

PATIENT: Well, I guess it is. How'd I get like that?

In this exchange, the patient indicates that he has the capacity to think about his feelings in a more objective, detached way than he had been aware of heretofore and that he can connect past emotions with his current situation. Mr. N demonstrates his curiosity to understand why he has these disturbing fantasies. Within this brief interchange, he has been able to connect his symptoms with fantasies that he has about himself and his family, and he has followed the therapist's exploratory leads by pursuing underlying thoughts. Over time, the therapist helps the patient to develop the ability to step back and look at his feelings and fantasies, a curiosity about how his mind works, and an interest in the therapist's ideas.

Treatment options and psychoeducation

Treatment options should be discussed with patients, although the relative values of various interventions are not a focus of this book (see introduction). The choice of treatment should be based on research findings and, importantly, patient preference. Psychodynamic psychotherapy can be encouraged if it is thought to be the recommended treatment (i.e., the patient has Cluster C pathology; Milrod, Leon, Barber et al., 2007).

In contrast to cognitive-behavioral treatments, psychoeducation is not a central focus of the psychodynamic treatment of anxiety. However, some psychoeducational techniques can be used to deepen exploration in this treatment. For example, an educational statement can be made to the patient during the evaluation about the patient's diagnosis and, if he expresses interest, the neurophysiological underpinnings of the disorder. However, our in-depth knowledge of neurobiological underpinnings of anxiety (Busch, Oquendo, Sullivan, & Sandberg, 2010; Gorman, Kent, Sullivan, & Coplan, 2000) is not specific enough to explain why at any particular moment a patient is experiencing distress and significant anxiety (Milrod, 1996). Therapists may make an educational comment such as, "You are fearful about a heart attack, but your doctor has stated there is nothing medically wrong with your heart." However, the PFPP-XR therapist follows this statement up with, "Therefore we need to understand why you continue to hold on to this fantasy."

It is important that the therapist behave in a calm and assured but empathic manner with the patient. In offering the previous information, the therapist states clearly to the patient what the problem is and how treatment will address it. A preliminary psychodynamic formulation (see Chapter 4; Viederman & Perry, 1980), including a description of the meaning of the anxiety, may be offered to the patient at the end of the evaluation. The therapist is active and educates the patient about how psychotherapy works: for example, that dreams, free associations, wishes, and conflicts are important mental constellations that can be used to explore the patient's unconscious fantasies, which contribute to anxiety symptoms. The twice-weekly treatment minimum is recommended to achieve a relationship of sufficient intensity with the therapist for transference interventions to convincingly carry emotional weight.

Relationship with the therapist

Anxiety patients can have special difficulties in the way they develop a therapeutic alliance. For many patients with anxiety disorders, the establishment of an alliance with their therapist can be experienced as the most frightening yet the most important part of the treatment. An alliance is established over time and is fostered by the therapist's openness and willingness to discuss patients' symptoms and concerns clearly as well as by the therapist's ability to mentalize the patient's mind and communicate this to the patient (Fonagy & Target, 1997). Questions about how the treatment works should be taken seriously and should be carefully explained. This is true at any point in the course of the treatment, although patient confusion about the process of psychotherapy becomes increasingly influenced by transferential fantasies as therapy progresses. It is against the backdrop of this helpful, professional yet friendly relationship that the evolution of transference must be observed.

Patients with panic and anxiety disorders are intensely anxious and often require a significant amount of reassurance that their problems can be effectively treated. The therapist should provide this reassurance, telling patients that anxiety symptoms typically respond well to treatment. Reassurance and psychoeducation are essential tools in all treatments, but these techniques are employed in psychodynamic psychotherapy to calm patients enough to permit exploration of the underlying meaning of symptoms.

Engaging the patient

Some patients readily engage in the psychotherapeutic process in an effort to understand the psychological origins of their panic attacks and severe anxiety. However, others show little interest, either due to character style, an inability to see the relevance of psychological issues to their panic attacks, or defensive denial. The therapist can often rapidly engage patients' interest and curiosity by demonstrating how anxiety symptoms may be related to their current and past mode of conducting themselves. The therapist can connect the anxiety and its associated fantasies with ongoing emotional concerns that patients have had throughout their lives.

Case example

During the course of her initial evaluation, Ms. O, a 28-year-old woman, said that she failed to see the relevance that her relationship with her mother had in connection with her panic attacks. This was striking, as she had described her mother as controlling and suffocating, and suffocation was a sensation that she experienced during her panic attacks. She lived alone with her mother and was in constant struggles with her. The therapist approached this topic with a careful exploration of the precise experience Ms. O had during panic episodes. Ms. O had mentioned that she would begin to scratch her skin.

THERAPIST: Can you tell me something about that experience?

PATIENT: Yes, I feel very upset at that point. But I'm not sure why I do it.

THERAPIST: Have you experienced this feeling or behavior at any other point?

PATIENT: Well, yes when I'm upset at someone and in a fight. But I'm not panicking then. I have it when I'm fighting with my mother.

THERAPIST: What do you think it means for you then?

PATIENT: Well, it gets her to be quiet. It's one of the only ways to get her to stop attacking me. Yes, that's quite interesting that it's the same as in my panic attacks. In some ways, I experience some of the same things when I'm fighting with my mother that I feel when I'm panicking, although I'm more angry than anxious. After the fight, my mother stops talking to me and I begin to feel like a terrible person. That's when the panic feelings start.

This was a beginning stage in the patient's new awareness of the connection between the subjective experience of suffocation and her rage with her mother and how both were related to her emotional state during her panic attacks.

Developing the patient's capacity to be psychologically minded is an important part of psychodynamic psychotherapeutic work. The therapist provides useful examples of psychological factors that emerge in the patient's panic and anxiety experience, as previously illustrated. Patients can generally make use of this material and usually elaborate on the formulations presented by the therapist, adding details, and altering the formulation to apply to their situation more exactly. This is part of the process of developing the capacity to reflect on one's symptoms.

The sense of humiliation about symptoms

A common source of difficulty in engaging panic and severe anxiety patients in treatment is the significant feelings of humiliation that they experience about having anxiety symptoms. It is not uncommon for patients with these symptoms to be invested in thinking of themselves as "strong" and to have very high expectations of themselves about having control over their feelings. This is often a reaction to the experience of anxiety and panic attacks creating feelings of incapacity, immaturity, and weakness. This emotional setup can prove to be a difficulty for patients in allowing themselves to become engaged in treatment, as patients often feel that they are too embarrassed to acknowledge the extent of their symptoms to anyone, including themselves or their therapist.

The therapist should be aware of the extent to which patients feel the need to deny their symptoms. Gradually, opportunities arise in therapy that enable patients to acknowledge how much of their lives is curtailed by anxiety symptoms that they have been attempting to avoid.

Case example

Mr. P, a 30-year-old man, had always seen himself as a "strong person." He felt that he needed to be strong and that any sign of weakness would be viewed as humiliating by himself and others. He felt that his parents had an expectation that he never demonstrate weakness. He described his father, whom he took as a model for his behavior, as "never getting upset or depressed." Mr. P's anxiety and panic attacks developed in the setting of a series of stressors, including his marriage and a promotion at work that entailed increased responsibilities.

He was frightened that he would be unable to perform at his new job and would be fired. As his anxiety mounted, he became increasingly worried that he would be rejected or abandoned by his wife for needing her help. This conflict added to his feelings of abandonment and panic, as he felt more alone and in danger of losing everything.

THERAPIST: How did your wife respond to your telling her about your anxiety?

PATIENT: Oh, really well. She was very supportive. But I had the sense that she would get sick of it, especially as I went on and on.

THERAPIST: You really don't feel she can handle your anxiety.

PATIENT: [*tearful*] No. Deep down, I don't feel she can. I just feel that she will see me as weak and lose interest.

THERAPIST: You seem to feel that when you need help there is no way to express it without risking being abandoned by others.

PATIENT: Yes, I think that's true. And I know that she is responsive to me. But, I don't know, I've always felt I needed to be strong. Maybe I can try to let that go a little.

Mr. P's panic attacks resolved after his first two weeks of therapy, although he remained in PFPP-XR to address issues related to his vulnerability to panic.

Case example

Ms. Q, a 21-year-old student, came to psychotherapy for a variety of pressing anxiety symptoms, including panic attacks and an embarrassing fear of being alone or driving a car. A tough-talking late teenager, she prided herself on always being rational, unlike her girlfriends or mother. Ms. Q was able to admit that her anxiety symptoms were highly embarrassing to her and were in fact the part of herself that she most disliked. She nonetheless had extreme difficulty talking about her scary thoughts and fantasies in therapy. The therapist had to ask about Ms. Q's symptoms often while Ms. Q smiled pleasantly and minimized their impact.

It remained difficult to gather much information about the fantasies underlying her anxiety for some time, as she said that she could not remember thoughts she had that were in any way connected with the symptoms. She remembered no dreams from any point in her life. Ms. Q said that she was in less distress since starting to see her therapist, but the reasons for this remained obscure. "I just need to keep coming," she said, "I don't know why." Her panic attacks had resolved within 2 weeks of starting psychotherapy.

The next month, she arranged plans to move to another city for a summer job to live with her best friend. Weeks in therapy were taken up with the details of her summer apartment and work. The therapist said to her that it seemed that she felt that the summer would liberate her from many of her concerns, including her school work, and her anxiety symptoms, which she continued to describe as having been in the past. The patient agreed merrily.

One week after leaving for the other city (2 months after her initial presentation), Ms. Q called her therapist, saying that she would be in town the next week and would like to see her. When she came to the office, Ms. Q said that things had "kind of gone wrong in [the other city]" and that she had been shocked by how upset and frightened she had been there. She had changed her mind, had given up her summer plans, and decided she would continue to live at home with her parents for the summer. She sheepishly said that she would resume therapy for the summer.

PATIENT: It's really not that big a deal, though; I just like it here.

THERAPIST: Well, it is rather a surprise. I know how much you were looking forward to your summer plans.

PATIENT: Yeah, I was, but I figured out that I just didn't want to be there. And it's no problem with Marcy. She's not mad. I helped her to find another roommate. So it's fine.

THERAPIST: I can tell that you don't want this summer retreat to be a big deal, but I really think it's important for us to look at exactly what happened in .... It seems familiar because we've just been talking about how so often you really try to hide the extent of your worries even from yourself.

PATIENT: Yeah, it is what we've been saying. [*laughs with bravado*]

THERAPIST: Well, I think that the sudden change of plans gives us the opportunity here to explore what happens for you when you get really scared. I know that this whole experience must make you feel very embarrassed, like you're a baby, right at a time that you've been trying to be more independent from your parents. I do think, though, that if we don't explore it better than we've done up to now that it will probably happen again, and I know you really don't want that.

PATIENT: I know. I just have to move out of my parents' house soon. This can't keep happening!

It was only after this point that the patient was able to become more actively engaged and curious about her own thoughts that were so frightening to her and was able to use her therapy in an exploratory manner in a more effective way. This case is particularly illustrative, in that the patient's panic attacks had disappeared almost immediately when she initially started her psychotherapy, although nothing substantive had been understood about them in the treatment. However, the therapist knew that this had been an apparent "cure" that was at risk of backfiring, given the extent of the patient's intolerance of the acknowledgment of the breadth of her symptoms and her unwillingness to confront the role played by separation fears in her panic onset. It had been predictable that when she interrupted her therapy, even briefly, her symptoms would reemerge.

EARLY SESSIONS

PFPP-XR initially targets the psychological meanings surrounding anxiety and panic disorder onset. Most commonly, patients begin early sessions with descriptions of anxiety symptoms since these symptoms are often compelling. Useful probes in this situation include the following: What occurs to you about the anxiety experience as you tell me about it now? Do you have any idea what you could have been worried about? What comes to mind about specific points?

However, if patients do not begin by describing their anxiety, the therapist should eventually pursue the symptoms and attempt to relate the material presented to anxiety or panic states. Primary areas of focus in treatment include feelings and circumstances surrounding anxiety onset, the meanings of individual anxiety symptoms, and the feelings and thoughts accompanying anxiety episodes. In the course of psychotherapy, patterns emerge as to particular stresses and thoughts and feelings that precede anxiety states that the therapist must communicate to patients. Brief connections may be made such as, "So at the time of your first symptoms you were dining with a friend at a restaurant that called up specific memories," or "At the time of your first panic attack, you were alone in your room reading something that stirred up a specific disturbing thought."

Stressors preceding anxiety onset

Patients with anxiety disorders often present their symptoms as having come "out of the blue" with no clear origin. However, studies indicate that meaningful life events typically precede panic onset (Faravelli, 1985; Klass et al., 2009; Roy-Byrne, Geraci, & Uhde, 1986). From a psychodynamic perspective, the patient's view of the illness as coming "out of the blue" represents a defense against the intense emotions that the precipitating events engender. The therapist must explore with patients significant life events that contributed to anxiety and panic onset and their potential emotional significance. An example of eliciting this information from patients is presented in the following case example of early treatment.

Case example

Ms. R, a 16-year-old mother of a 1-year-old, presented to the hospital emergency room with the complaint of the sudden onset of "confusional events" over the past 3 weeks. On evaluation, which included a neurological workup because of Ms. R's choice of focus in describing her symptoms, it emerged that she was having panic attacks for the first time in her life. The attacks included prominent feelings of loss of balance and tachycardia as well as a sense of impending doom. Initially, Ms. R could think of nothing different in her emotional life that could have been responsible for these changes.

THERAPIST: So, you really can't think of any way your life is different or has changed since you started having the panic attacks?

PATIENT: No. There's nothing. I just sit at home with my daughter. I have a boring life.

THERAPIST: What are your plans?

PATIENT: Well, actually, I've been thinking of joining the Army lately. I've gotten all the material. I just received it in the mail last month. It looks great: They'll pay for me to go to college and graduate school. It's really going to be the only way I can afford to do what I want.

THERAPIST: What'll happen to the baby?

PATIENT: I can leave her with my grandmother during the week and see her on the weekends. It's not ideal, but of course it was ridiculous for me not to get an abortion given my age.

THERAPIST: What does your husband think of your plans?

PATIENT: Oh, he's hysterical, actually. He thinks he'll lose me. He wants me to stay home. I'm sure that's why he wanted to get me pregnant in the first place, come to think of it. But this is my *life*! I have to go. It will break my heart not to be around the baby, but in the end it's for her.

THERAPIST: And your grandmother?

PATIENT: [*laughing*] She's pretty upset too. They love me. They don't want me to go away. I've never been away at all, ever.

THERAPIST: When was all of this to take place?

PATIENT: Well, before I got sick, I was in the middle of applying. It was supposed to be for next month. I've had to put it off now.

THERAPIST: With all of this in the air, I'm particularly struck by your saying that nothing's different in your life.

PATIENT: [*laughing*] So you really think this is connected?

THERAPIST: Yes.

PATIENT: Well, I hate to admit it, but I guess I've been a little scared lately. Things were suddenly going so fast. The idea of not seeing the baby almost kills me.

The psychological meaning of symptoms

Patients with panic attacks and anxiety disorders vary with regard to their symptomatic profile and the content of their anxious thoughts and fantasies. Minor individual variations in symptoms often carry specific psychological meanings for patients. Each symptom should be explored in depth with regard to its origins and psychological meanings. Some examples of this follow.

Case example

Ms. S experienced what were described as "typical" panic symptoms of shortness of breath and palpitations. She feared that she would suddenly die. Both of her parents had died at relatively young ages—her father in a car accident and her mother of cancer. The patient's profession, which entailed work with terminally ill patients, aggravated her lack of sense of safety about her body, with the feeling that it was prone to sudden deterioration.

PATIENT: Maybe having death so near at hand gets me more frightened. The scariest feeling is the shortness of breath. As soon as I experience that I begin to panic.

THERAPIST: What does this experience bring to mind?

PATIENT: Well, when my mother was dying from cancer, she became very short of breath. It was terrible seeing her that way, because it was at that point she realized that she was going to die. She became very tearful. I couldn't bear it.

THERAPIST: Had you ever seen her like that before?

PATIENT: No. Not quite like that. But after my father died she cried frequently. She was very helpless, and I had to take over things around the house. That was a terrible time for my siblings and me. It's interesting because I also feel helpless when I have a panic attack. I wonder if my shortness of breath is so scary because of what happened to my mother.

The panic attacks occurred after the patient had recollections of her mother, triggered by cleaning out her parents' home to sell it. This experience, along with other losses at that time, led to memories of the painful experiences of losing her mother, at first emotionally, when her father died, and later through her death. In fantasy, Ms. S had recreated these moments repeatedly during her panic attacks.

Case example

Ms. T described that one of her greatest fears during her panic attacks was that she would choke and suffocate while drinking. She revealed that when she was angry at other people, she often experienced the sense that she was physically suffocating. In therapy, she recalled early intense angry struggles during her childhood at the dinner table about her not eating and drinking enough.

PATIENT: I remember I wouldn't eat my food or drink. My father would get very angry and scream at me to drink. I felt forced to do it, like I might choke. I was really mad and crying.

THERAPIST: Did it feel anything like the experience of choking in panic attacks?

PATIENT: Yes, I guess it did, but I don't think I was panicking then. My father and I were always fighting over the years, and I often had that feeling.

These experiences became part of a combative, exciting, sadomasochistic relationship with her father that contributed to her anxiety. At the beginning of her treatment, Ms. T had described a hierarchy of frightening situations. Choking while drinking was at the top of the list. Ms. T had panic attacks, along with the feelings of suffocation, after experiences in which there were angry, exciting conflicts with her boyfriend.

Feelings during anxiety and panic

Although current definitions of anxiety disorders emphasize feelings of intense anxiety, patients often experience a wide array of feelings during anxious episodes. Several authors (Fava, Anderson, & Rosenbaum, 1990; George, Anderson, Nutt, & Linnoila, 1989; McGrath, Robinson, & Stewart, 1985) have described so-called anger attacks as a variant of panic attacks. Constellations of inhibited angry feelings frequently are an unconscious or conscious accompaniment to anxiety, and anxiety symptoms often carry other emotional valences. For example, they can symbolize an ambivalent longing for an absent other (Klass et al., 2009). Other common feelings during anxious periods include humiliation about one's perceived loss of control or feelings of confusion. The therapist should make efforts to parse the various feelings that occur during anxiety and panic attacks, as they form the emotional web that brings about the symptoms. This is illustrated in the following clinical vignette.

Case example

Mr. U, a 38-year-old, worried that he would leave his partner, even though he did not want to, because of his chronic and irrational feelings of jealousy. This was similar to what he had done in past love relationships. One evening, his partner did not seem to him to be as responsive as usual. Mr. U became frightened that his lover would suddenly end the relationship. He described a frightening feeling of potential loss. In this setting, he had a panic attack.

THERAPIST: Tell me more about what frightened you in the situation.

PATIENT: Well, I was very worried about how frightened I was. I felt crazy, and I was very embarrassed about it. I worried he would find out how crazy I was.

THERAPIST: And then what would happen?

PATIENT: Well, then he would reject me for how crazy I was, if he wasn't going to do it anyway. But rationally, I know there was really no problem at all. He wasn't about to end the relationship. Then later I was worried that I had offended him.

THERAPIST: In what way?

PATIENT: I asked him, "Why are you behaving this way?" I worried that offended him.

THERAPIST: You said it an angry way?

PATIENT: Yes, I guess I was angry at him. I don't like to admit that. I had a lot of different feelings. It was very confusing.

As the patient's feelings were explored further, he reported an increasingly complex array of emotions during his panic attack. Each feeling contributed to the experience of the panic state. Exploration in psychotherapy helped to reveal multiple roots of the patient's intense fears of loss and doom. This example demonstrates the complexity of possible transformations of anger. This patient had frequent thoughts of leaving his partner because he was jealous, yet he interpreted his partner's unresponsiveness as anger at him, which led him to fear that he would be abandoned. This common defense mechanism of projection, which serves to undo the passivity of dependent feelings, also functions as a punishment for conflicted fantasies of straying or for angry feelings.

EARLY TREATMENT: A CASE EXAMPLE

The following case is presented as an example of the first several sessions in the psychodynamic treatment of a patient with panic disorder. Ms. S, the patient referred to earlier in the chapter under "The Psychological Meaning of Symptoms," presented with panic attacks for which she had a full medical workup. The medical examination was negative, but she still was not fully reassured that she was medically safe. At first, the therapist reassured the patient about the nature of her illness.

THERAPIST: Your symptoms are consistent with panic disorder, which is a treatable psychiatric illness. The symptoms you describe—shortness of breath and palpitations—are part of this disorder rather than signs of a medical disease.

PATIENT: Well, that's very reassuring to know. It seemed as if I must have been having a heart attack.

THERAPIST: We want to try to understand what might be happening with you emotionally that might have triggered your becoming so fearful about your health.

This educational step had a calming effect on the patient, and the therapist was able to proceed to explore the situation at the time of panic onset. Ms. S said that she did not understand why she had panic, as there were no particularly difficult problems going on in her life at that time. In response to the therapist's questions, however, she revealed that she had been cleaning out her parents' house to sell it but had been "too busy" to let it bother her. She also reported that she had realized that a 15-year relationship with her boyfriend was "not going to go anywhere" but that this was no "boohoo."

She initially denied having any problems at her job, although she later said that she dealt with critically ill patients in her work (an "emotional drain") and was on the verge of changing jobs.

THERAPIST: What was it like closing up your parent's home?

PATIENT: Well, it was very busy. We didn't have time to think of anything.

THERAPIST: When was your first panic attack?

PATIENT: The day after we closed the house.

THERAPIST: Did cleaning up the house bring up memories of your parents' death?

PATIENT: Oh yes. We all talked about it. My father died suddenly when I was age 18. It was very hard on my mother, having to care for all of us. I couldn't stand seeing her like that. Later, I became very angry with my father; he left us with a lot of debts. [*The patient began to cry*] Then my mother died of cancer when she was only 55. It was terrible to see her when she realized she was going to die. It was very, very sad.

Later, the therapist discussed the patient's relationship with her boyfriend:

THERAPIST: Well, I'm not sure I understand completely. You've been going out with him for 15 years, and you act as if your realization that it is over is not significant.

PATIENT: I haven't been thinking about it. But I guess it is sad. I mean, my life is completely different now.

THERAPIST: In what way?

PATIENT: I'm not hanging around with any of the same people I usually do, but I'm still busy.

THERAPIST: It seems as if for some reason it's hard for you to acknowledge the impact of this change.

PATIENT: [*Crying*] Yes, I guess it's much tougher than I thought. It's very sad, after all this time. Do you think these events were connected to my developing panic?

THERAPIST: Yes. Patients often experience losses preceding the onset of panic attacks. We need to understand more about the impact of these losses on you to help reduce your panic attacks. It seems as though it's difficult for you to acknowledge feeling very sad about big losses.

Early in treatment, the therapist made educational statements about panic disorder that were intended to reassure the patient about her symptoms and reduce her anxiety level. However, as in any psychodynamic psychotherapy, the therapist's goals were to encourage the patient's exploration of the origins of her panic attacks on a psychological level. The patient was using denial to defend against the emotional impact of the recent losses in her life (see Chapter 10 on defense mechanisms). With gentle confrontation, the therapist was able to demonstrate her denial by questioning the patient about how it was possible that she could not be affected by the termination of a 15-year relationship. In this confrontation, the therapist invited the patient to become an observer of her own mind, with the goal of increasing her capacity for self-observation, mentalization, and curiosity about herself. The meaning of the loss of her boyfriend and the loss of her parents brought up by selling the house were overwhelming to her in a way that was not yet clearly understood. Her panic attacks permitted her to focus on her body and to avoid acknowledging the magnitude of her losses and her feelings about them.

In Ms. S's case, there was evidence of ongoing characterological problems that contributed to the patient's vulnerability to panic. For example, the question of what had led her to be involved in a problematic relationship for 15 years and what had led to the realization at this point that it was not permanent that required exploration. The fact that the patient needed to deny her emotional states, causing her to have inadequate information about how she was reacting to stresses, also remained an important element in her predisposition to develop panic. Ms. S's panic attacks rapidly resolved, and she became more curious as to the origin of her current symptoms. Ms. S terminated her treatment after 3 months of weekly psychotherapy in a panic-free state.

Chapter 9

Common psychodynamic conflicts in panic and anxiety disorders

Through exploration of the circumstances and feelings preceding anxiety and panic onset, the therapist and the patient are able to develop an ever increasing understanding of the unconscious conflicts central to the genesis of the patient's panic attacks and anxiety. Themes that emerge over time in therapy often involve conflicts about separation and anger, the role of guilty self-punishment, and sexual conflicts. The therapist helps the patient to elucidate how these conflicts lead to anxiety symptoms. These conflicts are described in greater depth.

SEPARATION AND AUTONOMY

Fantasies surrounding separation and autonomy are often areas of conflict for severely anxious and panicking patients. There is indirect support for this ubiquitous clinical finding in the literature from several epidemiological sources. Weissman, Leckman, Merikangas, Gammon, and Prusoff (1984), in the Yale Family Study, found that the presence of panic disorder in parents conferred more than a threefold risk for separation anxiety disorder in their offspring between ages of 6 and 17. In both retrospective studies of the childhood histories of adults and prospective studies of children at high risk for the development of anxiety disorders (one or both parents have agoraphobia), there appears to be a relationship between separation anxiety disorder in childhood and the later development of agoraphobia in adulthood (Leonard & Rapoport, 1989). Studies suggest that children with behavioral inhibition (BI) to the unfamiliar are at risk for the development of separation anxiety disorder, agoraphobia, social anxiety disorder, panic disorder, and other anxiety disorders (Biederman et al., 1990; Kagan et al., 1990; Rosenbaum et al., 1988). Behaviorally inhibited infants and children "manifested long latencies to interact when exposed to novelty, retreated from the unfamiliar, and ceased play and vocalizations while clinging to their mothers" (Biederman et al., 1990, p. 21). Rosenbaum et al. (1988) found that 85% of offspring of parents with panic disorder and agoraphobia demonstrated BI at significantly greater frequency than a comparison group of children of probands with other psychiatric disorders. This risk may represent genetic or psychological vulnerabilities, or both. Biederman et al. (1993) found higher rates of multiple anxiety disorders, separation anxiety disorder, and agoraphobia in behaviorally inhibited children compared with children without behavioral inhibition at 3-year follow-up after initial assessment.

Patients commonly report that life events preceding panic disorder onset involve real or fantasized loss or separation. Reactions to interpersonal loss and separation are a common antecedent to panic disorder onset. Our group found that 73% of patients presenting to a psychotherapy clinical trial with primary (*DSM-IV-Rev.*; APA, 2000b) panic disorder had panic onset within 6 weeks of experiencing an interpersonal loss event, defined as death of a close attachment figure, breakup of a serious relationship or divorce, or miscarriage/abortion (Klass et al., 2009). Thoughts accompanying panic attacks and anxiety typically involve fear of being alone and abandoned, often with the fantasy of being unable to care for oneself. Patients feel incompetent and as if they cannot survive alone. A phobic companion is often felt to be necessary to protect against this and other dangers, consistent with the well-known association between panic disorder and agoraphobia (APA, 2000a; Deutsch, 1929; Freud, 1895, 1926; Klein & Gorman, 1987).

A psychodynamic psychotherapy of any anxiety disorder must therefore investigate patients' fears of separation and autonomy and their sense that they cannot function by themselves. These fears have their roots in conflictual childhood events and are connected to ongoing interpersonal difficulties. Early temperamental factors, such as BI, and emotional precursors, as described by Busch, Cooper, Klerman, Shapiro, and Shear (1991) and Shear, Cooper, Klerman, Busch, and Shapiro (1993), set the stage for a separation-individuation process riddled with disappointments and conflicts and for future (later childhood and adult) difficulties with modulation of anxiety and interpersonal intimacy. In addition to separation fears, they can develop conflicts about dependency, with both intense wishes to be taken care of and a tendency to suppress such wishes, which can be experienced as being overly needy or humiliating.

These issues necessarily arise in patients' developing relationship with the therapist. For example, many anxiety and panic patients worry about becoming "overly dependent" on their therapists, as they have felt in other important relationships. These fears can make it difficult for them to become engaged in psychotherapy, and they may frequently find reasons to miss sessions. Other patients become quite dependent on the therapist and respond with mounting terror or intense sadness or anger to changes in meeting times, therapist vacations, and looming termination; they may come very early before sessions. The therapeutic setting, by its very nature, provides many natural inroads for exploration and reemergence of this important set of conflicts.

Case example

Ms. D, the 34-year-old woman discussed in Chapter 3, first developed panic disorder while driving herself from one city to another, en route to her 21st birthday party, which she had conceptualized as her "final independence" from her family. Prior to her first panic attack, she had been terrified and excited that this birthday meant that she would become an adult. During her initial panic attack, she had to pull off the road and was unable to continue driving. In her panic state, she felt she needed her mother to come and pick her up. For the next 8 years, Ms. D had multiple daily panic attacks and was unable to go out alone, to hold a job, or to continue in school. In ironic contrast to her fantasy that her 21st birthday party symbolized her independence from her mother, this event ultimately marked the beginning of her being totally unable to function in the most basic ways without her mother.

Not surprisingly, when she did enter psychotherapy years later, Ms. D's conflicts about independence and intimacy immediately came to the fore. She frequently canceled sessions or forgot them, which was ultimately understood as being connected with her very mixed feelings about not wanting to need help yet desperately feeling that she needed to be assisted by someone else, feelings that were reevoked in intense form as she started her psychotherapy. As in her relationship with her mother, the patient expressed fears of becoming dependent on the therapist and feared that if she did, the therapist would not respond to her needs. One month after the patient began her treatment, the therapist told her, "The last thing you want is for me to become important to you. I think you believe I'd never be there for you if that happened, and you'd be hurt and frightened by how angry it makes you."

"You're right," Ms. D replied. "Sometimes I feel it would kill me."

This interchange helped the patient to understand her acting out and enabled her to attend her sessions more regularly. This set of understandings, related to Ms. D's resentment of, yet equally strong desire for, autonomy, touched on the conflicted interpersonal and transferential nature of some of the meaning of her panic symptoms.

ANGER

Clinical observations suggest that patients with anxiety and panic disorders have intense difficulties tolerating and modulating their angry feelings and thoughts (Busch et al., 1991; Shear et al., 1993). Fear of anger and the conscious and unconscious vindictive fantasies that accompany these feelings when they arise are frequent precipitants of panic attacks. The therapist must approach the patient in a manner that facilitates exploration of angry feelings and the accompanying fantasies that are perceived as dangerous. A nonjudgmental stance is important as these patients often need, for a variety of defensive reasons, to see themselves as "not angry." Helping patients become aware of unconscious anger and to explore why they are afraid of it is an important tool in anxiety resolution. Helping patients distinguish fantasies from realistic concerns and handle anger in an effective way are also crucial parts of PFPP-XR.

The way patients' families historically managed anger can be informative. Familial difficulties with management of rage or hostility are manifested not only by a history of overt family acrimony and violence. Parental expressions of anxiety can also be understood by children as an expression of rage. For example, parents may be consumed with fears about their children's well-being and safety at times when children break rules, such as coming home late after curfew, which they know angers the parents. Patients' unconscious childhood understanding of the often unstated significance of parents' anxiety symptoms becomes incorporated into fantasies about the meaning of the expression of their own rage and anxiety symptoms. A child can intuitively understand his parent's reaction formation, and this awareness can develop into a pervasive way anger is understood and processed.

Common fantasies are that rage or its expression will result in abandonment or loss of the people on whom one most depends. Unconscious homicidal fantasies in the context of loving feelings can be central in patients' difficulty in mastery of intimacy and separation. These fears are not necessarily connected to actual experiences of childhood but can nonetheless represent compelling childhood fantasies.

Conflicts about tolerating anger can make it difficult for patients with anxiety and panic attacks to discuss their feelings and fantasies directly in their treatment. For example, some patients have observed uncontrollable anger in their parents and have been frightened that they would be harmed. These fears necessarily translate to the current psychotherapeutic relationship and can contribute to patients' reticence about expressing anger. Thus, historical factors must be incorporated into the therapist's understanding of the meaning of patients' anxiety and panic attacks and in the timing and structure of therapeutic interventions. Inhibitions in discussing these topics in psychotherapy often can be noted in relationship to patients' fear of acknowledging angry feelings toward the therapist, who necessarily serves as a model for their important, conflicted relationships.

Case example

Ms. V, a 42-year-old woman, presented for treatment of her second episode of panic disorder after a 4-year respite from panic attacks. A review of the history of her more recent panic episodes indicated that conflicted, and at times unconscious, rage at people she loved often preceded the onset of her symptoms.

PATIENT: In the fall, I felt like I had all the burdens for the family. My husband was particularly busy at that time, and he was never around to help me.

THERAPIST: How did you feel about that?

PATIENT: Overwhelmed at times. Particularly when he complained about something I did, when he didn't even try to help me with the decision.

THERAPIST: Did that make you angry?

PATIENT: Yes, it did. And then, in addition to that, my mother was ill, and she and my brother expected me to take care of her. I don't see why I had to take care of her, particularly when my brother was closer to her. But I still felt I had to do it. I was infuriated about that as well.

THERAPIST: What happened then?

PATIENT: Well, I began to withdraw from them and felt increasingly alone and angry. I began to have anxious periods. When I was anxious I didn't feel angry, just frightened. My son became an increasing burden. He clung to me instead of playing with other children. He kept waking me up at night, and I couldn't get a full night's rest.

THERAPIST: Were you angry at him as well?

PATIENT: Oh no. He's a child. He can't help it. But it did become frustrating.

The patient had been struggling with similar stresses and conflicts at the time of her first episode of panic disorder, which occurred shortly after the birth of her son 4 years previously. Her husband, a prominent lawyer, was particularly busy with his work, she was struggling with the demands of her new baby, and her mother had been ill. Notably, she routinely denied being angry at her child, although she experienced him as quite demanding. Instead, she said that he was "frustrating." This is typical of this patient's and other panic patients' struggle with angry feelings at people to whom they feel particularly attached (see Chapter 10 on defense mechanisms).

Consciously, this patient saw anger as a "waste"; nothing useful was accomplished by it. This was a conscious rationalization she used to protect herself from the distress she experienced when she became aware of her violent fantasies. She feared that her anger was uncontrollable and described a series of incidents in which she had either physically hurt people or feared that she would. For example, she had "found herself" brandishing a knife during a fight with her first husband. She said that her mother had reported "breaking her" of her anger in childhood, but the patient could not remember this.

Ms. V described a pattern of "indignities" that triggered the rage that often preceded her panic episodes. Typically, these were demands by others for her to take on chores or responsibilities that she did not want to do and that she found demeaning. For example, she felt that her family was unfairly demanding that she take care of her ill mother and felt guilty about being so angry at them. She also was worried that her mother might die. Exploration in psychotherapy revealed that these thoughts were in part related to "indignities" that she experienced at the hands of her mother early in life, when her mother had become very restrictive of her activities during her adolescence after ignoring her as a prepubertal child. When she became angry with her mother, her mother totally ignored her, leaving Ms. V feeling alone and abandoned.

In psychotherapy, Ms. V was able to see a connection between her anger and her panic attacks. She noticed that she began to have a limited-symptom attack after feeling increasingly angry with a colleague during an argument. An opportunity arose to explore these feelings in the transference, as Ms. V felt angry that the therapist was not able to prevent her anxiety, which had increased to near-panic levels in the setting of new stresses at home and work. The therapist told her that he thought she was enraged about the recurrence of her symptoms and felt abandoned by him too, just as she experienced her husband and others as being not caring and unresponsive about helping her, precisely as she had felt her mother had ignored her as a child. As she began to acknowledge her anger and as she reexperienced it in the transference with her therapist, her anxiety diminished, and she was able to be more assertive with her husband in seeking help in caring for their child.

GUILT AND SELF-PUNISHMENT

Guilty self-punishment and reactions to feeling guilty are core components of the dynamics of panic and anxiety disorders. Patients often experience guilt about a variety of unacceptable emotions and fantasies, including those surrounding anger and dependency. Many patients feel it is wrong or bad to experience such feelings, leading to denial or compensatory efforts in the form of undoing and reaction formation. Patients often feel they should be punished for these fantasies. Guilt and the urge for self-punishment can arise even when precipitants of guilt remain unconscious. Severe anxiety and panic attacks can often serve the function of self-punishment for guilt in the limitations and discomfort they bring. In addition, feelings of guilt can interfere with appropriate assertiveness with others, and patients' acceptance of hurtful and withholding behavior of others can serve as another form of punishment.

Case example

Mr. W, a 42-year-old high school counselor, presented for PFPP-XR after having struggled with panic attacks that began two years previously. At that time, he reported that he had increasing problems with his job, which involved work with adolescents from troubled homes who had drug or school attendance problems. He felt increasingly frustrated about the limited impact of his work. He believed that the adolescents he was responsible for did not have the value systems they would need to change their behavior and that their parents expected him to change their children by taking on the role of parenting not provided by often absent fathers. He felt compelled to play the role of a "miracle worker" and worked long hours. Expectations at his job had increased due to cutbacks in staffing at the school. Mr. W described "internalizing" his frustration with the job, as he felt that complaining to others at work would just create more problems for him or would be useless.

Mr. W described significant anger, regret, and disappointment over the limited relationship he had with his father growing up. He had five younger half-siblings (different father) and regretted not having played more of a paternal role with his siblings. He said that his mother's relationship with men was problematic and that he observed verbal and physical abuse of his mother by his stepfather. He described a traumatic turning point when his mother moved them to a nearby town to move in with his stepfather when the patient was age 11. At his new school he had few friends, was bullied, and his academic work suffered. He was reprimanded for being too aggressive, which he felt was necessary to protect against bullying. He was and remained angry at his mother for the move and at the lack of attention she paid to his problems at school, although he again said he "internalized" these problems and did not tell his mother about the extent of the bullying. The therapist pointed out that what Mr. W was calling "internalizing" his feelings seemed to serve the function of his avoiding dealing with them.

In PFPP-XR, Mr. W identified his emotional reactions that preceded his panic attacks, aiding his capacity to mentalize rather than "internalize" or deny his feelings. Upon exploring the precipitants of his panic episodes, it became clear that they were often triggered when he felt angry at the adolescents and families with whom he worked. He feared that his anger would become out of control, as his stepfather's had with his mother. It emerged that Mr. W also experienced intense guilt at those times, because he felt disgusted by his anger at students he was trying to help and because of his inability to help them. Thus, his panic attacks represented both his fear of his angry feelings in the setting of working with his students and guilty self-punishment: In the end, it was he who suffered such terribly debilitating anxiety. The therapist worked to further define the formulation based on the patient's past experiences.

THERAPIST: I wonder if you are trying to provide these students with the kind of parenting that you didn't receive.

PATIENT: Well, I never thought about it that way, but it makes a lot of sense. That may be part of why I get mad, because they won't take advantage of my efforts. I wish I had had someone like this to help me. Then I feel bad about getting so angry at them. They're just kids.

THERAPIST: Yes. And you respond to that by pushing yourself further to help them and get even more frustrated and anxious.

PATIENT: And you're saying that's when I panic—when I feel even more pressured, angry and guilty. I need to think more about that.

In this case, Mr. W's anger and guilt led to the defense of reaction formation, but his redoubled efforts at work only added to his feelings of frustration and sense of helplessness. The inadequacy he experienced and his sense of pressure with students and families were similar to feelings he had within his own family. Articulation of his anger at his students and how guilty he felt about it helped him to feel less frightened and self-punitive. He began to accept more of the limitations inherent to his job and pressure himself less, setting more appropriate limits with students and their families. He felt safer sharing his frustration with colleagues at work. In this context Mr. W experienced a resolution of his panic.

SEXUAL EXCITEMENT

For some patients, anxiety and panic attacks can take on a significance of their own, beyond the commonly experienced, manifest panic thoughts of being ill and dying or becoming "crazy." The anxiety and panic episodes themselves can be inherently arousing and may be closely tied to sadomasochistic sexual fantasies and conflicts. These patients frequently present complaining about their panic attacks but may be reluctant to be rid of them. Patients say that without the constant anxiety with which they have been living, life would seem "boring." The attacks provide excitement, which becomes a core segment of their identity ("It's part of who I am and it defines me"), and for some they consciously represent a distraction from more disturbing thoughts and fantasies.

Panic attacks, like any symptom, may take on various intrapsychic meanings for patients at different times. It is not until these secondary dynamic reinforcers of the symptoms are also articulated in therapy and alternative methods are found for the patient to cope with the underlying conflicts that the symptoms can be successfully relinquished. In the therapeutic setting, these dynamics may emerge in arousing struggles, often engineered unconsciously by the patient, with the therapist.

These issues can best be illustrated in the following clinical examples.

Case example

Mr. K, the 19-year-old man discussed in Chapter 7 who had multiple daily panic episodes, kept himself close to a panic state at all times by drinking quarts of strong coffee. When this was explored in psychotherapy, the patient reported that he "loved" the feeling of being so "wound up" that he was always close to a state of panic. "It's exciting," he said.

This patient became extremely anxious at times when he felt passive, "unmanly," or vulnerable. His early childhood history of having been sexually seduced by his mother was intimately connected with his fear of being passive. Staying close to a panicky, ultra alert state served to protect him from the disturbing passive longings that were unconsciously enacted paradoxically in the sense of dependency he experienced during his panic attacks.

With his therapist, Mr. K frequently initiated struggles about who was in charge, with the conscious feeling that he always wanted to be, even though he often begged "to be ordered" to do things, such as his homework. It was initially hard for him to acknowledge that he did this, but, as is often the case, a pattern of interactions that he engaged in with others was easier for him to appreciate when it was explored in the transference with the therapist's help. This example came from the second month of his psychotherapy.

PATIENT: Tell me what to talk about. I'm not going to talk about anything till you tell me what to say. I might talk about things that are unimportant and waste my time here.

THERAPIST: It sounds like you want me to order you around so much that you won't even talk without my prior approval.

PATIENT: Well, I don't know what's important. You do. You just don't want to tell me.

THERAPIST: At the moment, what does seem clear is that you feel that I'm neglecting you, that I'm depriving you of my knowledge, and that you're angry at me. But it does seem that this whole process, of being in a struggle with me, happens over and over.

PATIENT: I know. [*He grins and giggles*]

THERAPIST: It seems like there's something a little fun about being in a fight with me.

It gradually became clear that Mr. K found these struggles intensely exciting. He brought them about repeatedly and grinned and became physically jittery when they occurred. Teasing out these exciting issues and their relationship to his anxiety in the transference became important in this patient's relinquishing his panic symptoms.

Case example

Ms. X, a 27-year-old woman whose mother was a concentration camp survivor with an undiagnosed psychotic disorder, experienced her panic attacks during fights with her boyfriend, whom she occasionally provoked into hitting her, and also during sexual intercourse. As she became sexually excited, this patient had conscious fantasies of knocking her boyfriend unconscious with furniture. These thoughts routinely preceded her panic attacks, yet she was unable to experience orgasm without these fantasies. During her psychotherapy, she came to recognize that she experienced her boyfriend's sexual advances as physical attacks and that this frightened but also aroused her. It kept her "on edge." Her panic attacks did not always bother her. Although she found them frightening at times, when she initially presented for treatment she did not think of the attacks as something she could or would even want to, change. "They're this crazy part of my life," she said. "They don't always bother me."

Chapter 10

Defense mechanisms in panic and anxiety disorders

Patients' defense mechanisms are important in the treatment of panic and anxiety disorders because of their role in anxiety management and the way they contribute to symptom development. Defense mechanisms are a set of intrapsychic functions that serve to help a person to avoid unconscious frightening affects and fantasies. Patients with anxiety disorders may employ any type of defense, but clinical research and our own observations suggest that these patients use certain specific defense mechanisms frequently (Andrews, Pollock, & Stewart, 1989; Busch et al., 1995; Pollock & Andrews, 1989). We present a brief description of the most prominently observed defense operations in anxiety and panic patients, a description of how these defenses may operate, and some guidance about how best to approach them in psychotherapy. Defense mechanisms found in research to be commonly employed by patients with panic disorder include reaction formation, somatization, and undoing (Andrews et al., 1989; Busch et al., 1995; Pollock & Andrews, 1989). In addition, we have found that anxiety patients frequently use the defense of externalization in a similar manner to which they focus on their bodies (somatization).

REACTION FORMATION

Reaction formation is a defense mechanism in which an affect is disguised as its opposite. For example, rage can appear as an excessive amount of caring or concern, or a romantic attachment can be manifested by "hating," or criticism. Reaction formation is an unconscious mechanism that is frequently found in anxiety and panic patients, because it works to solidify a tie to a significant other at a time when that tie is experienced as being threatened by anger. The therapist should evaluate whether reaction formation is present when anxiety disorder patients incongruously raise how positively or negatively they feel about someone. They unconsciously may be masking the opposite set of feelings, which can be fruitfully addressed.

The following example represents a patient's use of reaction formation and demonstrates how it can be successfully monitored in psychotherapy to help the patient to gain further control over his life.

Case example

Mr. Y was a 26-year-old man who presented with a 9-year history of panic disorder. At the times of his most extreme symptomatology, he had seven to eight panic attacks per day. The attacks were intense experiences for him, because he had the sensation that he was suffocating. Although his panic attacks were brief in duration, between attacks he remained quite anxious, without autonomic symptoms, and had an almost constant sense of foreboding that "something really scary" might happen. The scary thing remained undefined but seemed to have a vague connection with the idea of Mr. Y's hurting someone else.

Mr. Y grew up on a large farm in a Western state and, at the age of 17 after the sudden death of his best male friend from a cerebral aneurysm, joined the Air Force. He remained in the Air Force for 4 years and was involved in active combat overseas. It was in the Air Force that he began to self-medicate for his extreme anxiety, first with heavy alcohol use and later with marijuana and benzodiazepines, which he obtained illegally. By the time he presented for treatment, he was physically dependent on high doses of Xanax and was using daily marijuana, but he had stopped all alcohol consumption. Despite this cocktail, he continued to have a constant sense of foreboding and experienced several panic attacks per week. He was aware of being consciously frightened of his anger. When he presented, he told his therapist, "My terror of getting angry makes no rational sense because I've never hurt anyone. I don't even think I've been in a fight since high school." He had not fired a weapon during his combat experience.

At the time of presentation, Mr. Y was involved in the process of breaking off a 2-year relationship with his fiancée. He initially described his reasons for doing so as, "We're just wrong for each other; I love her as a person, but I'm just not attracted to her anymore." However, it gradually emerged, over the first several weeks of psychotherapy that Mr. Y was locked in a raging, high-stakes battle with her, her friends, and her family and that although he could describe the events clearly he seemed to live as though he was unaware that there was a battle taking place at all. He was loath to acknowledge any angry feelings toward his girlfriend, even though he had ample objective reasons to be enraged.

Mr. Y reluctantly told his therapist that his girlfriend had stolen several thousand dollars from him that he had been painstakingly saving from working in a variety of different jobs to put himself through his senior year of college. Interestingly, Mr. Y felt that he might be being "unfair and chauvinist" to feel any anger about this, and his response at the time that he had learned about the theft had been, "Oh, well, she really needed the money, and she's much younger (4 years) than I am. I can't reasonably hold her responsible. She's not a mature person."

Once this event had taken place, at a time when Mr. Y by rights should have been reevaluating how much he could trust his girlfriend, he found himself unaccountably compelled to give her more money for other things that she needed, and for the first time in their stormy relationship he permitted her to physically hit him.

The gradual exploration of this reaction formation and the unconscious rage at his girlfriend that it symbolized, as well as the emergence of very violent fantasies about mutilating her in retaliation that he was trying to ignore (and were what made him describe himself as "chauvinist"), was central in permitting the patient to finally disengage himself, 4 months after starting treatment, from what had been a very masochistic relationship. This exploration also made it possible for him to stop smoking marijuana and to gain more control over his anxiety symptoms.

UNDOING

Undoing serves a similar purpose to reaction formation: It reassures patients (and the individual to whom they feel attached) that any negative affect that becomes conscious or is expressed has been retracted and disavowed. The use of undoing presents an opportunity for the clinician to note to patients how negative affects often have to be immediately denied. This can help patients gain awareness of the intensity of their discomfort with the feeling they are tentatively expressing.

Case example

Ms. V, described in Chapter 9, frequently used the defense mechanism of undoing, as in the following dialogue.

PATIENT: I got to where I really hated my husband, and believe me, I really love him.

THERAPIST: I notice that whenever you describe your anger at your husband, you then say how much you love him. It's as if you are reassuring yourself.

PATIENT: Yes, you've mentioned that pattern before, and now I'm beginning to see what you mean. I guess I'm less comfortable with my anger at him than I thought I was.

In this example, the therapist had pointed out the patient's tendency to make a comment that served to undo her anger on several previous occasions. Only over time did the patient become aware that this was her pattern and that it was an important clue to her degree of ambivalence. She became able to take a look at her experience of anger at the point at which she felt the urge to undo it. She learned that she became anxious and guilty after expressing anger toward someone to whom she was close, with a fear that she would be seen as a "bad girl" and would be rejected. She would then become inhibited and submissive and felt frustrated that she had not been able to express herself in the way she wanted. Her increasing knowledge about her feelings helped her to feel safer actually experiencing and expressing her angry feelings. This steady accretion of understanding by examining a conflict in a variety of situations is part of the process of "working through" (see Chapter 11).

SOMATIZATION AND EXTERNALIZATION

Panic and anxiety patients, because they tend to somatize rather than to acknowledge inner feeling states, often have difficulty with the process of looking inward. This problem can be viewed as an inherent aspect of patients' defensive styles, the same defensive style that contributes to the panic attacks or anxiety. Focusing on bodily concerns (somatization) and focusing on the problems of others (externalization) represent means of attempting to avoid addressing emotional states and conflicts. When these defenses arise in psychotherapy, the therapist needs to address them.

Examples of somatization are found throughout this text. For example, Ms. M, in Chapter 8, focused on subjective experiences of suffocation and scratched her skin to avoid direct feelings of suffocation and rage that she experienced with her mother. Ms. Q, also described in Chapter 8, experienced shortness of breath rather than think of the painful memories of her mother's demise. These patients initially did not see the connection between their feelings and their symptoms but were able to understand them over the brief few initial weeks of therapy.

In the case of externalization, some anxiety patients begin their treatment by focusing on the problems of others. A useful strategy is for the therapist initially to let patients continue discussing other people, looking for patterns in the way they view others. The therapist can encourage patients to look at their own role in their relationships with other people. If patients persistently focus on other people's problems and anxieties, the therapist can note to them that they seem to feel more comfortable focusing on the problems of others and can invite them to look at this. Following this, a connection can be made to patients about their likening their own anxiety to that of their friend, or it can be pointed out to patients that talking about other people's anxieties makes them feel less anxious in the psychotherapeutic situation, where they are discussing frightening topics. Which technique is chosen will be determined by the clinical situation and by the intensity of patients' needs for denial of the severity of their symptoms.

Case example

Ms. Z, a 13-year-old with panic disorder and an elevator phobia, had begged her mother to get psychotherapy for her symptoms. Although her problems had been long-standing, Ms. Z was beginning to feel that being so frightened so frequently was becoming more difficult. Nonetheless, when she began her twice-weekly psychotherapy, after describing her symptoms in detail in the first session, Ms. Z seemed to be unwilling to return to the topic of her phobia or her panic attacks. Instead, she spent her sessions describing her friends' problems to the therapist in detail. In particular, she focused on the anxiety symptoms of a close female friend. She described her friend's fears as "stupid" but occasionally added that she, too, knew what it was like to be irrational. The following vignette comes from the second month of twice-weekly psychotherapy.

THERAPIST: I wonder if you've noticed that you often tell me about H.'s problems.

PATIENT: Yeah, I guess I do. But she seems like such an idiot, worrying about these stupid things.

THERAPIST: I'm beginning to think that maybe you feel like there's something "stupid" or shameful about the problems you're having. Maybe you've been telling me about H.'s problems because they remind you of some of the difficulties that brought you to see me.

PATIENT: I dunno. Maybe.

Because of the urgency that is experienced during panic and anxiety episodes themselves, many patients have a need to prove to themselves and everyone else, including their therapists, that they are indeed strong and capable. For this reason, it is often a relief to discuss others. As described in Chapter 8, it is not uncommon for patients to view their anxiety symptoms as deeply humiliating.

If too many interpretations are given about others, externalization is reinforced, thereby aggravating the difficulty with inward exploration. A useful technique is to refer to a "part" of the patient feeling hurt or angry, as Anna Freud pointed out (cited in Sandler, Kennedy, & Tyson, 1980). This helps to emphasize the idea of intrapsychic conflicts being responsible for the production of symptoms. Another technical maneuver would be a statement about the conflictual nature of wishes, such as, "You are afraid of your wish to injure or sexually use or hit or murder and therefore need to talk about others struggling with these feelings."

Chapter 11

Working through and termination

WORKING THROUGH

Working through (Freud, 1914) is a gradual process in which patients' acquired knowledge of their conflicts and psychic functioning is steadily applied to increase their understanding of the way these conflicts affect various areas of their lives and their symptoms. This phase is helpful in reducing patients' vulnerability to anxiety and panic recurrence, as various ramifications of central conflicts and contributing factors to this vulnerability are explored. In the psychotherapeutic situation, the process is marked by repeating similar and deepening interpretations as they apply to different manifestations of the same intrapsychic phenomena to help patients appreciate how this particular set of dynamics has affected them. Patients typically demonstrate improved functioning in work and relationships as they become more conscious of their conflicts and their impact.

It is essential that therapists be aware that patients rarely change in response to a single interpretation, no matter how central; a gradual accretion of clarifications and interpretations is usually necessary. In addition, interpretations may be rephrased and modified by patients, who bring them into closer approximation with their own experience. A negative response to an interpretation may not signify that it is incorrect, because patients may not be ready to hear the new formulation. Nonetheless, therapists are advised to pay close attention to patients' responses and to reconsider the format of the interpretation or formulation.

Because patients with anxiety disorders, by the very nature of their symptomatic profile, have some inherent difficulty connecting their often overwhelming feelings with intellectually understandable ideas in verbal form, the working through process is essential in making connections between different aspects of patients' intrapsychic experience and life.

One task that the therapist has is to determine what constitutes sufficient working through of a particular phenomenon. This determination is based on whether the change created by the interpretation seems to have been sufficiently reinforced by the working through process that it will not break down under predictable stress. In the case of anxiety disorder patients, this will be evidenced by patients' increasing awareness of the nature of anxiety triggers and a new ability to effectively manage the challenges and emotions brought up in these situations.

Working through occurs outside of therapeutic sessions as well as in the sessions, as patients ponder what has been said in treatment and recognize how it applies to their life. For patients with severe anxiety disorders, who frequently perceive themselves as disempowered or helpless during their episodes of anxiety, part of the working through process often involves a recognition of their passivity and dependence on others and a gradual mastery of their panic and anxiety by learning to take more active care of themselves. In addition, during the course of panic focused psychodynamic psychotherapy—eXtended range (PFPP-XR), anxiety patients often become increasingly aware of displaced or disavowed angry feelings. Increasing awareness and comfort with these feelings can lead to the experience of anger as being less toxic than it had seemed previously and to more direct and effective interactions with other people.

Case example

At the end of the vignette in Chapter 9, Ms. V recognized a connection between her anger and her panic attacks after becoming angry with her therapist. She became able to be more direct and assertive with her husband. Despite this early foray into assertiveness, Ms. V continued to be uncomfortable when angry in many situations.

Most prominently, she felt conflicted about acknowledging and managing her anger at her mother. Noticing that when she visited her mother she began to panic, she avoided her mother entirely and did not speak to her for several weeks. Although she did not experience anxiety during the time she avoided her, she felt guilty and was sorry about her mother's medical condition.

Upon visiting her mother again, Ms. V was intensely uncomfortable and recognized her feelings as those that routinely preceded her panic episodes. Her mother had complained about Ms. V's recent absence and appeared ill. Ms. V had recognized in the past that her mother purposefully did not take proper care of herself when she felt mistreated, which led to recurrent bouts of her medical illness. Nonetheless, she did not feel angry at her. Ms. V's guilt led her to take care of her mother even more at these times (an example of reaction formation), which further intensified her unconscious anger and anxiety, as she resented her mother's passive and self-destructive expression of rage at her. She did not confront her mother about not taking proper care of herself.

The therapist interpreted Ms. V's unacknowledged anger on several occasions, comparing it to anger she had experienced in other situations and now was able to recognize. She responded that intellectually she knew she must be angry at her mother, because at other times this behavior of her mother's infuriated her. She did not, however, experience any anger, and she felt frustrated about this.

At this time in psychotherapy, Ms. V recalled a shocking incident in which her mother had called Ms. V's married lover's wife to inform her about Ms. V's affair with the woman's husband. Ms. V had felt "stunned" rather than angry when she found out about this and had never been able to discuss it with her mother. In revisiting this episode in her treatment, she realized the audacity of her mother's intrusiveness, which she believed was common for her, and slowly recognized the murderous rage that she had felt in response to this and similar intrusions at other times. She recognized that the sense of being "stunned" made her feel confused and also served as an unconscious protective device so that she would be unable to acknowledge her anger or entertain fantasies of hurting her mother. This work allowed Ms. V to recognize that she was indeed angry at her mother in the current situation and permitted her to confront her mother about her manipulative behavior.

For Ms. V, aspects of working through included recognizing how she warded off her anger; acknowledging, experiencing, and accepting her anger; newly remembering old underpinnings of her rage; understanding the links between her anger and panic; and becoming able to express anger appropriately.

TERMINATION

Patients with panic and other anxiety disorders frequently have significant conflicts surrounding issues of loss, separation, and the establishment of autonomy. In PFPP-XR, these highly charged themes are frequently a focus of exploration. Separations from significant others recurrently emerge as precipitants of anxiety and panic attacks. In addition, separation and loss trigger angry feelings that are a further source of conflict. In the transference, perceived empathic failures by the therapist can be experienced by patients as emotional abandonments that bring these conflicts to the fore. Therapist vacations, as well as time between sessions, provide an opportunity for exploring patients' reactions to separations.

An important aspect of working through feelings about separation is being able to experience rage at the needed other, without this feeling becoming so frightening that the separation becomes intolerable. This presents a particularly difficult issue for patients with anxiety disorders and requires repeatedly addressing reactions to separation. Despite the unavoidable focus on these issues throughout the course of the treatment, the termination phase (phase III) with panic and anxiety patients often involves an intensification of feelings of being hurt and abandoned and anger at the therapist. In this way, termination provides a crucial opportunity for solidifying gains in the development of patients' sense of maturity, independence, autonomy, and competence (Tyson, 1996).

Sometimes, patients may wish to terminate their treatment quickly after the resolution of an anxiety episode. While occasionally this can be advisable, further therapeutic work is usually indicated to reduce vulnerability to recurrence of symptoms. Patients can be frightened by the possibility of addressing underlying affects and fantasies that have remained unconscious during anxiety episodes. For anxiety patients in particular, with their conflicts about intimacy, independence, and separation, the recommendation to establish an exploratory psychotherapeutic relationship can be particularly frightening. The opportunity to work through these core conflicts and address them with the therapist, including in a termination phase, can greatly increase patients' understanding and tolerance of these sources of anxiety.

The following case examples come from longer-term anxiety and panic focused psychodynamic psychotherapies. The long case in Chapter 18 provides an example of the termination of a 24-session PFPP-XR treatment.

Case example

Mr. AA experienced a resolution of panic symptoms after three sessions of psychodynamic psychotherapy. In an additional 12 sessions, he began to explore conflicts with his intrusive mother and his difficulties with angry feelings that were central to the onset of his panic attacks. The patient continued to have significant difficulties in his relationships, particularly with women, and tended to isolate himself rather than become closer to other people and risk what he feared would be potential rejection.

At this point, the patient expressed a wish to stop therapy. The therapist stated to the patient that, although his panic symptoms had resolved, his tendency to isolate himself led him to feelings of loneliness that in turn made him particularly vulnerable to panic recurrence. Alternatively, when Mr. AA attempted to become involved in a more intimate relationship, he became very frightened. He did not know why this happened. The therapist expressed the opinion that Mr. AA needed to explore further what inhibited him from becoming involved more intimately with others and suggested that these were precisely the fears that made continued treatment with the therapist seem unpleasant.

After some thought about the matter, Mr. AA agreed to this plan. His treatment continued for another 8 months, during which time he was able to permit himself to become more involved with others. Despite this progress, Mr. AA still shied away from intense intimacy. He had no recurrence of panic attacks or episodes of severe anxiety during this period.

Case example

Ms. M, discussed in the transference section of Chapter 7, had been in psychotherapy three times a week for 3½ years when she began to talk about ending her treatment. Her panic attacks, with which she had presented, had entirely resolved within 2 months of her starting treatment. She had spent the remainder of her time in psychotherapy exploring the thorny issues of her desperate desire yet ambivalence about becoming involved in a relationship with a man, her conflicts about becoming more independent from her family (she maintained a dependent, childlike attachment to an older sister who often took on a mothering role with her), her rage at her rigid and unpredictable father, and her mixed feelings about taking on a more self-sufficient role. This last conflict often interfered with her professional functioning in graduate school. All of these issues contributed to the genesis of her anxiety symptoms.

In the transference, Ms. M's relationship with her therapist had dramatically altered over the course of the psychotherapy. She had initially taken a childlike, dependent attitude toward the therapist, treating her as though she were perfect while actively whining that the therapist should provide more structure and care for her in her life. This relationship was very much in the mold of what the patient had described as being her way of relating to her mother when she was alive, and she continued a similarly structured relationship with her sister. As the patient's autonomous functioning improved with psychotherapy, her transference evolved, and she began to experience the therapist as being more critical. She had the fantasy, which she recognized as being unrelated to reality, that the therapist, did not want her to move away from her emotionally by establishing a romantic relationship with a man. She found herself enraged at the therapist for issues like this, and although she was able to explore the connection between these fantasies with fantasies she must have had about her mother when she was alive, the anger at her therapist often felt quite compelling.

In anticipation of her graduation from graduate school, Ms. M began seriously to consider moving to another city. She presented many reasons, but the most intense and conflicted of them involved the fantasy that if she were to leave her treatment and "escape" her therapist, she would be able to establish a relationship with a man. Although she recognized the unrealistic nature of this fantasy, during the therapist's 1-week vacation she aggressively pursued a job opportunity in a distant city and agreed to take the job on an emergency basis. As she told her therapist about her decision after the vacation, she became extremely anxious and tearful and felt trapped into going to her new job.

The contract she had signed with the new job did not permit her to alter her decision, which she almost immediately desperately wanted to do. The therapist pointed out to her that she must have arranged this situation to "make" herself go, given how conflicted and frightened she felt about leaving her therapist. Ms. M arranged to delay beginning her new job by one year and spent the remaining time in therapy discussing her long-standing fears of independence yet her growing awareness of her own competence and talents. "It's like I've spent my whole life avoiding these things about myself so I wouldn't ever have to sever any attachments. But I know I don't need to be in babyish relationships like that anymore."

In her last few months in the city, Ms. M began a sexual relationship with a man, something which she had not ever permitted herself to do. She acknowledged that the new relationship with the man helped to diffuse the intensity of her preoccupation with leaving her therapist. Nonetheless, the relationship itself represented a real and important achievement in the life of this restricted young woman. As termination approached, Ms. M became more nostalgic about her psychotherapy. She arranged to go to the new city, set up her apartment, and saw her therapist several times on a return trip. "I feel like I'm taking a little bit of you with me by coming back and telling you about my new life without you." Despite fears that she would be miserable and lonely (and miss her therapist), Ms. M negotiated a very successful move. She wrote the therapist several long letters about her new life in the course of the following year. She has not had a recurrence of her panic attacks in the 20 years since treatment termination.

Part III

eXtended range

Chapter 12

Psychodynamic approaches to agoraphobia and other phobias

Anxiety disorders are frequently associated with agoraphobia and other phobic symptoms. Agoraphobia is defined in *DSM-IV-TR* (APA, 2000a) as fear of situations in which escape may be difficult or in which help might not be available in the event of a panic attack or panic-like symptoms. As in its handling of panic attacks and anxiety, the focus of panic focused psychodynamic psychotherapy—eXtended range (PFPP-XR) is on parsing psychological meanings of phobic symptoms. The therapist explores patients' overarching irrational, magical fantasies about themselves and others that give rise to the compelling magical fantasy that some objects, activities, or places in the world are "safe" and others are "dangerous." The therapist identifies underlying frightening fantasies, thoughts, and feelings that are being avoided, at least in fantasy, via avoidance of real world experiences. Symptoms can be reinforced through alterations in relationships with significant others, including the presence of an ambivalently viewed phobic companion (Deutsch, 1929). Persistent phobic and agoraphobic symptoms call for an exploration of usually unspoken, passive, dependent yet controlling fantasies in relationship to other people. These problems inevitably emerge in the transference.

PFPP-XR differs from cognitive behavioral interventions for phobias and agoraphobia in that the therapist does not instruct patients to confront feared situations. Specific instruction would indirectly confirm patients' sense of incapability ("I need my therapist to tell me what to do") and significantly disrupts exploration of dependency wishes and fears in the transference. As therapy proceeds, patients typically begin to expose themselves to feared situations that they had previously avoided. If this does not occur, the therapist explores why patients are continuing to avoid reified expressions of magical fears, despite having gained some understanding of their underpinnings in therapy. Phobias are complex psychological constructions, and they are reinforced by both patients' complicated emotional (intrapsychic) needs as well as the interpersonal needs of both patient and phobic companion.

MEANINGS AND CONFLICTS IN PHOBIC AND AGORAPHOBIC SYMPTOMS

From a psychoanalytic perspective, several core meanings and conflicts have been described for phobias, which overlap in part with those found in panic disorder. Specific phobias have been viewed as developing from the ego's response to the threatened emergence of unacceptable aggressive or sexual wishes. When these wishes trigger signal anxiety, defense mechanisms are activated that repress and disguise these wishes (Gabbard, 2000). For example, in Freud's (1909) case of Little Hans, a child who developed a phobia of horses, Freud's analysis, accomplished through the mediation of Hans's father, was that horses had come to symbolically represent Hans's father. The child's fear of aggressive and competitive wishes toward his father was displaced (to horses) and projected: He was scared that the horse was going to damage him rather than that he was going to damage the horse (who represented his father). The anxiety that Hans experienced could be mostly avoided if he just avoided horses. In this way, the phobia symbolically replaced anxiety derived from unconscious, wishes, and the dangers—originating from his own unconscious, conflicted, intolerable impulses to destroy and replace his father—were externalized on to the relatively safe object of horses on the street. In this regard, phobias share a similar construction to dreams: They symbolically express intrapsychic wishes and fears, and their defensive elaborations are filtered through primary process symbolism (Lewin, 1952).

Deutsch (1929) viewed agoraphobia as an expression of intense ambivalence in central relationships. She focused on relationships with phobic companions, who are felt to be essential to relieve the patients' fears. Deutsch described these patients as being enraged at the companion yet unaware of it. The presence of the phobic companion serves the dual purpose of both managing dependent wishes and reassuring the patient that the needed, ambivalently held object has not been damaged by powerful, rageful fantasies. Milrod (2007) suggested that these patients lack autonomous structure in their self-representation, requiring the presence of others to feel safe. Thus, the loss of a phobic companion is experienced as a catastrophic loss of a part of the self.

In association with the need for a companion, agoraphobic patients have an underlying sense of inadequacy, a fantasy that they literally cannot manage on their own. In part related to the fearful dependency of panic patients, this need intensifies the danger experienced with any acknowledgment of ambivalent feelings about a significant other. In addition, patients become increasingly angry because they feel unable to manage on their own, and for this reason they have a heightened sense that others do not adequately respond to their needs. Finally, these patients may have a lack of curiosity, interest, or tolerance in thinking about their internal world that reflects their terror of any acknowledgment of the depth of their angry fantasies and how conflicted their own relationships really are. This disavowal and avoidance of such essential aspects of inner life comprises an ego deficit and sets the stage for a view of the world as a dangerous place, which in turn must be avoided.

WORKING WITH PHOBIC AVOIDANCE AND AGORAPHOBIA

A central approach to addressing phobic avoidance in short-term psychodynamic treatment is to focus on the magical quality of the phobia. To maintain the phobia's continuity, patients must sustain a belief apart from reality, to the effect that the world is artificially divided between magically "safe" and "dangerous" objects, activities, or places. The therapist explicitly identifies this magical organization for patients: The dangers are not "real" or truly dangerous in the real world (or at least have a very low risk of danger that is greatly overestimated). Instead, phobias represent emotional dangers that need to be delineated in therapy. The set of phobic assumptions (fantasies) must be actively explored in the following manner.

The therapist should have patients fully describe the architecture of the phobia; it is only in this manner that underlying fantasies can be determined. Which places, objects, or activities are safe? Why? Which places, objects, or activities are dangerous? Why does the patient feel they are dangerous? What determines the difference between "safe" and "dangerous"? Where did the patient get these ideas about safety and danger? The therapist elicits key developmental moments when patients first developed their phobias. Possibilities include particular developmental events (e.g., birth of a sibling) or a frightening experience (e.g., being stuck in an elevator, which might have occurred as parents were separating). The connections between patients' fantasies and significant others' overt or unspoken ideas about dangers should be delineated. If the onset of the phobia is traumatic, as in the elevator example, what was so frightening about the experience? If the phobia carries a symbolic link to a loss or sad event (e.g., "Since Mother died, I can never be alone in the dark"), the therapist should explore and help patients articulate emotional links between the loss or fear event and the phobia's persistence. Why are these feelings being reevoked in the present?

Patients' phobias may be inadvertently reinforced by a family member, and the therapist should explore whether this is happening. These reinforcements may be taking place in the present (e.g., "My husband stops yelling at me when I get frightened") or in the past (e.g., "Mommy and Daddy stopped fighting and took care of me when I was scared," or "I got to take special walks with Mommy, and that was the only time I was alone with her and she was nice to me"). If significant reenforcements are occurring, the therapist should point out to patients the active role others play in perpetuating the fears.

If patients remain avoidant, the therapist should also explore the gratifying aspects of the phobia's continuation, such as satisfaction of dependent wishes. The therapist should address with patients any avoidance of taking steps toward self-exposure to the phobic situation (e.g., attempting to take the elevator), particularly when they have come to understand and at least partly believe that the fear is magical and irrational. Often, as patients describe their fears of taking these steps, further underlying meanings of symptoms emerge. Understanding these additional factors can free patients to pursue a less avoidant life. In the case of an intractable phobia, the problem often revolves around patients' passive, dependent wishes with others, which will be mirrored in the therapeutic relationship in the transference. These wishes include a regressive desire that the therapist (like a parent) "do" something such as "make" the patient stop avoiding. Provoking the therapist into action may be part of a pattern of sadomasochistic interactions. Alternatively, the patient may incite the therapist to provide a magical solution consistent with the infantile, passive stance in which the patient hopes to avoid activity, including thought. The therapist should articulate these wishes as they emerge in the transference.

Case example

Ms. BB, a 47-year-old married woman, described a fear of elevators and would not enter the elevator in the therapist's office building. She was hesitant to talk about this phobia, indicating to the therapist that there was something about the fantasy connected to the elevator phobia that she found particularly threatening.

THERAPIST: Can you tell me more about what scares you about the elevator?

PATIENT: It's too tight and too close.

THERAPIST: Can you say more what you mean by this?

PATIENT: I can't really explain it more. Why is it important to discuss this?

THERAPIST: Well, since you know that elevators are rarely dangerous, I think it's important to understand what this means for you emotionally.

PATIENT: I'm worried you're going to make fun of me if I tell you, although I realize that's not going to happen.

THERAPIST: Why would I make fun of you?

PATIENT: I'm not sure. I feel very embarrassed about it. It's strange though. I also believe if you came with me in the elevator it would no longer be dangerous. I would feel safe.

THERAPIST: You seem to have some very mixed feelings about me at this point. First, it sounds like you think I'm going to criticize you, but then there's something magical about my presence. We should try to understand more about that.

PATIENT: I don't know why that is.

THERAPIST: Maybe you can tell me about what you recall about these experiences in the past, and that may help us to understand your fears and your feeling that I would make you safe.

Ms. BB went on to describe her first episode of intense anxiety at age 10 when going through a tunnel on a trip abroad. She recalled feeling very frightened and being comforted by her father. Another memory of an early episode of panic also involved her father, who rescued her after she became trapped in the garage in her home. Thus, her father represented a responsive man who was mirrored in the transference with the idea that her therapist was someone who would magically make the elevator safe. Ms. BB recalled her phobias as drawing her father's attention in a special way, exclusive of her mother. She viewed herself as her father's "favorite" of four children and felt he sometimes liked her more than her mother.

The memories of her mother were distinct from the experiences with her father, as she saw her mother as self-involved and frequently critical when she became anxious or phobic. Thus, Ms. BB was also experiencing a maternal transference to the therapist, fearful that he would attack or humiliate her if she revealed her discomfort. Ms. BB believed the threat of attack from her mother increased when her father showed interest in her. She also struggled with anger at her mother for her insensitivity toward her fears. Her phobias represented a compromise formation, expressing a demand for her father's attention that in some ways felt unacceptable and off-limits, specifically in relation to her mother, and for which she punished herself in the form of the phobia itself, and the personal limitations and embarrassment it imposed. The phobia also represented anger at her mother by taking her father's attention and irritating her mother because of her fears and a presentation of herself to others as helpless and needy. The symbolic meanings of enclosed places (e.g., fantasies of a frightening womb or a sexual wish) were not explored further at this time.

Case example

Ms. F (see Chapter 3) was a 45-year-old woman who described the onset of severe agoraphobic symptoms that interfered with her going to work and with many of her leisure activities. Exploration in therapy revealed the onset of intense guilt and self-criticism following an abortion one year previously, about 2 months prior to the development of her agoraphobia. She had been ambivalent about having children but was leaning toward moving forward with the pregnancy. Her husband told her that he absolutely would not support her having the child. Although she did not identify it at the time, she later came to believe that her husband's negative feelings about being married to her affected this attitude; about 6 months later he demanded a divorce.

A few weeks after the abortion, Ms. F's guilt had diminished somewhat, although she struggled about the decision she had made. At this point the Iraq War began. Ms. F reported being frightened about the aggression in the U.S. attack on Baghdad and became concerned about a retaliatory dirty bomb. She became fearful about going out of the house and experienced the onset of severe agoraphobia.

Ms. F was the youngest of three children and, as an adolescent, lived alone with her mother, who was having severe alcohol problems. She felt constantly criticized by her mother, particularly about being "fat," and feared her mother's vicious temper. She was also frightened that her mother would be severely injured or die, so she felt she needed to stay at home with her. She was very angry at her mother about her drinking and her temper but feared expressing her feelings out of concern that her mother would drink even more or scream at her. She also felt guilty about being so angry, as she knew her mother was in need of help but refused it. The therapist explored her feelings at the time of symptom onset in greater depth.

THERAPIST: Were you aware of feeling angry at your husband?

PATIENT: Not really. I mean, if he didn't want a child, I wasn't going to push it. The only thing is, when we were first married he said he wanted to have a baby, but he seemed to have forgotten it. The other thing is he was prone to depression, and I didn't know how he would do with children.

THERAPIST: I wonder if you had trouble being angry with him like with your mother, worried that he would become ill.

PATIENT: Maybe. I know I was angry at myself, and that does sound like what happened with my mother, when I would end up feeling guilty.

The therapist went on to explore the patient's reactions to the war:

THERAPIST: What did the war bring up for you?

PATIENT: I was so upset. I couldn't believe we invaded. I was worried they were going to get back at us. We were going to get it.

THERAPIST: I think you unconsciously feared your own aggression was getting out of control, as you felt guilty about the abortion and furious with your husband. You worried you would get attacked or damaged in return and get punished for your angry feelings and wishes, just like you felt with your mother.

PATIENT: I see the connection you're making. But why would I be worried about another country attacking me?

THERAPIST: I believe these feelings were so scary and uncomfortable you somehow switched them to a danger that was outside of you.

PATIENT: That makes more sense to me than the fear of a dirty bomb.

Helping Ms. F to understand how the magical safety of the house and the danger outside represented conflicts about her feelings and fantasies rather than reflecting real-world dangers helped diminish her agoraphobic symptoms.

Case example

Ms. CC was a 22-year-old graduate student with severe panic disorder with agoraphobia such that she could never be alone without a phobic companion. She could not travel anywhere alone or be alone at home, even for 5 minutes, without having severe panic and feeling as if she would die. She organized her life to avoid these experiences at all costs. She lived in an apartment with her girlfriend, Fran, but when her girlfriend was at work, her best friend from college, Nancy, stayed with her until Fran returned. Every time she needed to come to the city (Ms. CC lived in the suburbs), Nancy drove from her home on the opposite side of the city to pick her up and drive her to the place she was going. Nancy waited for her until her appointments were finished and drove her home. Ms. CC came to her first four sessions accompanied by Nancy, who waited in the waiting room. Gradually, in the course of those four sessions, several specific antecedents to this severe agoraphobia were clarified.

First, this specific crippling phobia seemingly evolved "out of the blue" one day when Ms. CC was spending time shopping with Nancy. While driving home alone in the rain, she suddenly had the fantasy that she was trapped in her car alone (the car felt like a tomb). She had a panic attack with the fantasy that she would never get out "and see my mother again." This fantasy mirrored an actual experience she had when trapped in an elevator at the time her parents were divorcing. At that time she had felt particularly frightened and alone, and her mother had seemed out of control and ill. The agoraphobia emerged as Ms. CC was awaiting the arrival of her ex-girlfriend, Sally, who was returning from Florida. Ms. CC's relationship with Sally was complicated and made particularly difficult because Sally "had a temper problem" and became enraged at Ms. CC, refusing to "share" her with any of Ms. CC's friends or even with Ms. CC's mother. In reality Ms. CC was facing a sad separation from her mother and her friends and was feeling trapped already by Sally.

Second, Ms. CC had a long history, dating from early childhood, of severe separation anxiety disorder from her mother. When she was in elementary and high school, she never felt comfortable having sleepovers, even with friends from her own building, and had to come home in the middle of the night for fear that her mother "wouldn't be okay" without her. As an infant and toddler, she had insisted on sleeping in bed with her mother every night, much to her father's dismay, and she cried terribly when separated from her mother throughout her childhood, even when her mother went to work. As she grew up, her mother encouraged Ms. CC to go out and have sleepovers and broaden her experience, but Ms. CC thought of these encouragements as "lies ... maybe," because her mother feared separation and was severely anxiously attached to Ms. CC during her very early childhood, and before the birth of her younger sister (5 years her junior).

Third, relationships with phobic companions (Nancy, and Sally before her) were fraught with both a sense of "safety" (i.e., "I felt they were really taking care of me") yet also complicated by feeling controlled, belittled, and trapped, "as if they encouraged me to feel incompetent."

In the course of identifying these antecedents, as well as her very mixed feelings about herself in relationship to her phobic companions, Ms. CC felt stronger and less panicky and was impressed with the idea that she did not necessarily need anyone else to help her to manage her life. The therapist focused on her real strengths compared with her phobic fantasy of herself as lacking any skills.

She came to understand how she had ascribed these capabilities to her phobic companions and gradually realized that neither of these women was more competent in reality than she was to handle situations as they arose. She became increasingly serious about treatment and "worked hard" to get well, which was associated with a rapid response. She began traveling to sessions and elsewhere on her own, announcing "because obviously I can do it." Her panic and agoraphobia rapidly remitted.

Chapter 13

Psychodynamic approaches to social anxiety disorder

Social anxiety disorder and panic disorder have similarities in certain areas, including clinical symptoms of anticipatory anxiety, panic attacks, and phobic avoidance (APA, 2000a). They also share a number of central dynamisms, including complicated emotional responses to separation from close attachment figures and difficulty tolerating angry feelings toward them. Consensus among psychoanalytic theoreticians and clinicians indicates that patients with social anxiety disorder also have prominent conflicted exhibitionistic and grandiose fantasies and wishes (Fenichel, 1945; Gabbard, 1992, 2000; Kaplan, 1972; Lipsitz & Marshall, 2001; Zerbe, 1994). Clarification of these dynamisms can aid in treatment of patients who suffer from social anxiety disorder.

Social anxiety disorder also resembles panic disorder in patients' temperamental fearfulness and terrifying perceptions of parents. An association has been found between both disorders and behavioral inhibition (BI; see Chapter 9; Biederman et al., 2001; Rosenbaum et al., 1991). Higher rates of social anxiety disorder have been found in children with BI than in noninhibited children (Biederman et al., 2001) and in parents of children with BI compared with parents of children without BI (Rosenbaum et al., 1991). Systematic assessments of social phobic patients' perceptions found that they viewed their parents as being less caring, more rejecting, and more overprotective than subjects without known psychiatric disorder (Arrindell, et al. 1983). Temperamental fearfulness and developmental stressors can lead these individuals to view themselves as inadequate, incapable, shameful, and easily rejected, while they often experience others as powerful, threatening, and critical.

DYNAMICS OF SOCIAL ANXIETY DISORDER

Patients with social anxiety disorder have a core feeling of inadequacy and low self-esteem related to feeling incapable of functioning autonomously. They feel unable to act autonomously for a variety of reasons, including a sense of shame about themselves. They have a pervasive belief that they are too incompetent and immature to formulate responses to external situations, and they worry that they will betray their close attachment figures by functioning more independently, such that autonomy could function as a terrifying threat to these relationships. Their feelings of inadequacy aggravate the degree of mixed emotions and conflict they experience in connection with fantasized dangers envisioned with separation from significant others. The threat to relationships is intensified by their fantasy that powerful attachment figures are required for love, organization, and coherence. These patients believe, often unconsciously, that socializing outside their family of origin will lead to the loss of important relationships, leading to regressive fantasies of helplessness, increasing social anxiety and avoidance of social situations.

Patients develop intensely angry feelings and fantasies toward others they perceive as rejecting and humiliating, and they fear that their anger will pose a threat to needed relationships. Denial and projection of anger are common defense mechanisms among patients with social phobia, increasing their chances of feeling rejected and criticized. Their anger is partly fueled by feelings of helplessness and incompetence, which represent a narcissistic injury, and can be blamed on others for undermining their sense of competence. The view of oneself as humiliated and inadequate can also serve to protect against a self-perception of being hostile and threatening, self-images that are believed to be a danger to close attachments.

Patients with social anxiety disorder often have grandiose fantasies, which at times can be linked to conflicted sexually exhibitionistic wishes and fantasies (Fenichel, 1945). These fantasies may derive from attempts to compensate for a sense of personal inadequacy. Grandiose fantasies, with an underlying belief that one should be treated as special, often lead to disappointment in real social situations, furthering distress in response to social slights. Patients typically feel guilty when exhibitionistic and grandiose fantasies are experienced consciously; they fear punishment, which aggravates their anxiety. Patients may avoid social situations to avoid these fantasies or to punish themselves for having them.

In summary, social anxiety and associated self-criticism in part represent complex compromise formations. Social anxiety disorder encompasses fears of inadequacy, humiliation, and rejection, and social avoidance aids in averting threats to self-esteem. Social avoidance can function to maintain a regressive dependency on significant others and to avoid pursuing adult relationships, which are frightening to these patients with the greater independence that they imply. Underlying social anxiety disorder are fears of the experience and expression of anger, and avoidance serves to ward off these threats, while it can also represent an unconscious expression of contempt. Social avoidance can allow the patient to maintain a secret sense of specialness that could be challenged by real responses of others. Thus, painful shyness may be an avoidant defense against frightening aggressive, sexually exhibitionistic, and grandiose wishes and fantasies and can also function as a punishment for these wishes.

PSYCHODYNAMIC PSYCHOTHERAPY FOR SOCIAL ANXIETY DISORDER

Initial exploration of fears

Patients with social phobia experience catastrophic fears that they are socially inadequate and will be painfully rejected and criticized. In Panic Focused Psychodynamic Psychotherapy—eXtended Range (PFPP-XR), the therapist's approach to social phobia focuses on the emotional meanings of specific symptoms, the stressors surrounding symptom onset and exacerbation, the patient's developmental history, and fantasies and feelings that emerge in the transference. In this way, unconscious and warded-off fantasies and conflicts that underlie social phobia are identified and explored. Patients become aware that their fears derive from feelings of inadequacy, conflicted aggression, attachment threats, and guilt-ridden exhibitionistic and grandiose fantasies. Social anxiety improves as patients become able to identify these conflicts and as their fantasies become articulated and detoxified.

The experience of therapy, with the nonjudgmental and empathic support of the therapist, can aid patients in the development of more benign or supportive representations of themselves and others, thereby diminishing the perceived danger of social interactions. As with the approach recommended for agoraphobia, the PFPP-XR therapist does not directly instruct the patient to confront feared situations, as this can inhibit the development of greater autonomy and distort the transference. As psychodynamic exploration leads to reduced fears, patients naturally become more willing to confront situations they have been avoiding. However, mired as these patients are in taking a passive role, struggles in the transference occur when anxiety rises as their wish that the therapist tell them what to do is not fulfilled. Articulation of passive wishes in the transference and inherent dangers patients experience in taking a more active role necessarily come to the forefront.

Case example

Mr. DD, a 32-year-old lawyer with social anxiety disorder, developed panic attacks when he was promoted at work and was newly responsible for public presentations. In PFPP-XR, it emerged that he expected attack or humiliation by others in response to the expression of power and competence demanded by his new role. He feared he would be inadequate at performing the tasks expected of him. Subsequently, therapist and patient also discovered that the presentations represented the realization of his conflicted exhibitionistic wishes to be admired and to be the center of attention. Associated with this were fantasies of domination over others at his firm. Panic attacks, which he experienced in the context of his social phobia when running meetings, symbolized the guilty excitement and danger he experienced from these exhibitionistic and grandiose fantasies, while also punishing himself for having these fantasies.

The patient described his mother as overprotective and said that she felt threatened when he was assertive. For instance, she became highly anxious about his safety when he learned to ride a bike. As a child, he began to see any demonstration of personal capability on his own part as being aggressive and dangerous, a potential threat to himself, his mother, and their relationship. This formed a component of his fantasy that his promotion and speaking opportunities represented a danger.

Addressing the transference

People with social phobia often believe they will be criticized or rejected by the therapist in a similar way to what they anticipate will occur in other social situations. Fears of humiliation or ridicule may cause patients to avoid or skip sessions or even to leave treatment. They expect criticism or punishment for their often secret grand and exhibitionistic fantasies, which they can be reluctant to reveal. Patients worry that they will be attacked for critical feelings and fantasies they have about the therapist (mirroring their experience in other relationships and their fears of the way they will be viewed by others). The exploration of the transference allows for more direct articulation of these fears and helps patients to identify ways their expectations of humiliation and criticism color relationships.

Addressing conflicted feelings and fantasies

An important component of PFPP-XR is helping patients to become aware of, more tolerant of, and more able to express their various feelings and fantasies. Because of the inherent danger patients with social phobia experience about assertion of any kind, rage is often felt to be disorganizing and threatening, and patients can find being angry intolerable. Nonetheless, anger frequently emerges as treatment progresses. Understanding the origins of these feelings developmentally, identifying the details of related fantasies and why it seems so frightening to be angry, and being able to safely experience this rage and disappointment in therapy allow for increased tolerance. Patients may be aware of having fantasies of grand power and being the center of attention but often do not connect this with their social anxiety disorder. They tend to minimize the importance of these fantasies, given their manifest preoccupation with feelings of inadequacy. The therapist identifies these wishes and conflicts about them as they emerge in treatment and highlights their importance. The patient can be informed that grandiose fantasies form a guilty backdrop of high expectations that trigger anxiety in social situations.

Countertransference

Therapists must be alert to feelings of being criticized or frustration that may occur in working with social phobia patients. Frustration can be triggered by these patients' level of passivity and dependency and by their difficulty in taking more autonomous steps to change their lives. Covert expression of angry feelings can lead to subtle criticisms by the therapist that can intensify patients' feelings of inadequacy. In addition, therapists should remain alert to their reaction to patients' sometimes contemptuous attitudes toward the therapist. Focus on the transference can help the therapist to address these conflicts. The experience of a nonjudgmental, helpful therapist, who nevertheless does not direct the patient in how to specifically approach feared situations, is critical in modification of negative, tormenting self- and other-representations.

Case example

Ms. EE, a 30-year-old nurse, was fearful of criticism by others in many situations. She felt that she was inadequate, that her shyness was evident to others, and that others would invariably be highly critical of her. In particular, she felt others would reject her for her small stature, which she felt made her appear childlike. Due to her shyness and what she saw as physical flaws, she was certain that men would reject her. She frequently avoided parties and dates, with the assumption that she would be ignored or rejected.

Ms. EE described her parents as pleasant but passive figures, not actively engaged in the children's lives or activities. Of foremost significance in Ms. EE's experience of shyness was being tormented over many years during childhood by an older sister, Sarah, who seemed to feel that it was necessary to "whip" the patient and her siblings "into shape." In Sarah's view, she had to take over the role of the parents, who were ineffective.

Sarah was harshly critical of the patient's capabilities, including both social and academic skills. Ms. EE saw no alternative but to submit to her attacks, although it emerged that she experienced revenge fantasies toward Sarah that triggered guilty feelings. Attacks by her siblings and father on her mother, who was viewed as "spacey," intensified Ms. EE's internal struggles. She felt bad for her mother and identified with her while at the same time was furious with her for not defending herself.

It only gradually emerged that Ms. EE was highly critical of others as well. For example, Ms. EE, who was strongly committed to her job, felt disdain for other nurses who she felt did not really care about their patients and were excited for the workday to end. Ms. EE had performed well academically, in part in response to her sister's constant pressure, and she was critical of others who were less well read and not intellectual. As she became more aware of her negative views toward others, Ms. EE was surprised about their extent.

It emerged that Ms. EE felt threatened by the idea of being assertive and successful at work and in her relationships, as she associated assertiveness with power and the destructive behavior toward others that her sister demonstrated. She unconsciously identified with her sister, viewing herself as potentially abusive and sadistic, and felt guilty about her wishes for power. This conflict affected her work, where Ms. EE avoided promotion in subtle, self-destructive ways that kept her from moving into nursing management, despite her hard work. In a compensatory effort to undo these fantasies, Ms. EE found it safer to experience herself as inadequate and downtrodden and as a protector of the downtrodden rather than as a leader.

Conflicted exhibitionistic fantasies of controlling men through sexuality emerged as the patient came to believe that the therapist could tolerate her wishes to be more powerful. These fantasies, in which men were tortured with longing for her, to which she was unresponsive, had become conflated with Ms. EE's feared sadistic wishes. In part out of fear of acting on these fantasies, she avoided meeting men and viewed herself as unattractive, a belief that was explored in psychotherapy. She was surprised yet had to acknowledge that she found self-criticism preferable to any alternative. This compensatory fantasy of inadequacy served to protect her against her dangerous and rage-infiltrated fantasies of domination.

An additional reduction in her self-contempt and social anxiety disorder symptoms emerged from further understanding of Ms. EE's history with Sarah. It was important for the patient to be able to vent her anger and hurt at her sister and at her parents for not intervening. Ms. EE identified herself with her mother and was particularly conflicted about this issue, since she also viewed her mother with disdain. She was critical of the family's attitudes toward her mother yet was strongly influenced by them. Untangling of these mixed loyalties allowed her more assertive social behavior and a reduction in social anxiety disorder.

Case example

Mr. FF was a 28-year-old physical therapist who presented with severe social anxiety disorder. Mr. FF regularly avoided social situations, which left him somewhat alone and isolated. However, he was capable of being witty and charming when not anxious. He was frustrated in his profession, which he had pursued after giving up an acting career. Mr. FF had had dreams of being a movie star and still felt disappointed and bereft that this did not work out.

As Mr. FF's anxiety was explored, it emerged that he was as fearful about making inappropriate hostile remarks as he was worried about others rejecting him. For instance, Mr. FF felt the urge to make a nasty remark about another person's clothes being "dorky" or to tell a pregnant woman, "I hope the child doesn't look like you." He experienced a disruption in his conversation when these thoughts came to mind and was concerned that others might be aware of his hostile feelings.

Mr. FF's mother had moved to another town with him when he was 12 years old, leaving his father behind. He was ridiculed in his new environment, where his accent and style were quite different from others'. He also missed the support of his father, whom he rarely saw. Ultimately, his mother married a man whom he experienced as highly critical and humiliating. In Mr. FF's view, his stepfather attacked every assertive effort the patient made, viewing it as poor judgment. When Mr. FF pursued acting, his stepfather gave constant lectures about how acting was not a practical choice.

Mr. FF's mother ignored the stepfather's attacks. She also appeared to have mixed feelings about Mr. FF's growing up, as she focused on his having enough to eat and supported him financially without any consideration about his having to learn to handle his own financial affairs. Mr. FF's fantasies of movie stardom in part related to feelings of specialness and entitlement he experienced with his mother and defended against her infantilization of him. He was frequently disappointed when he did not receive the attention he hoped for from others, and anxiety was triggered by anticipation of these disappointments. Helping Mr. FF better understand the complicated impact of his relationship with his mother and become more aware of the effect of his grandiose fantasies moderated his expectations and reduced his disappointment in social situations.

In addition, exhibitionistic wishes became conflicted because Mr. FF anticipated punishment, such as what he received from his stepfather. Fears of humiliation also related to the teasing he underwent when he moved at age 12 and functioned as guilty self-punishment for his gratifying, forbidden fantasies. Thus, Mr. FF struggled between wishes to exhibit his talents alongside intense fears of "standing out," which would lead invariably to a panic attack at times of social performance. At the same time, he feared his own criticisms of others, which were related to retaliatory wishes to humiliate others in ways that he had been humiliated. Exploring these wishes helped to diminish the anxiety he experienced when attempting to be assertive.

Exploration of the transference proved particularly valuable in relieving Mr. FF's anxiety. Critical feelings toward the therapist, including the therapist's posture, office furniture, and clothing, were accepted and explored for their meaning in relation to the patient's expectation of being attacked and retaliatory fantasies. Over time, Mr. FF felt safer revealing other talents, which were numerous, including building furniture, skiing, and surfing. He had viewed the revelation of these talents as "bragging" or potentially disturbing to the therapist. This concern included fears that the therapist would feel threatened by his abilities and would attack or undermine him as his stepfather had. The ability to safely reveal his criticisms and his talents helped to diminish his social anxiety in other spheres.

Case example

Ms. E, discussed in Chapter 3, was a 56-year-old widowed woman with a multiyear history of social anxiety disorder and panic disorder, particularly fearing returning to work, which she had put off doing for many years. When exploring her symptoms of social anxiety, certain highly specific features emerged. Ms. E was fearful of older men with authority, whom she believed had significant power that they could use to hurt her. This included not hiring her or firing her if she did get a job and doing so in a critical and judgmental way. She was particularly worried about executive lunches and meetings involving an authority who might view her as "stupid."

In exploring the origins of her anxiety, Ms. E alluded to settings where she had worked 30 years previously. She found this past job humiliating and disappointing, particularly as she had entered her industry as one of the first women and had expected to be treated as a professional equal. It reminded her of her advanced classes in high school, where she also was one of the only girls, and the boys had made demeaning and sexual comments. Therapist and patient were able to link these themes to those that later were prominent in her social anxiety,

Another strand of meaning in her anxiety was associated with men in her life who were temperamental and scary. Her father, a veteran with PTSD after combat experiences in World War II, had a terrible temper and sometimes threw and broke things in arguments with her mother. Her mother left him when the patient was 12 years old, and the home subsequently became calmer. Ms. E's husband, whom she had met at work, showed a similar pattern of recurrent bouts of rage whenever she asked him to take responsibility for chores in their home and with their children. In addition to verbal abuse and throwing things, he repeatedly left home, often for days. This contributed to Ms. E's feelings of vulnerability and her sense of being out of control with men.

These fears emerged quickly in the transference with her male therapist. Ms. E saw the therapeutic situation as very rigid (e.g., she resented the therapist's starting and ending sessions exactly on time). She was particularly concerned about appearing "stupid" to him, caught in the middle of a thought at the end of the session. Being unable to see the clock in the therapist's office left her feeling out of control, yet, as the therapist pointed out, she remained resentful and passive, making no effort to turn the clock next to her chair in his office to see it. Thus, she felt that the therapist disregarded her, leaving her feeling helpless and humiliated.

At the same time, she was intensely critical of the therapist. Ms. E thought that the therapist showed disregard for her when he announced his vacation plans to her several weeks in advance. She had concluded that the protocol in the PFPP study called for 12 consecutive weeks of sessions, even though she had not been told this, and had silently changed her plans accordingly. Thus, she felt hurt by the therapist when he gave her his vacation dates, feeling she should have been given more notice: "Even unimportant people have plans," she said. Therapist and patient were able to discuss how she quickly perceived herself as worthless and vulnerable when she was with a male whom she viewed as an authority figure. Gradually, Ms. E was more able to articulate and observe how she projected her negative expectations onto someone who did not behave critically or judgmentally.

Chapter 14

Psychodynamic approaches to generalized anxiety disorder

Generalized anxiety disorder (GAD) is defined in the *Diagnostic and Statistical Manual of Mental Disorders,* fourth edition, text revision (*DSM-IV-TR*; APA, 2000a) as "excessive anxiety and worry (apprehensive expectation), occurring more days than not for at least 6 months, about a number of events or activities.... The person finds it difficult to control the worry" (p. 222), and the worry is accompanied by restlessness, fatigue, difficulty concentrating, irritability, muscle tension, and insomnia. Panic attacks and panic disorder frequently cooccur with generalized anxiety disorder (Pollack, Smoller, Otto, Hoge, & Simon, 2010). Overlapping psychodynamic features of panic and generalized anxiety may facilitate comorbid treatment.

PSYCHODYNAMIC FACTORS IN GENERALIZED ANXIETY DISORDER

People with GAD commonly have the fantasy that they must maintain control and be vigilant at all times, or and what amounts to catastrophe will result. This hypervigilant state can develop from a persistent fear of the conscious emergence of unacceptable feelings and fantasies and an associated worry about loss of control. In GAD, defenses have been relatively ineffective at neutralizing or disguising unconscious wishes and affects, adding to this sense of ongoing threat. For instance, in the case of Ms. GG (see vignette to follow), rather than denying her feelings, the patient experienced persistent jealous and angry feelings that frightened her. Alternatively, somatization and worry about external events may operate as defenses against unacceptable feelings and fantasies.

Chronic worrying can emerge in response to early relationships or traumatizing experiences that come to form an internal psychological template in which attachments are experienced as fragile or easily disrupted. Such developmental experiences can then result in the vigilant anticipation of potential loss, anger, and a sense of needing to protect the caregiver to maintain the relationship (Crits-Christoph, Connolly, Azarian, Crits-Christoph, & Shappell, 1996; Crits-Christoph, Wolf-Palacio, Ficher, & Rudick, 1995). The need for control, fears of disruption in attachments, and defenses against important emotional cues have an adverse impact on current interpersonal relationships, exacerbating chronic worries.

Researchers from various backgrounds have arrived at conclusions that overlap with this psychodynamic formulation (Cassidy, Lichtenstein-Phelps, Sibrava, Thomas, & Borkovec, 2009; Crits-Christoph et al., 1995). Studies have found that patients with GAD show a high level of emotional avoidance (see Borkovec, Alcaine, & Behar, 2004, and Cassidy et al. 2009) and suggest that worrying is a means of avoiding emotions that are even more difficult to tolerate. In addition, studies have shown that people with GAD have unusually intense negative affects and difficulty regulating and identifying their emotions. Mennin, Heimberg, Turk, and Fresco (2005) found that, compared with controls, college students and patients with GAD "reported heightened intensity of emotions, poorer understanding of emotions, greater negative reactivity to emotional experience, and less ability to self-soothe after negative emotions" (p. 1281). Worry is employed as a less than adaptive attempt to regulate emotions. Due to such pressures, these patients lack access to interpersonal cues because of their constant preoccupations, leading to greater problems in their relationships. Cassidy et al. suggest that these difficulties develop from insecure attachment, leading to problems in affect regulation and fears about interpersonal relationships. They found evidence of insecure attachment in GAD patients, including a feeling that they needed to take care of their parents. These persistent fears and emotional difficulties lead to ineffective attempts to obtain security from others.

PSYCHODYNAMIC TREATMENT OF GENERALIZED ANXIETY DISORDER

As in other symptom targeted psychodynamic approaches to anxiety disorders, the therapist explores the content of patients' specific worries with the goal of determining the particular threatening unconscious fantasies they are attempting to manage or displace, in an effort to make their emotional reactions more understandable. Early life relationships and traumatic experiences are investigated to determine why the patient views the world as being unsafe. The therapist works with the patient to identify sources of the threat of loss of control if vigilance is not maintained at all times. Precipitants of accentuated GAD symptoms as may occur are elucidated, including an exploration of times that the anxiety symptoms intensify to the level of panic. The therapist identifies and explores defenses, including somatization, which are often triggered when intrapsychic conflicts are not admissible to consciousness.

Further clues can be obtained from experiences of anxiety in the transference. The therapy provides a safe atmosphere in which frightening unconscious wishes and conflicts can emerge, including with the therapist, and can be rendered less threatening. However, even in this "safe" atmosphere, patients with GAD can experience a sense of threat in the therapeutic relationship. This transference is based in part on insecure attachments and in part on fears of exposing unacceptable fantasies to the therapist. The experience of this threat provides an opportunity to more directly examine the patient's catastrophic fears of loss of control. Issues and themes of separation and attachment, addressed throughout therapy, can be particularly accessible and useful to address during termination.

Case example

Ms. GG was a 36-year-old executive secretary who suffered from chronic fears regarding her health and social relationships. Her primary worries included recurring concerns about having a serious illness, whenever she experienced minor somatic symptoms, and anxiety about being rejected by her friends.

Ms. GG developed panic attacks and a worsening of her chronic GAD symptoms in the context of her inability to become pregnant. She felt deprived, angry, and jealous of women she knew who were having children. She felt guilty about these feelings and was concerned that she would say something that would reveal her envy, potentially disrupting her relationships. Getting together with a friend who was pregnant or had a small child triggered her anger and jealousy, along with panic attacks. Arranging a baby shower for a pregnant friend led to facial sensations she interpreted as possible signs of a brain tumor, creating intense anxiety that slowly resolved after the shower was over.

Exploration of Ms. GG's background shed light on the dynamisms with which she struggled. She described her mother as "wonderful" and her father as demanding, temperamental, controlling, and critical. She said her father warned her "not to ever make a mistake." He yelled at her for many things, including forgetting her backpack and missing the school bus. Ms. GG was particularly distraught that he routinely became enraged at her when the bus was late arriving home, something over which she had no control. She came to believe she needed to do everything perfectly or catastrophe would follow. She felt safe in the company of her mother but experienced her father looming in the background in a frightening and disruptive way.

A source of relief from her fears were her social relationships, in which she routinely played the role of being the center of attention, in charge and a leader of her group of girlfriends. She felt safe being the one to make decisions about the group's activities.

As an adult, Ms. GG continued to feel it was essential to be the leader in her group of female friends but found this increasingly difficult, as her friends were much less likely to respond to her efforts to control activities. One significant source of her worries was the threat of not being the center of attention, which she experienced as equivalent to being rejected. For example, she became angry and anxious when two members of the group planned a birthday party for a third and did not include her in the planning phase. She believed that her friends becoming closer to each other would ultimately lead to her being ignored or excluded by the group in an ongoing way. In therapy, it gradually emerged that her social group represented a link to the safety of her mother. Threatened disruption of her role in the group symbolically represented her terror of falling into her father's control, thereby losing her source of protection and stability.

With her closest friends in the group, she believed that if things were not perfect, she would lose their friendship. This left little room to negotiate or tolerate even routine tensions. If a conflict with a close friend intensified, she would develop increasing worries about her body, such as a focus on headaches or gastrointestinal distress as signs of possible cancer. For example, when her closest friend Jane did not agree to a plan she had arranged for the group to get together weekly for dinner, she became furious with her and then fearful that she would be seen as "mean," leading to worries about rejection. She believed Jane was getting together with a friend of Jane's, who was not part of the group, at the same time and that Jane was therefore rejecting her. As her struggle with this friend persisted, she became preoccupied that ongoing neck pain might be a sign of cancer. Her jealousy of women with children in her group of friends intensified her perceived threat of disruption in her relationships, flooded as she was with rage and envy.

Ms. GG was intensely guilty about her anger, particularly her frequent fury at her father. When she became angry with him, she felt guilty about criticizing him and experienced an urgent need to make up for her thoughts or comments. The guilt was heightened by a sense that her father was in fact vulnerable and that her sister and mother had much more tolerance for him. For example, she became enraged when her father repeatedly criticized her for keeping the air conditioning at too high a level in her house when her parents visited. When she complained to her mother, her father said, "Don't turn your mother against me; she's the only one who cares about me," intensifying her guilt and the sense she had that her anger was unacceptable and dangerous. In addition, when she felt or expressed anger at her father or others, she worried that she was behaving like her father and became unrealistically self-critical. At these points she began to recognize that she expected others to respond to her requests just as her father did with her, such as demanding that they follow her social schedule. Her identification with her father made it difficult for her to experience any angry feelings without feeling guilty and anxious about losing control over her hostile fantasies and impulses, such as urges to confront friends about behavior she disliked.

In addition, it emerged that Ms. GG was unaware that she routinely behaved in ways that expressed her anger indirectly, provoking others to express their anger at her frequently. These angry reactions were unexpected and intensified her feelings of hurt and wishes to retaliate. This pattern increased her anxiety and caused further disruption of relationships. For example, Ms. GG was dismissive of Jane's wish to get together but then was surprised when Jane was angry at her, despite her own intense emotional reactions when Jane acted in the same way. Becoming aware of this covert hostility, although frightening for Ms. GG, reduced her sense of helplessness and provided a better understanding of why her feelings and relationships felt unmanageable.

The therapist and Ms. GG gained further understanding of her anxiety through detailed exploration of the experience of anxiety and the situtions in which it recurred. For example, the therapist was able to identify the pattern of increasing fears of having a serious health condition after she experienced angry feelings or jealousy, such as would occur after visiting friends who were pregnant or had small children. In therapy, these fears were linked to the threat Ms. GG felt that she would be criticized or rejected if her negative feelings were revealed. Another related trigger the therapist and patient were able to recognize was the danger of potential disruption of a relationship, either in fantasy or reality. Fears that being dizzy meant she was having a stroke developed after a girlfriend threatened to end their relationship, which she was ultimately able to understand in therapy represented her own anger at the friend and a neediness that she found difficult to control.

Ms. GG's worries about illness represented a compromise formation that served several functions. Her physical symptoms brought on by anxiety were emotionally understandable in part as being defensive, when her fantasies and fears reached intolerable levels, as it emerged that it was less disorganizing for

Ms. GG to imagine dangers to her health than abandonments by friends. The pain and distress caused by her somatic preoccupations also functioned as a self-punishment for her envy of friends and the anger that she routinely felt toward them and for acting, in her mind, like her father. Additionally, her somatic preoccupations and panic attacks made her feel helpless or potentially disabled (hence, a victim) rather than an angry threat to others.

Despite Ms. GG's presentation to therapy with what she described as a strong desire to have a child, it emerged through exploration that she also had fears about how a baby might negatively affect her life. She imagined that the baby would remind her of her father, constantly demanding and "at her" to get his or her needs met. She feared a baby would damage her body, a fantasy in part related to her fears of the baby and her father's aggression. She felt guilty about ascribing these threats to a baby and worried how she would handle being angry at a baby in general. She wanted to be the perfect mother, to compensate for these thoughts and feelings, and worried that a wrong decision or attitude would ruin her child.

Ms. GG's feelings of helplessness and lack of control in a variety of situations and her need for total control everywhere she went were linked to conflicted feelings and fears stemming originally from her relationship with her father as well as her identification with him. Her need to control others and to aim toward what she imagined were "perfect" relationships were understood as compensatory efforts to minimize the danger of her aggression in this context. The therapist pointed out to Ms. GG that her perfectionism was bound to fail and would inevitably leave her further disappointed, frustrated, and frightened. The therapist noted that perfection was not possible or necessary for relationships to work. Ms. GG began to acknowledge that people could have conflicts and express strong feelings without necessarily experiencing the kinds of threats and criticism she had with her father. She became more direct in her communications with others and less obliged to avoid or deny such feelings and thoughts.

Several of these themes and dynamics were identified and explored in the transference, providing an opportunity to address them more directly. For example, she felt that if the therapist was not perfect it was likely because he was hostile and uncaring. At one point, Ms. GG became angry at the therapist because she was still anxious. She believed that the therapist could not fully reassure her about her hypochondriacal fears. She felt guilty about expressing her disappointment and anger and worried she would be "fired" as a patient. She also feared the therapist would criticize her as her father did, in this case for not getting better or for not being a good patient. For example, at a later point in therapy after she improved signifciantly, she believed the therapist would be very angry with her when she wanted to discuss decreasing the frequency of her visits from twice to once weekly, even though the therapist had agreed that this reduction should be considered.

Over the course of therapy, Ms. GG's worries diminished in intensity and frequency and her panic attacks resolved. She increasingly recognized the links between her worries and her conflicts about being angry at and jealous of those she cared for and her neediness as it had initially surfaced in her relationship with her father and did now with friends and the therapist. She became better able to identify her somatic preoccupations as signals of increased emotional conflict, to observe her own anxiety and moods, and to understand why her worries intensified when they did. Improved access to her feelings allowed her to more directly address tensions with her friends. Ms. GG subequently became pregnant, easing her jealousy. Her fears of bodily damage were diminished by her having understood their link to her fanatasies about pregnancy and her relationship to her baby, and the psychological genesis of her physical symptoms.

Chapter 15

Psychodynamic approaches to posttraumatic stress disorder*

A number of clinical similarities exist between posttraumatic stress disorder (PTSD) and panic disorder. Symptom onset often occurs following exposure to traumatic events in both syndromes, although the relationship between panic disorder and stressors has not always been explicitly articulated. In PTSD, the traumatic event is defined as a severe trauma in which there is an actual or threatened death or serious physical injury or a threat to physical integrity of oneself or others (APA, 2000a). The panic attacks in panic disorder are often described as emerging "out of the blue," yet studies and clinical observations have demonstrated that life stressors precede panic onset. Indeed, in panic disorder, acute symptoms have been shown to occur in at least 50% of cases after antecedent actual interpersonal loss events (Klass et al., 2009; Milrod et al., 2004).

Clinical similarities between the two disorders include frequent panic attacks, a high degree of baseline anxiety, and the tendency to avoid distressing or anxiety-producing stimuli (North, Suris, Davis, & Smith, 2009). In clinical situations, anxiety symptoms can be difficult to untangle as "belonging" to one syndrome or another, because overwhelming anxiety can become free-floating and pervasive. This may be particularly true in people who survive catastrophic trauma (Cougle, Feldner, Keough, Hawkins, & Fitch, 2010; North et al., 2009).

The acute anxiety states that occur in PTSD can also be experienced as arising out of the blue. In these instances the content of the anxiety trigger becomes disconnected from the affect via the unconscious process of dissociation, a key defensive organizing feature of PTSD (Anderson & Gold, 2003). While patients with panic disorder are also prone to dissociation, it tends to occur with less severity than after catastrophic or life-threatening trauma. In both groups of patients, dissociation may be thought of as an adaptive response to relieve distress from overwhelming threats. This mode of "adaptation" ceases to be beneficial when the real threat and its associated risks recede. At that point dissociation becomes

* We would like to thank Marie Rudden, MD, for coauthoring this chapter with us.

an unsuccessful unconscious attempt at psychological avoidance because the fear-associated affects persist, now disconnected from the traumatic events. In both disorders, psychodynamic interventions focus on identifying the unconscious repressed mental contents and associated affects that contribute to symptomatology.

Case example

Ms. HH reported severe, daily, out-of-the-blue panic attacks for 3 years, ever since she had had an anaphylactic response to medicine a friend gave her for a headache. When she took this pill 3 years previously, she had gradually become hot and could not breathe. Her lips swelled, and when she was brought to the hospital the doctor told her (she could not speak) that she might die because her airway had nearly been cut off. The doctors managed to revive her, although she required an intensive care unit stay and a temporary emergency surgical airway. Ms. HH said she did not dream or really relive the event, although she had been "always on edge" ever since. Of importance, her daily panic attacks, which she said came out of the blue, were always accompanied by the fantasy that she was again having anaphylaxis, and she frequently went to the emergency room to make certain she was not.

While aspects of this case have the structure of out-of-the-blue panic disorder, Ms. HH had primary posttraumatic stress disorder: During her panic attacks, she relived the traumatic experience of her anaphylaxis. Her sense that the attacks derived from "nothing" is a clinical illustration of the defense mechanism of dissociation.

FACTORS CONTRIBUTING TO PRETRAUMA VULNERABILITY IN POSTTRAUMATIC STRESS DISORDER

Although most people (50–90%) encounter trauma during their lifetime (Breslau, Kessler, Chilcoat, Schultz, Davis, & Andreski, 1998; Kessler, Berglund, Demler, Jin, Merikangas, & Walters, 2005), only about 8% develop PTSD (Alexander & Anderson, 1994). Vulnerability to PTSD involves an interaction of biological diathesis, early childhood developmental experiences, trauma type, and severity. Childhood trauma, chronic adversity, and familial stressors have been found to increase risk for PTSD and for its biological markers after a traumatic event in adulthood (Koenen, Moffitt, Poulton, Martin, & Caspi, 2007; Otte et al., 2005; Resnick, Yehuda, Pitman, & Foy, 1995).

Attachment styles may increase later risk of developing anxiety disorders, including PTSD. Fraley and colleagues (Fraley, Fazzari, Bonanno, & Dekel, 2006) found that survivors ($N = 45$) with secure attachment who had significant exposure to the events of September 11, 2001, described fewer PTSD and depressive symptoms on follow-up than those with insecure attachment. Attachment was assessed with the 30-item Relationship Scales Questionnaire (RSQ; Griffin & Bartholomew, 1994). Twaite and Rodriguez-Srednicki (2004), who studied 284 New Yorkers affected by 9/11, found that history of childhood sexual or physical abuse increased the likelihood but that secure attachment decreased the likelihood of PTSD symptoms. Secure attachment protected against and potentially mediated the development of PTSD. Thus, premorbid insecure attachment and difficulty in establishing basic trust (Fonagy & Bateman, 2008), due to biological predisposition or early life experiences, including trauma, leaves individuals vulnerable to developing PTSD. These vulnerabilities inevitably surface in the therapeutic relationship.

A PSYCHODYNAMIC FORMULATION FOR POSTTRAUMATIC STRESS DISORDER

The impact of trauma on mind and self

Neurosecretory and psychological influences that occur during trauma experiences disrupt memory consolidation (LeDoux, 2002). Moments of terrifying clarity accompanying flashbacks alternate with disparate and often inconsistent impressions of the traumatic event itself, making a coherent narrative of the trauma difficult. Affective dysregulation ensues, with a patient's emotions emerging unpredictably and with a sense of perplexing discontinuity from regular life. This dysregulation, accompanied by the consequent traumatic disruption of the individual's sense of agency and physical cohesion, results in a profoundly disrupted sense of self for many trauma survivors. Boulanger (2002, 2007) posits that the disrupted sense of a continuous and predictable self is the central dynamism underlying PTSD symptomatology. Understanding and articulating these central elements of the traumatic experience is crucial to working psychodynamically with patients with PTSD.

Repetition, dissociation, guilt, and the counterphobic stance

A hallmark of PTSD and a central focus of the psychoanalytic understanding of trauma (Freud, 1920; Lindy, 1996), reflected in *DSM-IV-TR*

(APA, 2000a) criterion B of reexperiencing the trauma, is that of unconscious repetition. What has been overwhelming to survivors and remains unintegrated into their sense of reality becomes seemingly inexorably repeated. Thus, patients may experience an objectively dissimilar set of circumstances as a recurrence of the trauma or may unconsciously provoke an experience reminiscent of the trauma. In the psychoanalytic literature, this process has been described as "repetition compulsion" (Corradi, 2009).

Trauma victims defend themselves against the full implications of their traumatic experiences and the often unbearable feelings of pain, humiliation, rage, and helplessness that accompany them via various unconscious defensive maneuvers, often including the experience of dissociative states, in which patients feel disconnected from others, reality, or their own emotional states. Dissociative states can alternate with intense affects, including anxiety, triggered by reminders of the horror experienced. This pattern includes the reemergence of painful aspects of the trauma (intrusive memories, intense emotions, and flashbacks) and attempts to defend against the reemergence of the memory or its reminders through avoidance and dissociation (the avoidance of certain people or activities felt to be associated with the trauma and pervasive numbing).

Sometimes patients with PTSD continue to experience anxiety symptoms, not only as primary neurobiological discharge or as the result of defensive failure but also because it is connected to conscious or unconscious guilt and shame about some aspect of the traumatic experience itself or their role in it, for which they feel compelled to punish themselves. For example, traumatized individuals may have internalized the sense of dehumanization and disgust with which they were treated by a tormentor, rapist, or assailant, and may consciously still experience this as a part of themselves for which they continue to deserve to be punished or humiliated. Survivor guilt can occur due to conflicts about having survived a trauma when others died or were more severely injured (Krupnick & Horowitz, 1981). In addition, individuals can identify with the aggressor (A. Freud, 1946) or can find themselves with compelling fantasies/wishes of hurting others as they themselves were hurt. This internal effort to avoid the repulsive sense of helplessness engendered by being a victim of the trauma, and to replace this sense of helplessness with the fantasy of mastery, can also trigger intense guilt and self-disgust, as patients become aware of their wish to damage others.

Some victims maintain a vigorous counterphobic stance to deny the extent of the impact the trauma has had (e.g., a woman sexually abused as a child might become promiscuous both to ragefully punish men and to deny the knowledge that she carries with her that she was so helpless and victimized). This counterphobic behavior may result in the patient's repeatedly putting herself in harm's way again, making her vulnerable to revictimization, a common phenomenon in PTSD.

Additional factors affecting traumatic sequelae and the meaning of the traumatic experience

Specific elements of the traumatic experience can pose difficulties and can have particular meanings for the survivor that are important to consider in a psychodynamic psychotherapy. When trauma occurs as a result of interpersonal hatred and violence, survivors face a more difficult challenge than those affected by impersonal events, such as hurricanes. It was the neglect of the people in government toward Katrina survivors that was recounted as most traumatic, not the storm itself, as individuals struggled with feeling uncared for and enraged (Lee, 2006). Once victims become objects of vicious, dehumanizing, and humiliating behavior on the part of the victimizer, survivors plunge into a world of "psychic equivalence." That is, horrifying, disorganizing, universal unconscious fears or fantasies have actually been witnessed and enacted in real time and contribute to an uncanny sense of living nightmare and a lack of differentiation between reality and fantasy. Rules that normally govern human behavior have been suspended. These impressions do not end with the cessation of the trauma but rather serve to revolutionize victims' sense of relationships between people and their relationship to reality.

Past experiences of helplessness and aggression may substantially affect reactions to massive trauma. Those who have suffered trauma in their past or who have already felt personally insecure and unsafe prior to the traumatic event are particularly vulnerable to developing PTSD. On the other hand, past experience is distinct from the actual traumatic experience that engenders PTSD, and past feelings of trust or mistrust, safety, or vulnerability, can be modified substantially by having been through trauma. Prior trauma affects the meaning of current trauma and the underlying dynamisms in traumatized individuals (Caruth, 1996). The conscious and unconscious meanings ascribed by patients to their traumatic experiences are crucial in fully understanding individual reactions to trauma.

PSYCHODYNAMIC APPROACHES TO POSTTRAUMATIC STRESS DISORDER

The essence of a general psychodynamic approach to posttraumatic symptoms lies in linking the disparate symptoms themselves: those that torment survivors and those that leave them numb and withdrawn to their emotional antecedents. The need for integration parallels the integrating efforts of Panic Focused Psychodynamic Psychotherapy—eXtended Range

(PFPP-XR) in linking anxiety symptoms to emotional states and underlying intrapsychic conflicts. Particular somatic sensations, for example, may actually result from symbolic memory encoding of elements of the trauma itself. An example would be the mysterious sensation of chronic nausea following a trauma in which survivors had viewed a dismembered corpse. The sense of sickening repulsion may have endured via the nausea, although the symptom is no longer consciously associated with this horrifying experience and seems to take on a life on its own. Patients' sense of disconnection can be identified as deriving from the trauma and can be productively viewed as a failed protective mechanism; the mechanism has developed to disguise their experience of anxiety and pain yet in its pervasiveness serves to blunt certain emotions and to make ongoing anxiety and distress seem far more confusing than they need to be.

The traumatic experience itself acts like a lens through which to understand the patient's current experience, much like the somatic panic experience in panic disorder acts like a lens to identify areas of intense conflict and departures from the patient's ordinary relationship to reality and way of thinking. PFPP-XR's articulation helps individuals more clearly understand the specific ways the traumatic experience continues to affect their experience of the world and relationships to others.

In addition to establishing a comprehensible psychological context and narrative for what can otherwise feel like disjunctive symptoms, in psychodynamic psychotherapy, the therapist explores the meaning of various transferences to better understand the specific emotional significance of the trauma. The therapist may be viewed, for example, as a banal bureaucrat who cannot possibly understand or care about the trauma, as a cowardly bystander, as a horrified witness to degradation, as an abuser. Helping patients see these often unconscious reactions to themselves and others and to appreciate a dynamic understanding of the ramifications of the trauma's impact is essential in a dynamic approach to PTSD.

Addressing conflicts, guilt, and defenses (Identification with the aggressor and dissociation)

Addressing defenses and underlying conflicts is a key component of the PFPP-XR treatment of PTSD. Dissociation and identification with the aggressor are prominent defenses in PTSD that, when addressed clinically, aid the emergence of frightening and conflicted aspects of the traumatic experience, facilitating better articulation and improvement in symptoms. Guilt about angry reactions or about survival often emerges as feelings about the trauma are explored. The following is a brief clinical example of the unfolding of some of these dynamic elements within a psychodynamic treatment of a patient traumatized in adulthood.

Case example

Ms. II was 18 when she moved to New York from Florida to attend college. She had a long history of illicit substance abuse and binge alcohol abuse and had been diagnosed with attention deficit disorder (ADD) in childhood and treated with Adderall with some success. She also had a long history of chronic anxiety without panic attacks and sleep difficulties since early childhood, aggravated by severe depression, bulimia, and polysubstance abuse in her very erratic mother. Nonetheless, Ms. II had never had a panic attack until her freshman year of college after she was raped.

The patient had gone to a bar with friends and had been dancing with a man she met at the bar, whom she could only vaguely remember, in part because she had consumed a significant amount of alcohol. Later, in the emergency room, it was determined that the stranger had "dosed" her drink with horse tranquilizer. Ms. II "woke up" in an alley behind the bar, with torn, bloody underpants at her heels, nearly naked, and immediately recalled, as if through a dense fog, the man raping and beating her. She was treated in an emergency room for both HIV prevention and other sexually transmitted diseases but declined to press charges, as she recalled so few specifics about her assailant because of the drug. Her parents flew in from Florida and stayed with her.

That night, she had her first panic attack, feeling as though "the walls were coming in on me" and as if she could not locate her body on the bed. Her old childhood fears of the dark reemerged explosively, and she was frightened and panicky, feeling as though she would disappear or die if any lights were turned off. She could not be alone. Her parents stayed with her for weeks, but she could not return to school that semester because of an inability to focus and severe anxiety. She stopped taking her Adderall, which helped her to concentrate at school, and refused any medication whatsoever, out of an unstated fear that she might become foggy as she did the night of the rape.

When Ms. II presented for psychotherapy, 3 months after the rape, she reported her story in a monotone. Although she consciously described her current problems after she told the story of the rape, she also seemed surprised that the therapist linked her panic attacks, other anxiety symptoms, and dissociative symptoms to the rape. "But how could it affect me so deeply?" Ms. II asked. "I don't even really remember it because of the drug he put in my drink. And anyway, I don't ever want to think about it again. Ever. I'm not discussing it." She nearly left the office.

In psychotherapy, the therapist listened to Ms. II telling story after story about her current life, which featured ways she felt (and was repeatedly) mistreated by boyfriends. One boyfriend actually date raped her after she broke up with him because he had cheated on her. The therapist was only gradually able to show Ms. II in real time the way that she managed to repeat many key elements of the rape experience over and over: specifically, the feeling of being "loopy" and out of control (a key feature of her panic experience) and the surprising, out-of-the-blue vicious mistreatment by men she thought she could trust. It was only after her second rape by her ex-boyfriend that Ms. II was finally able to see that in fact she was "remembering" the rape constantly, over and over, without actually permitting herself to think about it consciously or discuss it in words. It was only at this point that she was able to begin to change the way she approached relationships with men and that her severe panic and PTSD experiences improved.

This example demonstrates some of the central psychodynamic underpinnings of PTSD: an ever present, often unspoken terror that the trauma might repeat itself, which often fuels a reluctance to recall and address it, an example of dissociation and avoidance functioning defensively. While thinking about the traumatic event can sometimes be avoided consciously, the patient's preoccupation with the events expresses itself intrusively, in this case in repeated reenactments and reexperiencing of key components of the rape. Ms. II felt a deep sense of humiliation and shame at having been rendered helpless, abused, and raped. She experienced an ongoing, all-consuming struggle to regain even a relative sense of safety and self-coherence; she was plagued by often unconscious, disruptive rage at the man who raped her, which spread to her feelings about men in general. As she became better able to describe her experiences with men in words, she gradually became aware of her tendency to pick almost violent, irrational fights with boyfriends as a routine way of interacting from the very beginning of her relationships. This pattern tilted most romantic experiences toward men who were attracted to such behavior and introduced violent power struggles into interactions from the start.

Ms. II suffered from a fairly clear sense of guilt about the rape in the first place once she was able to permit herself to discuss it. She was well aware that her "wild party" lifestyle was deeply irresponsible, and she blamed herself openly for what happened. "Well, I was just an idiot," she frequently said. Her guilt (over rage at her mother as well as her '"wild" tendencies) played a role in her unconsciously seeking punishment through the repeated reenactments of her rape. These reenactments were also fueled by her unconscious attempts to master the traumatic experience and to show herself and the world that she could never be so helpless and abused again. Such reenactments may also have been recapitulations of even earlier trauma when she felt unprotected by her intoxicated mother, and her drinking may well have been an identification with her mother.

This patient frequently functioned on a plane in which action reigned supreme, and she literally could not think about or understand why she did many of the (posttraumatic) things that she felt an urgency to do, an example of dissociation. Gradually putting her experiences into words and translating her seemingly inexplicable actions into an understandable frame of these experiences as a part of her emotional response to her rape permitted her to gradually gain distance from the rape experience itself and specifically helped her to become less anxious and frantic. By focusing on the transference, in specific on her chronic irritation with her therapist's focus on verbalizing her experiences, working through her traumatic response to the rape also enabled her to resurrect traumatic memories from childhood, including those of her traumatic attachment to her mother; she could also explore the possibility of new relationships in which she could allow herself to begin to trust another person in a different way.

Length of psychodynamic psychotherapy for PTSD

Some authors (Lindy, 1996; Kudler, Blank, & Krupnick, 2004; Weiss & Marmar, 1993) have emphasized that to fully treat complex PTSD an open-ended, long-term psychodynamic psychotherapy or psychoanalysis is necessary. This recommendation is based on the clinical experience that for multiply or deeply traumatized individuals a sufficiently trusting alliance often develops only over time due to the victim's inherent mistrust of others and that some of the most trenchant and hidden elements of the traumatic schemata are unlikely to reveal themselves within a brief treatment. Some authors (e.g., Gabbard, 2000; Krystal, 1988) caution that expressive and interpretive work exposing PTSD patients to the full affective force of their experience may be unproductive or even worse for patients with unstable relationship and work histories prior to their trauma and for those who do not have a capacity for insight or difficulty with self-observation (Rudden, Milrod, Meehan, & Falkenstrom, 2009). Clinicians need to perform ongoing evaluations of the patient's response to these interventions. Psychodynamic treatments can help patients to develop insight and mentalization capacities, key deficits that form a part of the core of the anxiety and posttraumatic syndrome.

Chapter 16

Psychodynamic approaches to anxiety-related personality disorders

Patients with primary DSM-IV (American Psychiatric Association, 1994) panic disorder with comorbid Axis II personality disorders, 80% of which were Cluster C disorders, were found to be significantly more responsive to PFPP than patients with primary panic disorder who did not carry this personality comorbidity in one study (Milrod et al., 2007). Cluster C disorders are dependent personality disorder, avoidant personality disorder, and obsessive compulsive personality disorder. Key traits of patients with these disorders include a heightened sense of dependency on others, general unassertiveness and passivity, separation fears, shyness, sensitivity to disapproval, avoidance, perfectionism, and overconscientiousness. Similar yet exaggerated and more global expressions of some of the psychological conflicts we have described in patients with panic disorder, including difficulty tolerating being angry at people they love, ambivalence about asserting themselves, and difficulty in developing appropriate autonomy, can contribute to the development and persistence of these personality traits. It is thus unsurprising that Cluster C patients did particularly well in PFPP-XR, as PFPP-XR focuses specifically on treatment of these features. This chapter identifies psychodynamic approaches for these personality disorders and traits and describes how interpretation of defenses and intrapsychic conflicts, and a therapeutic focus on the transference, can reduce symptoms and interpersonal difficulties related to these characterological predispositions.

While it might appear that similar underlying psychological conflicts would increase vulnerability to both panic disorder and to cluster C personality traits, only about 50% of patients with panic disorder also meet criteria for any personality disorder by SCID II (Milrod et al., 2007b). Below we describe specific personality disorders that comprise the cluster C spectrum and provide case examples of treatment of panic patients with these comorbidities. It should be noted that patients frequently carry personality traits from different individual personality disorders and clusters of disorders.

DEPENDENT PERSONALITY DISORDER

Dependent personality disorder is defined in *DSM-IV-TR* (American Psychiatric Association, 2000b) as "a pervasive and excessive need to be taken care of that leads to submissive and clinging behavior and fears of separation..." (p. 295). Criteria for this disorder include, amongst others, "difficulty expressing disagreement with others due to fear of loss of support and approval," (p. 296), "goes to excessive lengths to obtain nurturance and support from others..." (p. 296), "feels uncomfortable or helpless when alone because of exaggerated fears of being unable to care for himself or herself" (p. 296), and "is unrealistically preoccupied with fears of being left to take care of himself or herself" (p. 296). The *DSM-IV* does not concern itself with dynamic interrelationships amongst various character traits, nor does it note the connection between dependent personality disorder and more anxiety-ridden antecedents or Axis I disorders, such as separation anxiety disorder. However, even amongst the traits described, a sense of personal inadequacy, fears of separation, and fears of disrupting relationships if one were assertive represent core aspects of conflicts that are prominent in both panic disorder, and in many of the other Axis I anxiety disorders.

Fearful dependency has been described as playing a central formative role in the development and persistence of anxiety disorders: patients often believe that they are incapable of managing on their own. Conflicts surrounding dependency, which can include a feeling of humiliation about dependent wishes and a fear of rejection if these wishes are acknowledged directly, interfere with awareness of these feelings and needs, the patient's capacity to garner support from others, and ability to more actively care for him or herself. Thus, dependency wishes and fears become intensified. Panic attacks and severe anxiety symptoms can represent a disguised, somatically-expressed, powerful wish to be taken care of by others, communicated in a compelling, sometimes coercive, self-punitive form. Mixed feelings about dependency can be aggravated by conflicts about the wish to achieve autonomy. These conflicts include worries that autonomy will lead to loss of key relationships, or that competitive or assertive skills will lead to an uncomfortable disruption of relationships. Dependency and associated panic attacks and anxiety can be viewed as a regression from the challenging experience of being a competent adult.

Lack of assertiveness is a central feature of dependent personality disorder, with a fear of disrupting relationships. This trait is akin to anxiety patients' fear of being assertive with others. These patients have particular discomfort surrounding the experience or expression of anger. This struggle is often intensified by unconscious rage toward the people on whom they feel so dependent. Rage can stem from disappointment about not being cared for, or as a result of narcissistic humiliation about their perception of a need for care. Patients with anxiety disorders, as well as patients with dependent personality disorder, worry that their anger will disrupt close relationships, which are felt to be essential for well-being and safety. The regression to a more dependent position can be viewed as reassuring, yet also as a punishment. In the patient's view, the threat from aggression is reduced if he remains dependent, yet he also never gives himself the opportunity to function independently.

Case example

Ms. F, described in Chapters 3 and 12, met criteria for dependent personality disorder. She had a number of traits surrounding fears about being able to take care of herself, and frequently made demands on others to take care of her. She struggled, for example, with cleaning, organizing her apartment, and managing her finances, often relying on her boyfriend to help her with these tasks. She felt guilty about asking for his help and worried he would reject her, but at the same time feared losing him if she became more capable and competent. To her, being taken care of meant she was loved.

Ms. F experienced her family as more responsive to those who needed care. Her brother, for example, unemployed with alcohol problems, was supported financially by their parents. In contrast, Ms. F, who was consistently employed for many years, was told that money promised to her by her parents was needed to manage their own finances, including support of her brother. Thus, for Ms. F, autonomy represented a loss of parental care and attention. Her conflicted wish to be cared for emerged in the transference, as she sometimes bounced checks to her therapist or fell behind on payments. When this was explored, she reported great confusion about keeping track of her money, and said she could not understand how her financial problems occurred. Exploration revealed her anger at the therapist, as at her parents, for not supporting her financially. Her bouncing checks and delaying payment were expressions of this anger and disappointment, and they also represented a fantasy that the therapist would take care of her by helping her organize her life, like her boyfriend, and would not charge her.

As a child, Ms. F had experienced little in the way of emotional nurturing from her parents, which ultimately led to deep-seated wishes to be cared for laced with fury at her parents for not having done this, and guilty self-recriminations about all of her feelings. Her alcoholic mother frequently criticized her, particularly when she was intoxicated, cursing at her and calling her "fat" and "stupid." Her father was emotionally distant and ignored her mother's problems, and Ms. F reported that he was also verbally abused by Ms. F's mother. Ms.F felt pressured to take care of her mother, emotionally and physically, in part because she feared for mother's health and safety. In this context, Ms. F's own wishes to be cared for felt selfish to her, and she believed her own needs had to be subsumed by her mother's. In addition, any overt wish for nurturing predictably led to disappointment. Ms. F had trained herself to deny these wishes, which were inevitably expressed indirectly, as illustrated in her management of home and money.

Ms. F had come to view stating any wish for help from others as "being a bitch." This view emerged because of the connection between her acknowledgment of her own wishes and her mother's rage at her. She connected her own assertiveness with her mother's cursing and name-calling of her father and herself. As a result of this emotional maelstrom, she felt unable to ask her boyfriend to fix something on the computer he had set up for her, worrying that he would get angry and reject her (echoing thoughts surrounding her inability to ask him for financial help). She feared she would be seen as a "bitch" for not appreciating his efforts. In therapy, she became able to identify the intensity of her wishes to be cared for and to understand the threat she felt from expressing them.

She grew to recognize that her "confusion" about money and organization was the result of conflicted feelings and disappointment. She wanted to be independent, but believed if she were strong she would be forsaken. She wished to be taken care of, but felt this was unacceptable and selfish. As a compromise, she consciously avoided thinking about or acknowledging her dependency wishes, while unconsciously attempting to extract what she felt was her due in ways that could make others resent her, leaving her feeling inadequate and deprived. As she was able to clarify her needs and what held her back from getting them met, she became less uncomfortable expressing them directly. She recognized that others were unlikely to respond like her mother, and was surprised and relieved by the support she received.

As Ms. F was able to develop more supportive relationships and see that her needs could be met, she was less frantic that she would be uncared for, and was able to function more autonomously. Because her dependency conflicts contributed to both Ms. F's panic disorder and to her overall dependent personality style, the resolution of these conflicts was associated with a reduction in both her panic disorder and with her characteristic dependent behavior.

AVOIDANT PERSONALITY DISORDER

Symptoms of avoidant personality disorder show significant overlap with those found in social anxiety disorder. In *DSM-IV-TR* (American Psychiatric Association, 2000b) the disorder is defined as a "pervasive pattern of social inhibition, feelings of inadequacy, and hypersensitivity to negative evaluation" (p. 295). Criteria for this disorder include: "avoids occupational activities that involve significant interpersonal contact, because of fears of criticism, disapproval, or rejection" (p. 295); "shows restraint within intimate relationships because of the fear of being shamed and ridiculed" (p. 295), "is preoccupied with being shamed and ridiculed in social situations" (p. 295), and "views self as socially inept, personally unappealing, or inferior to others" (p. 295).

The dynamics of avoidant personality disorder also overlap with social anxiety disorder. Patients with social anxiety disorder have a core sense of shame and personal inadequacy and worry that others will humiliate and reject them. Core feelings of inadequacy and incapacity heighten worries about disruptions in relationships. Angry feelings and fantasies trigger further concerns about rejection, as attachment to significant others feels essential for a sense of security and safety yet feels easily threatened. Avoidance of particular social and occupational situations is employed, often unconsciously, to reduce the experience of intolerable feelings of personal inadequacy and rageful criticism of others. In these cases it is essential for the therapist to identify the specific emotional conflicts the patient is avoiding.

Case example

Ms. JJ, a 26-year-old woman with primary Social Anxiety Disorder (SAD) and avoidant personality disorder, had improved significantly in terms of her SAD symptoms in PFPP-XR, as she and her therapist focused on her guilty yet hostile relationship with a brother two years her junior. Her brother was born with a number of physical deformities and had always angrily blamed Ms. JJ for treating him with disdain. Ms. JJ acknowledged that she had briefly but intensely taunted him in early adolescence, and she continued to feel very guilty about her behavior at the time. Ms. JJ's brother blamed her for most of his life problems, including his loneliness and social situation, even though she clearly was not responsible for this. Her parents "humored" her brother, and no one openly disagreed with him, despite his chronic blaming of her and increasing temper tantrums, as they all felt so "sorry for him." "My brother's a freak, and it's my fault," Ms. JJ lamented.

Ms. JJ's social anxiety took the form of feeling extremely embarrassed and "on display" whenever she had to speak in public and worried unrealistically about being rejected and "looking stupid" in social situations, with occasional associated panic attacks. She tended to avoid these situations and speaking in front of other people, even at times when she felt she had things to say. In PFPP-XR, she began to recognize that the feelings of "looking weird" and "being on display" that she had at these times were intimately associated with her sense of guilty identification with her bizarre-looking brother. These fantasies and the associated anxiety, panic attacks, and avoidance that she suffered in social situations functioned to endlessly punish her for the way she had ridiculed him. Articulation of these antecedents helped Ms. JJ to make presentations more comfortably and to function better in social situations; her SAD essentially remitted.

Yet Ms. JJ remained chronically avoidant in less obvious ways without the massive anxiety attacks she had suffered before. She hated her job, despite being extremely well-liked, yet felt too uncomfortable discussing ways she could make changes there with anyone: her boss, co-workers, or even with the human resources director, who had offered to move Ms. JJ to another group within the business. She permitted her husband to minutely criticize almost everything she did, feeling unable to and uncomfortable in defending herself. "I'm a big wimp," she cried one day, "and I hate myself for it!"

Focusing on the fantasies she had when she knew herself to be angry and feeling "abused" in various situations permitted Ms. JJ to recognize how hurt and injured she chronically felt. She repeatedly found herself being very embarrassed because she was haunted by memories of physically bullying her brother when he was smaller than she was. She remembered pulling his hair and screaming at him. At one point in this discussion, she said simply, "So you see, deep down, I am a bad person."

THERAPIST: It does sound as though you were not a nice sister when you were 12.

MS. JJ: I know! It's horrible! I hate myself!

THERAPIST: I hear you. Actually, though, when was the last time you actually did anything like this with B?

MS. JJ: [*shocked*] When I was 12…no, maybe, 13. Why?

THERAPIST: The question is—will anything you ever do make this better?

MS. JJ: [*very surprised*] It's a funny question. Like on the one hand, it's so over. I really make a point of never being mean to him or to anyone else now. On the other hand, I act like I'm not done with this; I can see this.

Through a more realistic exploration along these lines, Ms. JJ gradually was able to feel less guilty about her adolescent embarrassment and rage at her brother and to take greater control of her life. She negotiated a better job within the company for which she worked and a more comfortable relationship with her husband.

OBSESSIVE-COMPULSIVE PERSONALITY DISORDER

DSM-IV-TR (American Psychiatric Association, 2000b) defines obsessive compulsive personality disorder as "a pervasive pattern of preoccupation with orderliness, perfectionism, and mental and interpersonal control, at the expense of flexibility, openness, and efficiency" (p. 296). Criteria for this disorder include: "is preoccupied with details, rules, lists, order, organization, or schedules to the extent that the major point of the activity is lost" (p. 296), "shows perfectionism that interferes with task completion" (p. 296), "is excessively devoted to work and productivity to the exclusion of leisure activities and friendships" (p. 297), and "is overconscientious, scrupulous, and inflexible about matters of morality, ethics, or values" (p. 297).

Patients with OCPD fear a loss of control over their emotions, including their angry and dependent wishes. In patients with obsessive compulsive personality disorder, the defenses of intellectualization and dissociation of affect, in which feelings become disconnected from actual thought content, function as defensive strategies to manage their fears. In PFPP-XR, one focus of the therapy is to help patients to identify and integrate warded-off affects. Patients' preoccupation with lists, rules, and organization can represent further defensive efforts to avoid feeling out of control. Addressing the patient's obsessional traits can help to identify the emotional meanings of symptoms. These patients' perfectionism, conscientiousness, preoccupation with order, and efforts at affective control can lead to struggles with the therapist about the framework and content of the therapy. These tensions provide opportunities to explore these characteristics and elucidate underlying fears in the context of the transference.

Case example

Mr. KK was a 39-year-old single freelance painter and photographer at the time of his presentation with new onset panic disorder and conversion disorder. He had a long history of preoccupation with his body and also chronically experienced physical symptoms at times of stress, although this history only emerged later in his therapy. Mr. KK said that he had been entirely well until one day while on vacation with a friend, when he was suddenly overcome with shortness of breath, shaking, numbness in his limbs, and an urgent sense of impending doom. He was medevaced to a hospital because he believed he was having a heart attack "or worse." It was only after extensive medical testing, including several medical hospitalizations, that he was diagnosed with panic disorder and conversion disorder by an internist and a neurologist, and referred to a psychiatrist.

Mr. KK was shocked to be advised that psychological problems led to his symptoms and subsequent "breakdown." Throughout the early weeks of his therapy, he recurrently worried that he must be suffering from a yet-to-be-diagnosed medical problem that was causing him such extraordinarily frightening physical symptoms. He initially reported that his life was going "fine," and for this reason, he could not imagine how his problems could be psychological. However, it quickly emerged that Mr. KK was in the throes of a life crisis that he had heretofore not acknowledged to himself. Having lost his job in the stock market several years before, he had decided to work as a freelance artist. He found that he needed to, but was unable to, force himself to execute the work he agreed to do, as he would become impaired by indecision as to how to proceed. He struggled with what he should be doing first: should he just do the photographs he was hired to do? Should he instead be trying to market himself to other people? This made him anxious, so he usually avoided his work altogether, devoting endless frustrating and ineffectual hours each day toward prioritizing his time rather than permitting himself to work.

Thus he was left constantly struggling to keep up yet feeling limited by "routines" he had established so as to avoid the chasm of anxiety that he experienced whenever he had "free" time. His romantic life suffered from similar difficulties. Seven years following a failed relationship with a woman, he wanted to date, yet felt unable to decide whom he should ask out. Mr. KK had always been somewhat aware that he was "mildly" anxious when he got "stalled" or "kind of locked" as he put it (into not doing things, but obsessing about them). Yet until the diathesis of anxiety that he experienced during the vacation and its aftermath, his specific "small-scale" preoccupations about particular items of work or particular social concerns had obscured his ability to evaluate the current course of his life in a more global manner. When he finally engaged in psychotherapy, he began to see that the entire process of becoming a freelancer was fraught with emotional conflicts for him, something that his obsessional symptoms had played a significant part in his avoiding.

Common emotional conflicts in patients with an obsessional personality structure include such an excessive focus on small details such that the larger picture of what is happening, or what the events really mean, can get lost. This is often accompanied by an emotional distancing or isolation of feelings from upsetting triggers of anxiety, whether they are thoughts, events, fantasies, or wishes. For these people, severe anxiety can arise in part out of these disconnections between things that happen and patients' lack of acknowledgment of their personal emotional significance. Anxiety can also appear when elaborately constructed schedules, such as Mr. KK's highly plotted plans to "work" (which he began to understand in therapy could equally well be described as his unconscious plans to "avoid work"), are disrupted. Such schedules are often constructed with more emotional interference than those that arise simply as a result of realistic difficulties with time management.

Chapter 17

Common clinical difficulties in practicing panic focused psychodynamic psychotherapy—eXtended range

PATIENTS WHO CANNOT ARTICULATE THEIR ANXIETY EXPERIENCE

Highly anxious patients are often overwhelmed by their anxiety symptoms and may be desperate for treatment. Thus, it can initially seem surprising, once they actually find a therapist and start therapy, that some patients can have considerable difficulty articulating what actually happens when they experience severe anxiety. Although symptoms can be clear-cut, patients sometimes report that it is hard for them to tell whether they are anxious or whether they have had a panic attack and, if so, exactly when. Difficulties in communication about various aspects of their anxiety can feel insurmountable, including an inability to pinpoint specific circumstances of their panic or anxiety symptoms, such as times that they became anxious, what they were doing and thinking when they got anxious, with whom they were, and what had happened earlier in the day. Although many panic and anxiety patients have difficulty immediately accessing actual fantasies and specific feelings that preoccupied them while they were anxious, these patients may have an insistent denial that there was any specific content to their anxiety.

Although panic focused psychodynamic psychotherapy—eXtended range (PFPP-XR) techniques target patients' defenses against knowledge of their feelings and fantasies associated with anxiety, the level of confusion found in these patients does not always readily respond to clinical recommendations of PFPP-XR outlined heretofore in this book (or to any other anxiety-specific psychotherapeutic approach, regardless of orientation). These difficulties represent an exacerbation of anxiety patients' typical defenses of denial and "not knowing." Such phenomena form the fabric of what we have described as *resistance*; in sum, they represent unconscious pressures that function to reinforce the symptoms and keep them alive. This disruption in the capacity to think about anxiety symptoms also highlights one aspect of the regression described in Chapters 3 and 5, in which highly anxious patients can struggle with thinking verbally about their emotional state. Nonetheless, in each situation in which the PFPP-XR therapist encounters what feels like a stalemate, he or she must try to understand the fantasies that give rise to the patient's seeming intransigence in the way one would with any resistance.

The basic psychodynamic principles outlined here can illuminate how best to proceed clinically in such situations. The inchoate quality of the panic and severe anxiety experience for these patients *forms a specific element of the meaning of panic and functions as a defense against the conflicts that gave rise to the anxiety.* The sense that the symptoms cannot be described can serve as a guidepost for the clinician in unraveling the emotional underpinnings of the panic and anxiety symptoms. If the inability to pinpoint what is happening during severe anxiety episodes has worsened since starting treatment, this phenomenon may begin to inform aspects of the transference that might have otherwise gone unnoticed.

Case example

Mr. LL, a 29-year-old Senegalese American hedge fund manager in a corporation hurtling toward bankruptcy, presented with overwhelming panic attacks that forced him to take a medical leave of absence from his job. Panic attacks occurred almost constantly, requiring multiple trips to emergency rooms. Mr. LL denied experiencing anxiety and was convinced that he was having a pulmonary embolism, a concern he developed after watching an episode of *ER* on television. Despite a negative medical workup, Mr. LL continued to focus on his bodily concerns. He could not distinguish between physical and emotional feelings.

"But it makes no sense that I have panic attacks because I just don't get anxious," he reported. Mr. LL also said that he had "never" experienced any anxiety of note before the 2 weeks prior to presentation, although he had noticed that he was "uptight" at work before he began to have panic attacks. Despite this statement, it rapidly emerged that he had been worked up for severe, debilitating headaches and dizziness on multiple occasions over the 3 years prior to presentation.

PATIENT: It's just so weird that everyone agrees that this is anxiety. I don't agree. I can't agree. And I'd rather have this be physical, believe me.

THERAPIST: Why?

PATIENT: Because at least that would be normal, or okay.

THERAPIST: How so? Having a pulmonary embolism is very serious. It can be fatal.

PATIENT: Right, but this is like I'm crazy.

It gradually emerged that Mr. LL had sought out the "toughest job possible," from his perspective, in part because of the degree to which it was important to him to be "strong and manly," a self-definition he felt was required to fulfill his father's expectations of him as his only son. "Being the only son is no joke in my culture," he remarked. Thus, the seeming inability that he had to even entertain the idea that he was anxious—"which is like being weak"—emerged as a central aspect to the meaning of his symptoms.

PATIENTS WHO ARE CERTAIN THAT NOTHING THE THERAPIST CAN DO WILL HELP

It is understandable that highly anxious patients who have had several disappointing experiences with different forms of psychotherapy or medication that have not helped their anxiety might approach a new treatment with trepidation. This is to be expected and should not be considered a formal "difficulty." Despite these worries, most patients become rapidly engaged in PFPP-XR and quickly feel empowered by the process of developing further understanding about underlying emotional meanings of their symptoms.

Nonetheless, a minority of patients complain continuously that therapy cannot be expected to help. Their therapists' comments may be interesting, they say, but in the patients' view they do not alter anything in their anxiety symptoms. They announce forcefully throughout the treatment that they will not get better. Many of these patients are also depressed. Such patients can be discouraging to treat. When such a situation arises, it is essential for the therapist to make a concerted effort to understand the overarching fantasy that patients have of themselves that they cannot improve. This fantasy forms a coherent piece of the narrative about themselves. Alternatively, patients can feel protected by their symptoms and sheltered from needing to address pressing life concerns. Such a fantasy can also highlight their ambivalence about anything changing in their life and underscores the attachment—albeit in an unhappy way—to the symptoms and the limitations they impose. These fantasies are compelling for a particular reason, and when it can be understood, patients can begin to experience relief from anxiety.

Case example

Ms. MM, a 41-year-old single Jewish immigrant from eastern Europe, had severe panic disorder that had lasted for over a decade since her immigration.

She had daily panic attacks and was frustrated because she often had to avoid making plans with friends, or even going out, because her multiple specific phobias and agoraphobia were overwhelming. She was also worried she would not have the opportunity to have a child. An only child of older parents who had remained in Europe, Ms. MM reported that she had felt "deep relief" when she moved to the United States because she was able to get away from their "miserable home." Her parents depressed her, she felt disconnected at home, and she never questioned her decision to leave Europe despite her crippling anxiety since arrival.

Ms. MM had failed two courses of cognitive-behavioral therapy (CBT) and three medication trials when she started PFPP-XR. She told her therapist:

PATIENT: I know this won't work.
THERAPIST: How do you know that?
PATIENT: Because nothing will ever work for me; no matter what you say, I am hopeless. It is genetic about me.

In an anxiety dream that she had early in the course of her therapy, she dreamed that she was donating her ovaries to a woman "who could use them." Although she was not suicidal and verbally endorsed a desire to get better, she often told her therapist that it seemed unfair that other women got cancer and she didn't "because I am hopeless and expendable." The therapist noted to her that her expendability seemed related to whether she would have a child, which was clearly a goal that felt like an emergency, given her age and single status. Ms. MM superficially agreed but said that this did not matter anyway.

While superficially interested in what her therapist said, Ms. MM never "gave another thought" to the underpinnings of her anxiety when she left the therapist's office, and she often spent time pointing out to him how nothing he said or asked about seemed related to her anxiety. Ultimately, the therapist found these comments distracting and discouraging, and in a countertransference reaction he found himself feeling almost as passive and helpless as the patient reported feeling.

The therapist began to ask Ms. MM about her often unstated yet pervasive image of herself as being "hopeless" and "expendable." Ms. MM had no idea what this related to (as she frequently felt in PFPP-XR), yet in the process of attempting to understand her family's expectations of her the therapist eventually asked her about her parents' wartime experiences as Jews in eastern Europe during World War II. Surprisingly, Ms. MM reported "never having thought about that at all," even though her parents clearly had been alive when her country was invaded by the Nazis. The therapist underscored for her how unusual he found it that she had never been curious about this central question about her identity:

THERAPIST: You're not curious about what happened to your parents during World War II under the Nazis, just like now you don't seem to be curious about your panic either.

"Despite myself—just to be nice to you as an experiment, doctor," Ms. MM asked her parents about their war-time experiences when she next spoke with them. They did not tell her much, but her father made it clear that he had had to hide in the forests, living on scavenged food and starving for a number of years. Her mother "mentioned" that she had given birth to a child who died and had been secretly buried near their home. Ms. MM recalled that she had been told these stories before, when she was a young child, yet had not really thought of it since. It all felt "familiar and uninteresting." Nonetheless, it seemed to her to be a fitting elaboration of her "hopeless, pointless home." She remained confused, as she had been when she was told about the existence of this dead sibling in childhood, about who was older, herself or the dead baby.

PATIENT: But so what? So I get reminded of all this sad stupid stuff about my family, but how does this relate to my life? I am here, far from there! And I have panic, and I am doomed.

Gradually, over the course of many sessions, the therapist was able to connect Ms. MM's pervasive feeling of being expendable herself to the fabric of her parents' lives and their enduring grief and the fact that nothing she could ever do or achieve could begin to lessen the pain of their tragedy and loss. In this process, for the first time, her panic remitted.

CONCRETE THINKERS

No matter what their educational or socioeconomic background, once engaged in a psychodynamic psychotherapy, most people do not have difficulty thinking dynamically or can readily develop this capacity, and most find this approach empowering (Milrod, 1996; Milrod et al., 1997; Rudden et al., 2003). Despite divergent habitual ways of thinking about feelings and symptoms, the language of unconscious motivations transcends specifics of culture and education (Freud, 1900; Dowling, 1995). This speaks to the continued poignancy and universality of great works of literature (Bloom, 1973).

As we have emphasized in this volume, it is characteristic for anxiety disorder and panic patients to displace internal conflicts with more concrete bodily symptoms or to avoid evocative situations rather than experiencing and acknowledging painful reactions and feelings. We have described how to help patients to translate these symptoms into underlying affects and emotional meanings. However, for some patients with severe phobias and agoraphobia, whose symptomatic constellation involves a concrete reification of internal psychological conflicts, beginning to think about underlying emotional underpinnings of symptoms can prove challenging. While some of this is expectable in this patient population, there is a small group of patients for whom any independent focus on emotional meanings of symptoms feels impossible. These patients tend to take a somewhat passive stance in their therapy and are often resentful of their therapist's suggestions about focusing on specific events that led to experiences of anxiety. They communicate the idea that they would prefer the therapist to somehow solve their problems without their active participation. Sometimes their stance toward their therapist can be somewhat provocative, almost daring their therapist to "do" something.

The approach that we recommend in such situations is to focus directly on negative and passive dependent aspects of the transference and patients' (necessarily disappointed) fantasies of having the therapist actively take care of them, as a parent might. In fact, any such real attempt on the therapist's part would likely be ineffective and would lead to disappointment and possibly further regression (see discussion of agoraphobia in Chapter 12). For some highly anxious patients, feeling lost and confused and unable to think for themselves constitutes a defensive posture toward their entire life, making a host of activities, including participation in any anxiety-focused psychotherapy, extremely challenging.

Case example

Ms. NN was a 20-year-old college sophomore when she presented to the PFPP study. She sought treatment after she had been asked to leave college for academic reasons (3 Fs and a D) after the first semester of her sophomore year. She reported having daily panic attacks that came out of the blue, with no specific clear content, but she had difficulty describing anything about what made them so frightening. She was entirely unaware of thoughts or fantasies that she was experiencing when she was having panic attacks. When asked, she whimpered in a small voice that they were "just very scary." Ms. NN had a history of a significant language-based learning disability as well as a processing disorder that had been diagnosed during elementary school. She had received extensive remediation and special educational interventions throughout her elementary, middle, and high school career. She continued to qualify for tutors and extended time in test taking. Her family was composed of high-achieving professionals; in this setting, Ms. NN, the youngest of three children, was treated by all members as if she were a small, irresponsible child who could never be taken seriously. This position was reinforced by her continued educational needs.

In PFPP, Ms. NN revealed extensive details about her learning difficulties early in her treatment. Yet once having communicated this information, she seemed to be comfortable thinking about her "problems" only in a very vague manner. She seemed clueless about most aspects of her emotional life and reported not being "upset at all" about having failed out of school. "I like staying home," she said, grinning. "I guess I could get a job at some point maybe. It's really comfortable for me, and my parents are nice and take care of me." She also reported that her anxiety was "a little better" since she had started therapy, but she had no understanding about why this might be, other than to say "Well, maybe being in therapy relieves stress." She had difficulty pinpointing what this stress might constitute, other than a separation from her live-in boyfriend from college, with whom she still continued to speak and visit frequently. The therapist's attempts to pinpoint emotional pressures leading to panic onset were generally met with forgetfulness and what appeared to be a genuine lack of interest in her own mind and the way it worked. Understandably, the therapist felt frustrated.

Nonetheless, when further articulation of anything surrounding the specifics relating to her anxiety seemed futile, the therapist began focusing on the surprising comfort Ms. NN reported feeling about "not knowing anything about what I really think or feel," which the therapist pointed out, must at the same time make her feel incompetent.

THERAPIST: Does it ever bother you that everyone in your family treats you like you're a baby?

PATIENT: [*laughs*] No, not really. I kind of like it.

THERAPIST: Why? What's so good about it?

PATIENT: I dunno. Well, I kind of guess that maybe no one gets mad at me for not doing well, or whatever. Like that. Like I flunked out of school, and no one's mad!

THERAPIST: And I still can't always tell what you think of it. Are you upset about flunking out?

PATIENT: I dunno. No. Well, kind of. Maybe. I dunno.

THERAPIST: That must be terribly confusing for you not to even feel like you know whether you're upset about flunking out.

PATIENT: Yeah, I guess it kind of is. [*cries very hard, very suddenly*]

THERAPIST: You suddenly look so sad about it now.

PATIENT: I know, it's weird, right?

THERAPIST: I'm starting to wonder how upset you get about a lot of things, but it seems as though you don't let yourself even try to know what's bothering you.

PATIENT: Maybe.

This session heralded a different tone in Ms. NN's therapy, in which she began to be able to articulate her feelings as well as the specifics surrounding her anxiety in a new way. Over time, she began to be able to recognize the comfortable, practiced, yet limiting defensive style she had always used in connection to her emotional life and how angry and humiliated she felt being "the dumb one" growing up in her high-achieving family. Her panic remitted in PFPP.

EMOTIONAL BONDS TO SYMPTOMS

One challenge in a brief, symptom-focused psychotherapy can be confronting the important role that anxiety symptoms per se play in the lives of some patients, and the way the content of the symptoms have come to occupy their minds. Symptoms often function to drive out more frightening, threatening thoughts and feelings, including depression and despair, and the experience of the emotional magnitude of losses of close attachments. Preoccupation with symptoms can also take the place of patients' experiencing the need for greater independence and self-assertion, even as expressed in terms of the development of specific intellectual interests. Patients sometimes report that they feel uncomfortable, "empty," and "bored" without their habitual constant preoccupation with anxiety symptoms, as if the symptoms themselves provide, in fantasy, both companionship (this is often a very specific fantasy) and occupation. It is essential that PFPP-XR therapists be aware of this set of dynamics and that they directly address and articulate them with the patient.

Case example

Ms. OO, a 20-year-old with severe agoraphobia and panic disorder, had lived most of her adolescent and early adult life carefully gauging how anxious various situations would make her and leaving her apartment only "when things looked good"—in other words, when the weather was good, when she did not have a stomachache, and when she knew that her mother was easily within reach either in person or by telephone. This emotional arrangement had led to academic failures and job losses. At the time of her presentation, she was being threatened by the administration of her college with termination, as she had failed multiple classes—largely for poor attendance—over 2 years. Much of her waking life, it emerged, revolved around her various fears and avoiding anything that might trigger anxiety.

Gradually, as Ms. OO's anxiety improved in psychotherapy and as her therapist began to link her panic symptoms and agoraphobia with her mother's chronic, severe separation anxiety from her throughout her upbringing, as well as with mother's severe depression, Ms. OO reported "feeling lost."

THERAPIST: How so?

PATIENT: It sounds really weird, but it's like I have nothing to think about now. I've spent so much of my time thinking about what I shouldn't do so I don't get anxious or feel bad, and it's not like that anymore. But ... I know it sounds weird, but I sort of miss it.

THERAPIST: What do you miss?

PATIENT: Well, things feel so empty and lonely now. It's almost like nothing matters. I don't know what to think about. It's like I'm on my own.

In effect, for Ms. OO, relinquishing her symptoms felt equivalent to giving up an iron tie to her mother and the intimate relationship they had developed around worrying.

Chapter 18

Vignette, part II

Psychodynamic formulation and therapeutic action

To illustrate the development and the content of the psychodynamic formulation, we return to the case of Mr. A from Chapter 1. We will look at information the therapist identifies to be core components of the formulation: triggers and symptoms of panic attacks and anxiety, patterns in current and past relationships, prominent resistances and defenses, evidence of conflicts and compromise formations, and transferences and countertransferences. We will trace the therapist's formulations, her interventions, the patient's responses, and the ensuing evolution of the formulation. Finally, we will describe the patient's personal and intrapsychic development and the course of his panic. Although this patient's treatment broadly demonstrates the three phases of panic focused psychodynamic psychotherapy—eXtended range (PFPP-XR)—identifying panic triggers early in treatment, addressing intrapsychic conflicts in midphase, and focusing on termination toward the end—it also demonstrates the degree to which these phases overlap (the identification of panic triggers and work on termination in the midphase; addressing intrapsychic conflicts throughout).

In PFPP-XR, panic triggers and specific anxiety symptoms provide pivotal clues as to the development of panic and anxiety and can be a good starting point for an initial psychodynamic formulation. Whereas in a longer-term psychodynamic psychotherapy, a therapist might take more time to develop a psychodynamic formulation, the PFPP-XR therapist must begin working on a formulation immediately. The therapist searches for patterns that span multiple areas of inquiry in an effort to discern which conflicts, defenses, or affects are most important in the development of panic and other anxieties. The therapist also employs information about the conflicts and defenses in anxiety disorders delineated in this manual but is careful not to rigidly impose them on the patient's material. Although certain dynamic themes and therapeutic approaches are common in these patients, the therapist needs to be flexible in the approach to the individual patient.

INITIAL FORMULATIONS AND INTERVENTIONS

In her effort to start "building" a psychodynamic formulation, the therapist looked at Mr. A's panic triggers, his reasons for entering treatment, and his demeanor in the room with her. As the therapist listened in the first two sessions to the circumstances that made him anxious and panicky, she considered several possible dynamics involved in his anxiety:

- She wondered silently whether the episodes might have been related to Mr. A's feelings about separation because he said they came on when he was leaving home and was "between places ... outside of a safe cocoon" and worsened when his daughter Isabel was growing more independent.
- She considered a relationship between Mr. A's fear of his inadequacy and his panic: his attacks came on when he believed he had to perform, when he felt inadequate as a provider, and when he described as feeling "like a little boy posing as a man."
- The therapist wondered what role Mr. A's anger played in his panic attacks, as his grabbing Isabel's doll and the ensuing terrible panic attack were the ultimate spurs for Mr. A's seeking treatment. Panic attacks were often prompted by his resentfully having to do things at other people's behest that he did not want to do.
- The therapist noticed how distant Mr. A seemed from his emotions at times during these early meetings. His story was very sad, but his affect seemed muted, prompting the therapist to contemplate whether the panic attacks were connected to Mr. A's discomfort with letting himself be aware of the depth of his feelings, particularly as he reported that his anxiety and panic worsened when his mind was free to wander, and abated when he was distracted by details or chores.

ADDRESSING MR. A'S DISCONNECTION FROM HIS FEELINGS

Mr. A spoke in the first few sessions about feeling "ungrounded": lost, inadequate, and numb after his mother died. He said that he had rarely cried about losing her and that he had forgotten a lot of details about his early relationship with her. Although he commented on how numb he felt even in the session, he became momentarily a bit tearful when speaking about losing her. He talked about trying to appear manly but looked much of the time as though he was playing the role of an ebullient boy. He spoke about feeling "fake." The therapist was struck by the depth of the sadness of Mr. A's story, the vehemence with which he warded off the sadness, and the complexity of the layers and paradoxes in Mr. A's early account of his life story. The therapist began to track these themes and details and to look for aspects of her understanding that Mr. A would be comfortable hearing. She believed Mr. A's denial of sad and frightening memories, emotions, and fantasies fostered the feelings he described of being "fake." She also believed his panic was in part being fueled by his sense of emotional disorientation and not knowing his own mind.

Rather than delving further into details of Mr. A's history, the therapist chose first to address his disconnection from his emotions and the discrepancy between what it appeared he was feeling (from his tears) and what he said he was experiencing (numbness). She did this not only because she thought this resistance was connected with panic but also because she believed that until she explored his evident distance from his current feelings and his apparent need for such a distance, this defense and resistance would hinder Mr. A's ability to remember, to associate, and to comprehend the emotional meaning of everything else he said. The therapist pointed out to Mr. A the contrast between his almost tearful recollection of the devastating events around his mother's death and his experience of numbness, past and present, and noted to Mr. A that he seemed to be warding off pivotal feelings of grief and loss, using humor and a façade of bravado.

Mr. A was surprised to hear that his sadness "showed." As he turned his attention to the defenses the therapist had identified, a number of themes emerged. He described his profound and overwhelming experience of loss and grief when his mother died and said he felt lost and frightened. His associations indicated that these emotions triggered a sense of vulnerability, fragility, and inadequacy and that he sought to hide these feelings behind a pseudo-secure, humorous veneer in an attempt to convince himself and others that he was neither frail nor inadequate.

Mr. A said he was never allowed to talk about his feelings. He reported the fantasy that no one cared about his emotions and that they were unspeakable. The family had avoided talking about anyone's feelings from the time his mother had fallen ill, and Mr. A had inferred that the way to handle them was to steel himself against them and manage them on his own. As a consequence, Mr. A often experienced numbness and confusion. The therapist inferred that Mr. A's repression of sadness, grief, and fear as well as his steadfast silence about these feelings made him vulnerable to the emergence of these emotions in the form of panic attacks, which may have been the only way he could allow himself to express any frustration, fears, or wishes to be cared for.

The therapist highlighted how Mr. A connected sadness and weakness and commented that allowing himself to experience sadness and neediness seemed to make him feel inadequate and anxious. She noted that warding off his emotional states from himself and that joking, posturing, and sparring to deflect others from becoming aware of his sadness appeared to be attempts to make himself feel strong. When this resonated, she broadened her observation to weave in a panic trigger and suggested that Mr. A might have experienced a similar anxiety when his mind was allowed to wander, as at these times he could not help feeling more intensely. She drew a parallel between his brushing away sadness with jokes and his pushing other emotions away by trying to distract himself with busywork. Mr. A said that this made sense and became more curious about the way his mind worked.

When the therapist felt that Mr. A had begun to understand these defenses and part of his need for them, she delved further into some of their ramifications. His joviality and efforts to busy his mind and suppress his emotions reduced his sense of vulnerability briefly but left him feeling fake and alone, and ultimately more anxious about being lonely. The therapist pointed out that Mr. A's efforts to ward off anxiety in one way brought on new anxieties and increased his vulnerability to panic attacks. Mr. A agreed that this explanation made sense, and he found it somewhat comforting. Listening to himself describe his own associations to his family's way of handling loss and sadness gave him an idea of some of the origins of his choice of how to handle his own. Especially in light of his increasing understanding of the complex function of these defenses, he could allow himself to contemplate handling his feelings differently.

The therapist recognized that the comforting effect of these early explorations occurred in part because they reconnected Mr. A with his emotions, even ones that made him feel frightened, weak, and out of control. The therapist's interest in Mr. A's mind and her encouraging him to tell her about his experiences was also comforting. Recognizing his own possible role in his panic allowed him to imagine the possibility that the therapy might give him a greater sense of control. These interventions targeted the compartmentalizing impact of Mr. A's defenses, which was in part connected with his surprise that the therapist could see his sadness. His surprise at her awareness mirrored the common experience of panic as coming "out of the blue."

As they talked about his attempts to avoid experiencing his emotions and looked at the consequences, Mr. A suggested that perhaps his panic filled a void. The therapist thought that Mr. A's observation signaled his capacity to appreciate that panic served a purpose for him and that it was not merely something induced by external circumstances, such as something "in the water." It also showed him collaborating with the therapist in a search for the meaning of his anxiety. His ability to view panic as serving an underlying emotional need also let the therapist know that Mr. A was ready to begin to explore some of the warded-off aspects of his life that were even more emotionally threatening to him than panic was and that were in part responsible for the panic itself.

Mr. A's insight spoke to a growing awareness of his own emotional role in his panic attacks. Once he could see himself as unconsciously preferring the attacks, as horrible as they were, to experiencing other, even more unpleasant aspects of his emotional life, then he could begin to appreciate that he might be unconsciously employing panic to manage some of his own intrapsychic needs. He could also view himself as developing the capacity to find new and more adaptive ways to satisfy those needs. Mr. A's flash of awareness that his panic filled a void brought with it an unspoken hope that if Mr. A and his therapist could understand that "void" and help him fill it in other ways, he might be able to live without his panic.

Thus the therapist's first interpretive efforts were to address a salient resistance directly and early. Mr. A naturally associated to origins of this particular defense in his early experience (not talking so as not to upset his dying mother or recently widowed father) and was able to look at this habitual choice newly through adult eyes. Old adaptations and ways of resolving conflicts were ones he had chosen unconsciously at an earlier stage of life, when he had a more limited repertoire at his disposal. His adaptations bore the stamp of his childhood ways of thinking. He could see that suppressing his feelings had become a reflex even though it was maladaptive and rooted in the limited repertoire of childlike defenses. Looking at how his defenses protected him in some ways and backfired in others opened the possibility of newer, more mature and nuanced adaptations to intrapsychic pressures, ones less likely to engender panic. These realizations introduced Mr. A to how PFPP-XR works. It also diminished his sense of isolation, gave him hope for building relationships, and helped him feel more grounded, all contributing to a lessening of some prominent ongoing contributors to his anxiety.

ADDRESSING MR. A'S CONFLICTED ANGER

As this work unfolded in the first few sessions, another set of feelings emerged in parallel—that of Mr. A's pervasive anger. As early as the first session, Mr. A had asked the therapist a personal question. The therapist had replied that she did not think it was helpful for her to answer such questions directly. When he got annoyed, she empathized with his frustration and explained that the reason she did not answer such questions was that answering could obfuscate their being able to better articulate what led to his asking this question. Focusing on his feelings and fantasies about the therapist, rather than on her answer, would yield valuable information. She encouraged Mr. A to use his questions as a tool to understand his thoughts and concerns more fully.

In the session following this explanation (number 2), Mr. A came in and exclaimed, openly irked, "OK, let's get the ground rules straight!" In the context of getting annoyed with the therapist, Mr. A told the story of his being outside playing in the water when his mother, already ill, called him to do his homework. When he told her he did not want to, that he was "busy practicing diving," she blurted out, "You are my son. I love you, but sometimes I wish I had Alberto [Mr. A's friend] for a son!" Thus, Mr. A associated expressing his anger with an expectation of being rejected.

The therapist was aware of her own countertransference from the outset of the treatment. She felt sad about Mr. A's devastating loss and was mindful of an urge to comfort him. She admired him and found him likable and engaging. Despite these reactions, she was also aware of being easily caught up in minor power struggles with Mr. A and felt torn, as she wanted to focus on his need for comfort and empathy. She felt this tug many times throughout the treatment and often experienced him as interrupting her. As time went by, she found herself increasingly vociferous in stopping him from interrupting her but then inadvertently gave him extra minutes at the end of sessions. As she explored her own reactions, she became aware that Mr. A pulled for extra nurturance while also warding off the therapist's more tender feelings, and she was able to see her response in relationship to Mr. A's disavowal of his neediness (which they had begun to discuss) in his effort to feel strong. She could recognize how he engaged her in mini-battles for control as he engaged everyone in his life in these struggles. As she experienced her empathy derailed by his cantankerous behavior with her at times, requiring extra efforts on her part to regain it, she recognized from his stories that he had a habit of antagonizing others and depriving himself of the comfort he so wanted. She understood his compromise as one of the underpinnings of his chronic sadness and loneliness as well as of his panic and used her unspoken awareness of her countertransference to guide her in her search for multiple connections between this global way of relating and his anxiety.

The therapist believed that Mr. A's anger over "the rules" was conscious enough to be accessible, and the emergence of Mr. A's anger in the room made the therapist feel it needed to be addressed quickly so it did not impede the progress of the treatment. This battle for control that welled up with immediacy in the transference over "the rules" also emerged in Mr. A's memory of this fight with his mother, in the rage he described with Isabel that scared him enough to prompt him to seek treatment, and in his descriptions of various interactions in his daily life. As his temper was one of Mr. A's reasons for seeking therapy, the therapist felt he would be receptive to an exploration of his angry response to her. The therapist went on alert for themes related to management of anger.

In sessions 3 and 4, Mr. A spent a lot of time talking about angry tiffs with extended family. He was working his fingers to the bone trying to refurbish his brother-in-law's cabin cruiser. He felt no one else was carrying any weight or appreciating his skill or diligence. At one point, Mr. A said he wanted to be able to express his opinions openly and directly and relate to other men as an equal, not as a falsely deferential little boy. He said, "I want to be with them man to man, adult to adult, side by side, hand to hand." The therapist heard this as a slip—it seemed that Mr. A meant "hand *in* hand," but the pugilistic connotations of "hand to hand" were filed away in her mind as Mr. A's associations to being an adult. She felt addressing it at that time might interrupt other material that was at least as fruitful, as his associations were along the same lines of his viewing relationships as opportunities for battle. This slip was indicative of Mr. A's struggle with angry feelings, as his wishes to be manly were tied to aggressive fantasies that he found frightening.

Mr. A described numerous ways his anger distanced him from his extended family (and others) and undermined his efforts at connecting with loved ones. Tying these observations together with a statement Mr. A made about his having been too rebellious and difficult for his parents to tolerate, the therapist turned Mr. A's attention to his anger and noted to him that he seemed to be keeping his anger to himself out of fear of expressing rage and being "too difficult for [others] to bear."

PATIENT: In a conversation, something I might say might be offensive to somebody. I don't walk around worrying that I'm going to walk up to someone and say, "Hey, you fat slob. Get off your duff!"

THERAPIST: It sounds as though you're concerned that if you let your true feelings out, especially when you're angry, that other people will respond to you angrily—that they'll belittle you, hurt you ... and even abandon you. When you let your mother know how angry you were with her, she told you she wanted a different son. Soon after that, she died. I can see how concerned you might be about letting your anger out. One of the repercussions is that you don't say things that might change the situation, like asking your sister and her husband for help. You're concerned that you wouldn't be able to say it in any way that's not very angry, so you don't say it and then you remain furious and alone. You bottle things up, and you get even more anxious about your anger.

PATIENT: You said it!

This is an example of an early panic-focused formulation. Although the therapist did not mention panic per se, she was making a connection between Mr. A's fear of his anger and his ongoing anxiety, a connection that laid the groundwork for understanding the ties between fear of his anger and his panic attacks. The main intervention here was that the therapist turned Mr. A's attention to his rage and began to give him a way of speaking about it and a sense that his feelings could be discussed with her rather than buried. She highlighted his fear of his rage and linked it to an early scenario with his mother, identifying its origins. She proposed to him that he might have connected his feelings of rage at his mother with her death, as she died soon after the fight he remembered. Finally, she turned his attention to the impact that his defensive suppression of his anger had on his attachments. Without framing it yet explicitly to him as a conflict, the therapist essentially addressed Mr. A's difficulty expressing his "true feelings"—in this case anger. His wish was to be able to express anger; his fear was of harming the other person, as he felt he had harmed his mother, and of being unlovable and abandoned or attacked, as he had felt when he got angry at his mother and she said she wanted a different son. His (imperfect) solution was to hold his tongue, isolate himself, or get into struggles that did not effectively express his anger. The therapist helped him to see the consequence of this particular way of resolving this conflict (he inevitably felt lonely and isolated). She showed him that this resolution of his conflicting needs represented a choice, thereby tacitly giving him the option to consider more adaptive choices in whether and how to express his authentic feelings.

As Mr. A saw that his therapist tolerated his rage and did not distance herself because of it, he became more comfortable talking openly in therapy about his anger at his mother. He felt his mother did not love him unless he was meek and compliant. He always tried, therefore, to be "loving, kind, and helpful" so she and others would not reject him because of his rage. The therapist suggested to him that although suppressing his rage and acting helpful (an example of the defense of reaction formation, see Chapters 3 and 10) enabled him and others to see him as kind and lovable, it left him feeling trapped, disempowered, and even more enraged. She indicated that his pretense contributed to his sense that he was "faking it," which left him feeling alone, as had his attempts to deny his sadness by brushing it off with jokes. This use of reaction formation, the unconscious motivation of which was to enable Mr. A to stay attached to his mother in fantasy and to others, ultimately left him feeling more alone, and therefore even more vulnerable to panic. This set of interventions encouraged Mr. A to begin to accept his feelings more and to feel progressively freer to be more authentic. This work sparked a discussion of ways Mr. A might be able to express needs and even anger without alienating others.

In this context, Mr. A asked the therapist what she wanted him to talk about. The therapist saw this as an enactment of an aspect of the power struggles they had been discussing, one in which Mr. A was passive and submissive, or "meek and lovable," rather than taking the initiative to bring up what *he* wanted to discuss. She pointed out to Mr. A that he had handed the reins to her in choosing the topic.

PATIENT: There *is* something I came in wanting to talk about. Anger. I feel anger, and I keep it in. I don't speak what's on my mind.... Instead of getting it out, I keep it inside.

THERAPIST: You began the session doing the very same thing [*referring to his deferring to her*].

The therapist noted Mr. A's inclination to comply with her wishes, when he struggled so much with his desires to get his own needs met and his own voice heard. She pointed out how the themes of rules and power struggles seemed to emerge in all of his important relationships—first and foremost with his mother, also with Isabel, with Sylvia (his wife), and now with the therapist. His view of a dyad entailed the notion that either he could be compliant and loved by the other person, in which case he would be resentful and seething, or he could take control and risk rage, abandonment, and retaliation by the other person. The elucidation of the underlying inevitable rift between himself and the important people in his life at all times helped him recognize more clearly why he felt so chronically lonely and unlovable. She framed it this time overtly as a conflict.

THERAPIST: You would like to follow the rules.... You want to be so good and do everything right. On the other hand, you want to do things your way—"loosen your tie" [*Mr. A's words*]. You feel you can't do that [for reasons explored earlier].... You suppress your own needs and comply with others ... and that leaves you feeling angry. You even got angry with me over that. I think this struggle underlies a lot of your anxiety.

They looked at how this conflict set up interpersonal situations in which he could see that "either way I lose." This interchange opened the door for them to explore his fear that his anger might disrupt their relationship as well.

In this example, building on their earlier work on Mr. A's anger, the therapist chose a set of feelings that were central to Mr. A's panic, ones that made up a pivotal conflict she thought he would be able to tolerate discussing with her She delineated his wish (to get his needs met and his true emotions heard), his fear (his feelings might kill people, or at least make them angry and disgusted), and his unconscious defense against the wish (holding his tongue, being compliant). She showed him how the defense warded off the feared consequence but carried consequences of its own (his feeling inauthentic, unlovable, lonely and resentful, and "numb"). She then seized on the first clear evidence of that conflict in the transference and delineated how it was alive in their attachment. She linked this particular way of relating as well as the attendant fantasies and feelings toward others more broadly with many other relationships in his life, both past and present. The explanation of the resistance in terms of the transference fantasy, the development of the resistance, the fantasy's roots in early experience, and the connection of these fantasies with other relationships is an example of the integrative linkages so important in PFPP-XR.

A central feature of PFPP-XR is to demonstrate conflicts underlying panic and anxiety, because the phenomenon of feeling torn between two equally unsatisfactory options—with the resulting sense of lack of choices or control—contributes strongly to anxiety. An understanding of each branch of the conflict is key, but the overview of how the different emotions and fantasies fit together in such a way as to make the patient feel trapped and without choices offers a particularly important tool for understanding panic. A fuller understanding of how this fear arose originally (Mr. A's mother died while he was a budding adolescent in a state of rebelling against her, and his early teenage mind assigned a causal connection between his self-focus and rage at her and her death) offers even greater perspective on the fantasy life underlying his case of panic disorder. A fuller understanding of his defenses offered a similar deepening of this perspective. Mr. A and the therapist understood together later that his "not talking" was a repetition in his adult life of what he thought his mother wanted from him ("being meek and lovable"), which paralleled his belief that he had been tacitly instructed not to talk about his emotions so as not to disturb the tenuous family equilibrium when his mother died.

Mr. A led a disjointed and compartmentalized emotional life. His defenses served to shield him from conscious awareness of the full panoply of his emotions and left him feeling variably mystified, fragmented, incoherent, fragile, and inauthentic. Contextualization of his relevant wishes, fears, and defenses, and some of their origins, as well as the links across relationships throughout his life, in treatment and out, offered Mr. A a chance to integrate disparate components of his inner mental life into a more cohesive understanding. As this process took place, Mr. A began to see a glimmer of hope of feeling more at home in his inner world, with diminution in anxiety and panic. He became increasingly adept at making and identifying these connections and, despite his resistance, readily accepted the value of these efforts. Although other patients with anxiety disorders may require more guidance in understanding the usefulness of linking their feelings and fantasies to their anxiety symptoms, the techniques described here in helping Mr. A will also be valuable in these cases.

ADDRESSING MR. A'S GUILT

As they discussed the consequences of Mr. A's setting up power struggles and his avoidance of more mutual interactions, he talked about his guilt about his anger, particularly at his mother. Mr. A spoke passionately about how sorry and guilty he felt that he was not kinder, more understanding, and more nurturing to his mother when she was ill. The therapist understood the emergence of this material as an association to Mr. A's not allowing himself to enjoy closer loving connections and inferred that the guilt he was talking about was partly responsible. He spoke about the torment he felt trying to figure out whether he had been just a normal budding adolescent, stretching his wings and rebelling, or whether he had been selfish and cruel to his dying mother, killing her with his rebellion.

The therapist pointed out that much of Mr. A's anxiety arose in connection with guilt and a struggle to forgive himself for how he behaved as a young adolescent facing a catastrophic loss. She urged him to consider how terrified he must have been and how unsure he seemed about how to assuage his grief. He felt soothed by the therapist's inquiries and acknowledged that the behavior he felt had been so deplorable was merely that of someone who "was just a little kid." In the next session, Mr. A said, "After last session I found myself as an adult speaking to the little kid in me, saying it's okay—you were just a little kid, trying to find out what independence was all about."

Mr. A grew increasingly able to reflect on his own, to step back and examine his own actions and motivations, and to search for underlying emotional reasons for recurrent puzzling behavior. The therapist believed that some of the changes that enabled him to begin to use PFPP-XR techniques on his own were as follows:

- Identifying how the therapist heard his emotions in a way he had not experienced before
- An increased recognition and tolerance of his anger and other feelings that allowed him to more safely examine his emotional state
- A reduced sense of guilt and fear about the destructiveness of his rage and the fantasy he had killed his mother
- A recognition of new ways of relating

As he was able to make sense of some of his feelings and fantasies, he was able to begin to soothe himself, a new capacity represented in his image of his adult self now able to comfort the devastated child in him.

ADDRESSING THE LOSS OF HIS MOTHER AND THE NEED FOR STRUCTURE

In the context of this work, a new aspect of Mr. A's proclivity for power struggles emerged. He talked about his wife as a "strong Latina Mama," commenting on how responsible and regimented she was. The therapist pointed out his implication that it was important for him to have married a strong woman.

THERAPIST: You're saying it was important for you to marry a woman who was strong and anchoring [a mama] who would pull a family together ... pull you together with your family ... give you a certain structure you feel you are missing.... It's related to your feeling that you lost that solid grounding when your mother died.

PATIENT: No question about that!

The therapist pointed out that Mr. A seemed to look to her in sessions as well for that kind of grounding. What should he talk about? Was he using such-and-such word correctly? She built on her earlier delineation of the conflict over rules in the therapeutic relationship to identify how important the "rules" were in allowing Mr. A to feel safe. On one hand he resented them tremendously, and on the other hand he craved their structure.

THERAPIST: In fact, many of your anxiety attacks occur at a time when you're leaving areas of—

PATIENT: Structure!

As they looked at this new angle of his conflict and how feeling torn among numerous options, all troublesome, fueled his anxiety, Mr. A became aware of this previously unconscious aspect of how he experienced rules and grounding. The therapist reflected that his panic attacks took place when he was "neither here nor there," and the patient mused that that was exactly how he felt after his mother died. This interpretation enabled the patient and therapist to link Mr. A's panic attacks to his emotional experience of losing his mother. The therapist suggested that a panic attack could be in part a reliving of that traumatic loss, a way of grieving a loss that he had not previously permitted himself to grieve.

In PFPP-XR, when a recurrent thought, belief, fantasy, or way of resolving conflict seems to fuel panic or anxiety, the therapist must find ways to loosen the patient's tie to that fantasy, thought, or feeling. In the process of working through, the therapist works with the patient to uncover the multiple meanings of anxiety symptoms as well as the various purposes the symptoms may serve and reasons that anxiety is the patient's resolution of the conflict rather than something more adaptive.

PATIENT: It's almost as if I want that grounding but am afraid to go back to a place I was when my mother was alive.... I'm afraid to experience those emotions—I'm afraid to let myself feel a sense of security, because I might lose it again. What if I lose it again?

As Mr. A began to see his need to deny his insecurities, he allowed himself to recognize his need and insecurity about being able to perform and began to discuss his fear of inadequacy. Throughout the therapy, Mr. A often described himself as helpless, childlike, and inadequate. This view of himself was connected in part to a terrible longing he had for his capable, tender, and nurturing mother, whom he had lost at such a young age. Mr. A's opportunity to have a mommy was cut short painfully, and he had never allowed himself to feel his deep sorrow. His ongoing view of himself as debilitated was in part a memory of the helpless state he experienced at the time of his traumatic loss. His "little boy" posture was also a way of hanging on in fantasy to his mother, whom he missed so badly. It allowed him to act like the person he thought his mother loved, as he felt she liked him better when he was meek (like Alberto). At the same time, relegating himself to being "meek" made him feel emasculated, humiliated, and enraged. Seeing himself as a strong man, however, was also fraught with the danger of feeling motherless and alone. Any of the options he experienced were associated with anticipation of destruction or abandonment, and he began to understand more fully how this constellation of views left him so prone to panic. Clarifying these fantasies permitted Mr. A to begin to evaluate new possibilities, including allowing himself to take the risk of feeling close to others. These efforts also laid the foundation for work on these conflicts in relationship to his father.

After these first eight sessions, Mr. A's panic attacks, which had occurred two or three times weekly, for up to 45 minutes at a time (sometimes longer), had dwindled to much less frequent episodes and for much less time. He did have feelings of panic, but they were not sustained for more than a few minutes. When he had anxiety, even panic, he felt able to "put it into perspective."

In session 9 he came in and said that his attitude toward his anxiety was, "It's just an anxiety attack, and it'll pass!" He said he was letting his family into his life more, enjoying his children more deeply, and feeling his love for his wife and children in a more intense way. He described watching them play together and said, "It's just the miracle of life ... a wonderful, wonderful thing." He felt enough growth in his confidence that he was "strolling the streets" before session, a big achievement given his agoraphobia.

The therapist pointed out to him that his sense of feeling more rooted in his family, more confident, more willing to venture out, and less panicky were all connected. Bringing the focus to panic, she reiterated that his panic attacks took place when he literally "ventured out" of one place on his way to another and that the venturing out had a meaning to him (being motherless and incapacitated) and that he was now experiencing that venturing differently, permitting himself to stroll outside freely and fearlessly. He admitted that he was afraid that by talking about his new sense of well-being, he would jinx it. The therapist focused on his persistent anxiety, saying that the change in his internal state represented a kind of venturing out from an old way of being to a new one. It stood to reason he might be anxious about that change as it implied a separation from the safety of his known and familiar, even if excruciating, feeling state. This interpretation indicates the connection PFPP-XR therapists make between fears associated with panic attacks and agoraphobic symptoms and the patient's experience of his inner world.

As Mr. A better understood the connections between his sense of impotence and his rage, sadness, and panic, and as he saw his therapist tolerate his ongoing anger and increasing autonomy, he managed anger differently in all of his relationships. He was more able to express anger as it arose, so it did not reach terrifying proportions in his fantasies. He felt more comfortable asserting himself and less frightened that he was inadequate. He felt he deserved love in a different way and allowed himself to feel happier, more loving, and less numb. The "void" previously "filled" by panic was now being filled by richer experiences with loved ones. Reviewing what he and his therapist had discussed, he began to make his own connections more readily when he noticed himself becoming anxious and found that he was able to soothe himself more quickly. The intensity of his anxiety decreased substantially.

IDENTIFYING AND COPING WITH FEARS OF SEPARATION AND LOSS

At the end of the session 9, Mr. A revealed he had been furious with Isabel and that he had disciplined her in a way that frightened both her and him and that made him feel guilty. As he left for work, he was plagued by the thought, "What if this is the last time I see her?" As he described this to the therapist, he commented, "I have no idea where that came from. Where does that idea come from?" As the therapist urged him to try to answer his own question, Mr. A and the therapist could relate this fear to his being taken by surprise when his mother died and his painful realization that he would never see her again. His not seeing how obvious a connection this was is another example of the heavily reinforced defensive disconnection typical of anxiety patients.

Mr. A related how he made sure to hug and kiss Isabel and tell her he loved her before he left. Initially Isabel rejected Mr. A but then kissed him and told him she loved him as well. He said he wanted to make sure his daughter would never suffer the same torture he had of his mother's dying while they were angry at one other. The therapist suggested that he got to "heal a hurt" with his daughter that he had felt with his mother. They examined how these repeated fights and reconciliations were a way of keeping his mother with him and of reliving his childhood memory of separation and then undoing the rift. He not only was leaving his daughter as his mother left him but also was recreating a situation in which his daughter was angry with him in the way his mother had been. This time, however, he got to tell Isabel he loved her, as he wished he had told his mother, and she told him she loved him, which he wanted desperately to hear from his mother. Mr. A and the therapist focused less on his maternal "transference" to his daughter than on his identification with his mother. Mr. A saw that he was recreating an old relationship for very specific reasons and that, although his repeated actions met certain unconscious needs, they were maladaptive and fostered unnecessary contention with his daughter.

Acutely aware that these unresolved feelings in Mr. A's relationship with his mother were such salient sources of his anxiety, the therapist urged him to go back and talk more about the hurt he was trying to heal concerning his mother. She asked him what he would have wanted to say to his mother. He said he would have wanted to comfort his mother in her pain and fear. The therapist pointed out ways he had tried to do that before she died and added that comforting his daughter now seemed to be a way of doing something he did not get a chance to do long ago. He talked about the pain of not getting a hug from his mother and not fully kissing her goodbye, in part out of a "false expectation" that she would get better and in part so as not to upset her with the notion she might be dying. The therapist asked him what he wished his mother had said to him. He said he had wanted her to comfort him; he would want her to tell him that she loved him and would always be thinking of him, that she'd always be there for him and with him.

He wondered how his mother could not have said to him that she loved him. The therapist acknowledged Mr. A's pain that his mother did not speak those words to him and asked if he believed that the only reason she did not say them was that she did not feel it. He talked about his feeling that there was "no greater pain than leaving your children" and wondered whether it might have been just too painful for her to acknowledge that she was going to die and to say the things he wished she had said. The therapist noted his awareness of the possibility that even though she did not say those words she might still have felt them deeply. He seemed relieved after this interchange, as he had not permitted himself to comfort himself with these thoughts previously. Part of the reason Mr. A could not soothe himself earlier was his guilt over how angry he had been and his worry that he had killed his mother. Pain, panic attacks, and loneliness were self-inflicted punishments for his fantasized crimes. As he began to gain a fuller, more adult perspective on the events leading to his mother's death, he began to forgive himself for his angry adolescent rebellion. He started to allow himself to think, feel, and comfort himself in ways previously off limits.

The therapist remembered a slip Mr. A had made in one of their early sessions. Instead of saying "when my mother died," as he meant to say, he had said, "when *I* died." They had not had a chance to explore it at that time. Thinking about the current session as well as this slip, the therapist brought up Mr. A.'s belief that the painful terror Mr. A felt when he left home in the morning in a routine way (even though he could be fairly certain he was coming back) was an experience much like the one he believed his mother had of being forced to leave him and his siblings. From this connection, the therapist suggested that Mr. A was experiencing what he imagined his mother had felt and that this might be a means of reuniting with her in fantasy. It could also be an unconscious way of undoing in fantasy what he wrongly perceived as his abandonment of her. The therapist underlined how pain and anxiety seemed to be powerful connections with his mother. He acknowledged that he felt he was constantly playing a dual role with himself. He was at once a person in pain and also the nurturer trying to get himself through the pain. The therapist pointed out the parallel with panic attacks and delineated how the attacks themselves were a way of identifying with his ill mother. He said, "I wonder if panic attacks are like a sickness I can get better from." "I relive my mother's illness through these attacks, but I recover in a way she never could. This way I have some control." As he talked himself down from each attack, he could rescue himself as he wished he could have rescued her. Panic attacks were a way of holding on to his mother and rescuing her in fantasy. This insight brought significant relief from panic as well as from sadness and general malaise.

Instead of putting the vast realm of his feelings about his mother into words, he had been handling them by enacting them through panic attacks. In this segment of the therapy, Mr. A talked about extremely painful emotions he had not had a chance to acknowledge or process, to have someone else understand them, and to understand them himself from a more adult perspective. This work allowed him to feel the love and intense desire for his mother he had warded off. The awakening of an image of his mother within him ushered in a new set of fears and fantasies.

IDENTIFYING STRUGGLE AND ILLNESS AS A MEANS TO AVOID LOSS

In the next session (10), Mr. A talked about his wife's having the flu. He also yawned and spoke about how yawns are contagious. Fear of illness and death were powerful underpinnings of Mr. A's panic and anxiety. Although there were many other themes to address, the therapist followed these associations and asked if Mr. A recalled any fears of catching his mother's illness as a child. He denied the fear but immediately associated to childhood fears of losing his penis and commented that he did not see why this memory was "welling up from nowhere." The therapist pointed out that they were talking about his anxiety, particularly about contagion, an anxiety that seemed to heighten after his mother lost body parts. He said, "It seems so obvious now," and talked about how confused he was after his mother's surgeries. He was able to recognize how he must have had so much fear and so many questions, but "I never verbalized them; I never talked about them at all."

The therapist related these newly remembered fears to Mr. A's anxiety in the previous session about feeling calm, open, and joyful. She had in mind that Mr. A's panic was in part born of a conviction that he could and would never get his needs attended to and that he would be condemned to a life of fulfilling the needs of those around him, feeling resentful and enraged, fearful of his anger, lonely and depressed forever. For his panic to remain at bay, he would need to understand how he himself kept his needs from being met and why he behaved in a way that perpetuated the painful, recurrent interpersonal situations that so distressed him. If he acknowledged how good he felt, it would be taken away from him, just as he felt his mother got sick just after they moved into a big, beautiful house. The therapist remembered his statements that he was arrogant and "on top of it all" as a young child and suggested that he believed that his feeling strong and confident was tantamount to being "cocky." He unconsciously warded off the feelings of confidence and security he so desired and missed, and of preempting anything, including relationships from being lost or "chopped off." He added, "Because of my fear of losing it.... I don't give it a chance to develop." His reaction was, "I'm angry that I'm not allowed to feel good. I'm angry that I'm not allowed to feel secure." Yet he was beginning to understand that he was in charge of the "allowing," and he was not permitting his own happiness because he was too conflicted about the potential dangerous consequences.

The therapist began next to turn her attention to Mr. A's steadfast avoidance of keeping his panic diaries, which was required by the PFPP study. Although she had no specific formulation in mind, she believed that this was a continued enactment of something she and Mr. A. had understood only in part, as the behavior persisted. Anger and rebellion had proved so central to their understanding of Mr. A.'s panic, and she believed this was a related resistance. This behavior represented the emergence of a more global maladaptive defense in the specific context of the transference, which promoted unsatisfying attachments that ultimately fueled Mr. A's panic. The therapist pursued this by asking him how he understood his avoiding keeping the diaries. When he said angrily that he wanted to be left alone about them, the therapist focused on their relationship, pointing out that Mr. A seemed to feel attacked and angry at the therapist's explorations of his not bringing in the diaries. He indicated that he felt yelled at, as though he were being told he was irresponsible, and confessed that he actually liked the feeling, as it felt "like the old days, when I used to get yelled at a lot ... familiar.... It seems mothering, almost." He associated to his wife's yelling at him, and said, "Maybe I like fighting."

Mr. A came to session 12 with an irate diary entry. "Driving home from the session, angry at the world. ... Get the fuck out of my way. What's the point of following the rules? ... I was good, and you still died. Fuck you." The therapist commented that he seemed to direct his anger at everyone but her and that it seemed very hard for him to allow himself to feel anger toward her in her presence. She commented that he demonstrated this anger with her a lot more than he realized, disguising it in humorous quips and barbs in sessions. As he reflected on this, he referred to the fantasy that the therapist would kick him out of treatment and that he would have to get his needs met in another treatment, which he dismissed as an off-the-cuff remark of little significance. The therapist emphasized that she believed this was a very significant expression of an important feeling. She believed that as they were on the verge of entering the second half of the treatment, Mr. A was responding more acutely to the approaching end of the treatment. She framed his remark about her kicking him out of treatment as an expression of his anger about the short-lived, time-limited treatment. She commented that for someone who lost his mother so young and so abruptly, with as much pain and anxiety about separating and as much insecurity about being loved and attached as he had, it was likely that he would have powerful feelings about ending the treatment. He responded, "'It resonates true,' to quote you." He expressed how helpful he had found her in enabling him to understand himself and to feel more deeply and said how sad and upset he would feel when the treatment ended. He said that this was like his earlier loss of his mother "in miniature." He volunteered that not doing the panic diaries might be a way of staving off the end of the treatment.

The therapist picked up on Mr. A's conjecture and generalized it by suggesting that Mr. A's provoking power struggles in many ways on a frequent basis seemed to be a way to keep the therapist engaged, as his struggles with his mother kept her engaged and as his anxiety and panic attacks kept his mother alive in fantasy with him. She summarized that for Mr. A, as long as he was in a struggle, he was (in fantasy) not alone. She added, "You're afraid you can't keep me with you. You're afraid that the only way you can keep me with you is to have a fight going on or for you to be sick." The therapist was looking for new ways to help Mr. A diminish his panic and find strength. Often midway through the treatment, the PFPP-XR therapist develops a feeling that there are certain feelings that must get addressed for the patient to be able to continue anti-anxiety work essential for his recovery on his own. Being able to hold on to a positive connection with close others was something the therapist felt was an essential capacity she had to help Mr. A address and develop.

ADDRESSING CONFLICTS OVER COMPETING WITH HIS FATHER

At this time, the therapist was aware that she had heard almost nothing about Mr. A's father. She had a hunch that that relationship was likely of importance to Mr. A's panic, as his very first panic attack had taken place in a setting, the only detail of which Mr. A reported was that he was with a male authority figure he described as a "father figure," just after a vacation alone with his father. She was curious about the absence of material thus far about his father. She wondered about the possible role of competitive struggles with his father, in light of Mr. A's conscious castration anxiety, the possible emerging erotic transference (seen in a recent slip when the patient said to the therapist "since we got together," referring to the start of treatment), the apparent inhibition in Mr. A's love life, and Mr. A's slip in session 3 when he said, "man to man, adult to adult, side by side, hand to hand."

The therapist noted to Mr. A that he had hardly mentioned his father at all. Mr. A spoke about how wimpy he felt his father was when he was a child but how he saw now how strong his father was in the way he held the family together and how free of anxiety his father seemed. In the context of this discussion, Mr. A revealed a panic trigger he had not previously reported: he had panic attacks in hotels, especially when he had to pay. As the therapist asked him to associate to this trigger, Mr. A said the attacks occurred when he looked around the hotel and saw other families enjoying vacations. This reminded him of vacations he enjoyed as a child with his family. When the therapist probed further, he answered, "I'm a grown-up family man now ... but I still feel like a kid." Being the head of his family felt like a daunting responsibility that was brought into high relief when he went to pay the bill, as "that's what fathers do."

In part responding to Mr. A's anxiety about how to handle his panic after the treatment ended, the therapist summarized for Mr. A: "You were asking me last week about what to do when you have anxiety. This is the kind of thing we can address. We know that there is something about being in a hotel that revives a memory for you of being a carefree kid on vacation with your family. Now you pay. You've earned the money. You're the boss, but you still feel like a little kid, not up to the task of running a family. That feeling makes you panic." She indicated to him that understanding more fully how and why that feeling made him panic could be a powerful antipanic tool.

In the ensuing session (13), Mr. A talked about how angry it made him to feel like a little boy. The therapist highlighted in contrast how anxious Mr. A also was about functioning as an adult man and "doing what fathers do." She built on her interpretation that he warded off fears of having anything "chopped off" by limiting his pleasure in relationships, unconsciously employing anger and panic. She emphasized Mr. A's conflict about being a man: "If you assert yourself and are not 'meek and submissive,' you're afraid that will make your mother or your wife angry. On the other hand, you're also afraid of outdoing your father and incurring whatever reaction you might anticipate from him." He responded, "I make three times as much as he ever made." He continued, "I'm afraid to feel good. I'm afraid of feeling anxious and ... losing things." The therapist added, "Losing people and body parts! As hyperbolic as this sounds, we know this is something you've consciously been terrified about. If you've got it to lose, you could lose your penis. If you're out there enjoying your success, and your strength, enjoying your loving relationship with Sylvia, and your fatherhood of Isabel, then you could lose it. It's easier to be the little boy cowering in the corner." Mr. A replied, "Which is, quite literally, what I do!"

After several exchanges in which the therapist reiterated how dangerous it felt to Mr. A to feel strong and successful, possibly more strong and successful than his father, Mr. A commented that the therapist was bringing up a new subject—that of a son's rivalry with his father for his mother's attention. He connected this to a huge fight he had with his father when he was a teen. The fight was about his having had sex with a girl who was the daughter of a business competitor of his father's. Mr. A's father felt this connection was inappropriate, and Mr. A said he was fighting against his father's edict to end the relationship. Mr. A reported swearing at his father in Spanish (to be especially insulting) and storming out of the house. Furthermore, the girl was known in the neighborhood to look like Mr. A's mother, and she had the same name as his mother. The therapist worked with Mr. A for several sessions to show him how conflicted he was about being a strong, desirable, sexy man and how panic served to protect him from feeling this way. On one hand he desired the pleasure, but on the other hand it meant to him that he was competing with his father and incurring the dangers of his father's wrath, or, possibly worse, the danger of beating his father and causing his father's demise. She connected his fear with the castration anxiety he had described experiencing as an 8-year-old. She said that his associations were evidence that these scenarios were playing out in his unconscious mind, which does not operate like our rational minds (secondary process) but more like dreams—intense, phantasmagorical, and illogical (primary process). She explained that as these conflicts played out in his mind, he responded emotionally as if his fantasy dangers were real. His responses were either to avoid being the strong, sexy man, which he did in many ways, or to venture toward success and then panic in response to his fear of the consequences. The therapist also interpreted that the panic attacks themselves were a way Mr. A castrated himself.

In the session following this interpretation and the talk about his being strong, successful, and sexy, he came in and reported that he had driven his brand-new jazzy red boat through two wooden pilings while docking it. He managed to squeak through, but the opening was narrow enough that he scraped the paint off both sides of the boat. He was arriving for a gathering of friends and family, and he had hoped to "make a splash" so everyone could admire his boat and his skilful maneuvering. At first he was skeptical when the therapist said she thought this act was yet another way Mr. A castrated himself, but he listened intently, beginning to see the mounting evidence. In his effort to grapple with conscious thoughts versus unconscious ones and concrete thinking versus his symbolic world, he said, "We seem to keep coming back to my fear of losing my penis, but that was only consciously a concern when I was 7 or 8." The therapist answered, "These are all manifestations of the same fear. I think this fear underlies a lot of your fears about your body. When you're wondering during a panic attack if you're going to lose your eyesight, or you think something's wrong with one of your limbs because it's gone cold and limp.... These are ... all related to a root underlying fear."

She pointed out that part of his feeling so vulnerable to attack was that he felt he deserved to be attacked for his competitive and destructive impulses, and he consistently provoked people to fight with him. When the therapist asked more about his relationship with his father, Mr. A said that in general he was fairly unrestricted growing up and rarely got punished. "I could get away with murder." Of course, the therapist drew Mr. A's attention to that expression and used it to illustrate why Mr. A consistently was compelled to punish himself, given that he felt like a murderer. His understanding of his need to limit his success helped him to see his "inadequacies" in part as his own doing and lessened his fear that he would "fall short." As his fear of not being up to performing contributed to his panic, his understanding of the defensive aspect of his underperformance led to a lessening of his fear of inadequacy and of his panic.

Mr. A brought up another trigger of his panic they had not yet discussed, which had emerged only in the setting of their talking about his struggles with his father. He panicked when he was putting on his tie in the morning. He mused, "The vision that shoots up from my mind is standing in front of my mirror, my father's mirror—all right. So there was a slip. I meant my father's mirror. What does that mean that I said 'my mirror'? I'd watch my father put on his tie. When I'm putting on my tie in the morning and have a panic attack, I have a vision of watching my father put on his tie ... and I think, 'Here I am making a transition from *child* at home being taken care of to adult parent putting on a suit to go out into the world to be a provider.'"

The therapist added that the slip making his father's mirror his own was a symbolic way of taking his father's position, an act she suggested was one of the main reasons being a grown-up was so terrifying to Mr. A. She asked him if he saw a connection between this memory and his feelings in hotels, which he did.

THERAPIST: Being a grown-up means that you've knocked him out of the picture ... and it sounds as though you fear he was kind of easy to knock out of the picture.... That's a scary thing for you.

PATIENT: You mean physically? Literally knocked him out of the picture? Taking over the role of head of the house?

THERAPIST: You've taken over the role of Father. You're the daddy now. You're the breadwinner. You're the person paying for the hotel. You're the guy putting on your tie in front of *your* mirror. And wearing a tie in and of itself has to do with being a man. ... And every time you put on your tie, it's a reminder that you are a man. In your memory of being with your dad, you say, "This is my mirror." Symbolically you've knocked him out of the picture. ... But the fear you feel at those times when you are the father is *as if* you had knocked him out literally.

PATIENT: Killed him?

THERAPIST: Yes.

PATIENT: Died.

THERAPIST: Yes. And that's why I think you're so anxious.

Mr. A pondered further and asked, "Am I the reason he was not more successful?" He and the therapist were able to explore Mr. A's guilt that he had done his father in—and "gotten away with murder." As Mr. A and the therapist worked through this guilt, Mr. A had an effusion of memories and associations about close friendships with male friends as a teen, and sexual explorations and experiences with girls, about many of which Mr. A felt guilty and ashamed.

As this material emerged (session 18), Mr. A voiced a feeling of sadness and loss about being an adult and "giving up my childhood—that childhood part of me." The therapist asked what he wanted to hang on to. "Being nurtured, being taken care of, being comforted, receiving compassion." The therapist pointed out to Mr. A that he did not have to be a child of the age that he was when his mother was alive to get nurture, comfort, and compassion. As he talked about how hard it was for him to "leave that stage of my life," he also described how effective and productive he felt he had been over the weekend in some of his work projects. He felt he had "acted like an adult." He told the therapist, "It was almost as if ... you were taking away a certain nurturance ... making me give up my childhood ... and I don't want to do that. ... This is an environment where I know I can get compassion and the deepest of understandings anywhere. ... Nobody anywhere will put in as concentrated an effort to understand me and help me understand myself." He talked about feeling uncertain about how to open up to others in his life in a way that would make him feel so deeply understood. The therapist reflected that he was processing how he could do this for himself when he had to do without her, feeling she was "kicking him out" of treatment.

THERAPIST: I think you're talking about ways you're taking over a lot of what we've been talking about. You're putting it into action, with some success.... When you talk about my "kicking you out of childhood," you are keenly aware that our sessions are numbered at this point. Are you aware of how many we have left?

PATIENT: [*shaking head*] No. I haven't stopped to think about it.

THERAPIST: If you stopped now to think about it, what would your guess be?

PATIENT: Six? Off the top of my head. ...

THERAPIST: Exactly. ... Do you see how carefully you might be keeping track, how aware you are without being aware that you're aware! Pretty astonishing, isn't it?

Mr. A's acute sensitivity to and hyperawareness of impending threat and separation reflect a trademark of people with anxiety and panic attacks. This sensitivity contributes to anxiety-inducing factors patients avoid by compartmentalizing their understanding of their emotional lives, leading to the "out of the blue" sensation.

ADDRESSING CONFLICTS OVER SEXUAL FEELINGS

In the next session (19), Mr. A reported a panic attack as he was undressing the previous evening. When the therapist asked what he believed had triggered the attack, he said he did not know. He associated to a television newscast 2 days previously in which a little girl had informed the authorities about her stepfather whom she thought was being physically inappropriate with her. Mr. A also spoke about a dream he had had the night of the television show about an adorable lamb wearing a pink bow. He was cuddling the lamb close to his bare chest. He mused, "It felt so good, it's gotta be illegal." The pink bow reminded him of one he and his wife had just bought for their younger daughter, Ana. He said the bow was similar in color to the shirt the therapist had worn in the previous session.

When asked, Mr. A did not readily see the threads of his associations and their connections to the panic, although he was aware that the sensual feeling with the lamb was connected with his desire to be an appropriate father to his girls. The therapist clarified this by showing him that once again he was riddled with conflicted feelings. She pointed out that on one hand he had a wonderful feeling, an impulse to be close to this lamb (associated with his daughter) in a physically intimate way. On the other hand, he was concerned his desires might be inappropriate and harmful to his daughter and that the authorities might punish him (the news show the day before the dream was an association to the dream and part of the fabric of the dream, called the "day residue," Freud, 1900). She added that as he undressed he remembered how good it felt to be unclothed in the dream. She asked, "Is it any wonder what triggered your panic?!"

She continued, "You have had trouble telling the difference among a thought, a feeling, a fantasy wish, a dream, and an intention or action. So sometimes, once you've thought or felt an urge, it feels to you as though you've actually committed a sin in its most dire form." This emotional experience of fantasy as if it were reality is a frequent one among people with anxiety and panic. This tendency may be connected with the cognitive style of experiencing feelings as if they were somatic realities and with a vulnerability to concrete thinking seen in these patients.

Toward the end of this session, the therapist picked up on Mr. A's associations and reflected that he was describing having feelings of closeness and mutual love that frightened him. She pointed out that he had been speaking in the previous session about how close he felt to the therapist and how deeply nurtured he had felt by her. The therapist said she believed that he was struggling with how close to allow himself to feel and how ashamed and guilty he felt about his yearnings for her as he had felt with the lamb in his dream.

As these feelings and conflicts were elaborated over the remaining sessions, the therapist delineated the many ways Mr. A tried to manage his guilt about his desire for both intimacy and sexual contact (which he experienced as being linked) by depriving himself of these satisfactions. Seeing himself as a little boy, provoking contention in relationships, not taking the time to explain his needs and feelings to his wife in a way she could hear them, and consistently colluding with his wife in allowing their younger child to sleep in their bed whenever she cried were some of the many ways Mr. A short-circuited his pleasure in closeness and joy of his own successes. They could see his contentious connections as a way of engaging others in an intense, fraught struggle that mimicked his connection with his mother. The therapist questioned whether panic attacks might serve a similar function. The panic attacks permitted Mr. A to feel an intense, dizzying, breathless excitement that felt almost sexual and that at times got people to be intensely involved and concerned about him. At the same time, just as the sparring had, they allowed him to keep a safe distance from others. The pain of the panic attacks also provided a built-in punishment for what he felt were forbidden and "impure" desires. Mr. A and the therapist worked on these issues for the rest of the treatment.

ADDRESSING TERMINATION WITH FURTHER MOURNING OF THE LOSS OF HIS MOTHER

The therapist focused on how acutely, even if not consciously, Mr. A was keeping track of their time together and further discussed his "forgetting" of the time remaining. She linked this "forgetting" to his difficulty holding onto her, which she suggested heightened his anxiety about separating from her. He said, "I don't remember [the details of our work], just as I don't remember my mother." He connected this with feeling fearful of letting new people in as well. "I'd have to open myself up … letting go. … There's a world of possibilities out there … and I'm scared. …" As he spoke about his worries, the therapist highlighted a fear Mr. A had revealed throughout the treatment: to see himself as responsive and accessible meant that he was a wimp. His consequent posture was often cantankerous and "stubborn" to avoid feeling open and vulnerable. This echoed his view of relationships as "hand to hand" rather than hand *in* hand and explained in part his reliance on anger and contention to demonstrate strength.

As he voiced his fears of relinquishing his stubborn stance, he reported feeling more comfortable with tenderness and vulnerability. He related several anecdotes about new ways he was relating to his wife and daughters. He mentioned that he had disciplined Isabel in a way that let her feel nurtured and supported and that got her to calm down from a developing tantrum. He also described his wife's response to something he told her, a response that was empathic and admiring. He was helping Ana fall back asleep in her own bed when she awakened in the night, and as a result he and Sylvia were having more time in bed and enjoying a resurgence of their sensuality and sex life together. The therapist commented that Mr. A's telling these stories was evidence that he believed that there was room for these relationships to grow and that he felt able to promote that growth.

As the end of the therapy approached and the therapist and Mr. A discussed what Mr. A forfeited by making the compromises he made, he talked about the sadness he felt about the treatment ending. He identified the fantasy that if he allowed himself to feel like a mature man, the therapist would let him leave treatment. Mr. A viscerally recalled how angry he was at his mother for dying, something he had not permitted himself to feel since he was a child. He saw how terrified he was of losing and of loving. It became clearer to him that his boyish stance curtailed the depth of his relationships and the pleasure he felt in them and was part of his ongoing unconscious effort to avoid the pain of loss. Articulating these feelings led him to see how broadly he deprived himself for reasons pertinent to his childhood way of thinking but not relevant to his adult life.

As they explored Mr. A's fears of allowing himself to feel vulnerable and as they shored up his sense of confidence about being able to function more independently, he was more comfortably able to talk about how sad he felt about leaving the therapist and how it felt as though she were going to die. "It's sad that I won't be able to enjoy someone so caring. It's very sad." The loss rekindled memories of losing his mother, and he talked about how he did not cry as a boy at his mother's funeral and about how he spent so much of his life blocking out emotional pain. He continued to say how good it felt that he got to cry at his uncle's funeral a few years previously. He experienced a real catharsis in letting go. Although he said he felt only a little bit like crying in the session, the therapist could see in his face that he experienced relief at being able to talk about his sadness, something he felt unable to do with his mother for fear of upsetting her.

In the last session Mr. A presented the therapist with a gift. He had wanted to find something more humorous but could not find it, so he came up with this gift instead. Upon opening the box, the therapist found a lovely, translucent, pale green chiffon scarf. The therapist thanked him and commented that it was very beautiful. She asked how he felt about the gift. He said, "I didn't know if it was appropriate ... thinking about you in it, since it goes around your body and it's kind of see-through." As it was the last session and the therapist felt too pressed to explore in an open-ended way, she took the opportunity to impart a message she believed was important in obtaining lasting relief of his anxiety. She replied, "It is appropriate for you to think, feel, and say anything in here. It is your private space, just as your mind is your private space. It is safe to talk and think openly to yourself about those ... intense angry, loving, sexual feelings...."

Mr. A had been talking a lot about his sadness over losing the therapist and the grief over his mother that this separation rekindled for him. The therapist believed all along that an important part of the ending of this treatment was allowing Mr. A ample opportunity to say good-bye in a way he felt he never had with his mother. The therapist had not expected his erotic feelings for her to emerge so readily in this last session. As the impending separation had evoked these feelings so intensely and as his conflicts, guilt, and shame over his sexual and erotic feelings were such potent sources of anxiety for him, she felt they needed to work through them more. She invited, "I think it would be helpful, even in the small amount of time we have left, even in the '24th hour' for us to talk more about these feelings." He said it made him anxious and asked in a mock-sheepish tone, "Couldn't I just crawl behind this chair?" The therapist answered, pointing to a characteristic defense she had addressed before as central to his panic, "Sure! You're a master at finding other ways of hiding [from these feelings] without crawling behind the chair!" "Humor," he volunteered. "Yes. Humor, and being a little boy. I think your desires get blended together ... your desire for me as a mommy to hold you, soothe you, rock you, to make you feel strong and secure, and your sexual desires to hold me in a different way, and to embrace me with the shawl. These feelings are confusing to you."

He described more of his fantasies about her and remarked that he had never talked so openly about feelings about someone with that person, and it felt good and scary at the same time. He talked about his sense that he had to draw the line (by not talking more about those feelings, for example). The therapist pointed out that one of the ways he would set limits was by experiencing himself as a sick little boy. She suggested that by doing this he turned a capacity to love and have pleasurable relationships into a crime, for which he was constantly punished himself. She conjectured that he was working through feelings about his mother that he had not had a chance to resolve and that he had been very involved with his mother's body.

Mr. A remembered that one day when he was 8 or 9, before his mother was ill, he walked into her bedroom, catching her by surprise. She was undressed. The therapist asked what he remembered. He was able to remember feeling excited. He said, "I looked at her body. She was really pretty. That's the last time—she knew I was looking at her differently than as her little boy. She was never without clothes in front of me again." He mentioned that his mother grabbed a garment to cover herself, a pale green, translucent chiffon nighty. When the therapist asked if he saw the connection to the gift, he said, "You just won't let up, will you?!" and smiled, as though he felt relieved.

He and the therapist were able to talk about how terrifying it was for him to acknowledge and expose his feelings. He desperately wanted people to hear and understand him but described how much easier it was to hide. "All those people seeing me." The therapist added that it could also be a relief for him to share his emotions and allow himself the vulnerability he needed to feel understood. They spoke about how being honest with himself could give him a sense of authenticity he sought and a sense of grounding he lost when he lost his mother. They also discussed how sharing his feelings with others could allow him to feel loved and could ease his sense of isolation as well as the pain and panic he experienced at the thought he would forever be alone.

As they discussed this, Mr. A shared that he had begun looking around for a bigger boat that the family could stay in together for longer trips. His wife had wanted one for a long time, and he had surprised and delighted her with the news that he had started looking. The therapist pointed out that Mr. A seemed to be allowing himself to grow and make room for his family to grow together in new ways. She wrapped up by saying, "It seems as though you feel ready to explore uncharted waters!" Mr. A smiled calmly and said he did.

* * * * *

The therapist noted several themes as she initially listened to Mr. A's panic triggers, panic symptoms, chief complaints, and salient history. She identified the transferences that emerged with Mr. A feeling alternatively like a needy, compliant little boy wanting a mommy to love, admire, and nurture him (with resultant shame) and like a contentious and assertive man taking a stand but anticipating retribution (with resultant terror). She could see the prominence of his conflicts over expressing anger, allowing himself to be successful and allowing himself to love. His struggles with profound loss, grief, rage, fear, and despair were evident.

When the therapist identified two early prominent resistances in the treatment, she addressed them quickly and, when possible, in the transference. An exploration of Mr. A's disavowing and not talking about his feelings led to a memory of his sense that it was too much for his mother if he talked about his emotions and too much for his father to tolerate after his mother died. Through adult eyes, he was able to see how much he needed to do this and to "hear" his own feelings and identify them. He could also recognize how his defenses isolated him and contributed to a sense of aloneness that underlay his panic. As he let himself speak more freely, he became aware of suppressed anger. As his conflicts about anger were explored, including how they emerged between Mr. A and the therapist, he was able to understand the original reasons and fears about his anger in his relationships with his parents that gave rise to his inhibitions about experiencing and expressing anger. As he understood his anger better, his terror and guilt about its potential destructiveness dwindled, and he was able to find ways to relate to others more lovingly and honestly, including expressing anger in a way that allowed relationships to survive and to grow.

As he began to experience more loving and sexual feelings, from which his anger had distracted him, the emergence of these emotions (including in his relationship with the therapist) permitted him to remember old feelings that evoked profound guilt for him in his relationship with his father. He could see the childlike nature of the fantasies that underlay his fears of outdoing and destroying his father and was able to allow himself to feel more comfortably sexual and successful. The fantasy that he could never perform well consequently abated, as did the panic that accompanied that fantasy. Termination provided the opportunity to resume the mourning for his mother in a way that he could not as a little boy and allowed him to experience an array of unresolved fantasies about his mother. The resolution of some of these conflictual and previously unacceptable emotions removed the discomfort he had had about wishes to be close to his mother and enabled him to keep a loving image of her in mind without experiencing guilt or shame. As he understood these connections, his panic and depression remitted. His adult perspective released him from old guilt and from his need to punish himself by limiting his joy in life and by panicking. He was left freer to find better compromises and to fulfill his wishes for nurturance, love, sexual gratification, and success without panic or fear of venturing out (agoraphobia).

Throughout the course of the treatment, the therapist helped Mr. A to identify as many meanings of panic and functions that his panic served (see Chapter 4). Among other formulations, he understood the meaning of his panic triggers in terms of his grief over losing his mother and his sense that he could not function without her (dizziness, "ungroundedness," feeling lost between places), his fear his rage could kill others as he believed it had killed his mother (panic when he was angry at being told what to do), his terror he would be alone forever, and his conflicts over being a father and a sexual, successful man, as he had the fantasy this meant destroying and replacing his father (panic when paying for hotels or putting on his tie in front of "his" mirror). He understood that symptoms of panic functioned as memories (feeling ungrounded and dizzy between places expressed his unspoken grief about his mother, feeling as though he might lose his numb limbs related to his memory of being afraid he might lose his penis) and as a means of connecting (wanting to be taken care of as a sick little boy). He saw the role panic played in keeping his cherished mother with him (by identifying with her illness) and as a defense against his fear of being too strong and successful (panic stopped him in his tracks and punished him for his "sins"). Panic itself had in part served a soothing role for him ("it filled a void"). Finding new ways to meet the many psychological needs served by his panic, agoraphobic avoidance, and traumatic reenactments allowed him to grow and enjoy his life with many fewer symptoms.

Despite the complexity of this case as presented here, no formulation can be fully complete. For example, there was almost no exploration of Mr. A's relationship with his siblings in this treatment. Mr. A's treatment addressed enough, though, that there was a significant reduction in his panic, agoraphobic avoidance, and traumatic reenactments. His increased psychological understanding allowed him to find new ways to meet his psychological needs and to increase his enjoyment of his life.

Afterword

In our original *Manual of Panic-Focused Psychodynamic Psychotherapy* (Milrod et al., 1997), we concluded, "Systematic research is needed to ascertain the efficacy of psychodynamic psychotherapy for the treatment of panic disorder. In the meantime, we believe that the focused psychodynamic approaches suggested in this book can help therapists treating patients with this complex and disabling illness" (p. 98).

Our original manual enabled systematic outcome studies of psychodynamic psychotherapy for panic disorder that demonstrated efficacy (Milrod et al., 2007). So far, Panic Focused Psychodynamic Psychotherapy (PFPP) is the only psychodynamic psychotherapy to have demonstrated efficacy for any *DSM-IV* (APA, 1994) anxiety disorder. Patients have generally remained well. PFPP has been transported to four other sites and is now being studied in New York, Philadelphia, Washington, D.C., Germany, and Sweden. We believe this revision of the manual has more clearly articulated our psychodynamic formulations and the specific focused therapeutic strategies that have been of value in our clinical and research work in panic disorder and its associated comorbidities.

Panic disorder is the anxiety disorder with the greatest morbidity and highest suicide rate (Kessler, Sonnega, Bromet, Hughes, & Nelson, 2005). Other anxiety disorders similarly cause great social and occupational impairment, share high suicide rates (Kessler et al., 2005), and take a tremendous toll on their sufferers and those around them. We have therefore distilled our observations about our successful treatment using Panic Focused Psychodynamic Psychotherapy—eXtended Range (PFPP-XR) on anxiety disorders other than just panic disorder and agoraphobia and have extended our psychodynamic approach to a broader assortment of anxiety disorders and associated characterological symptoms, highlighting this treatment's transdiagnostic utility.

Our functional magnetic resonance imaging (fMRI) studies, directed by Brad Peterson and Andrew Gerber (Gerber, A.J.; Junior NARSAD Award: Neuroimaging Study of Three Psychotherapies for Patients With Panic Disorders, 2008) are underway at the New York State Psychiatric Institute and Weill-Cornell Medical College to examine neurobiological changes associated before and after treatment with PFPP in patients with primary panic disorder. At the time of publication of this revised manual, these data are still being collected.

In the future, our research enterprise will continue to evaluate commonalities and differences in dynamics among different anxiety disorders and to refine our understanding of "response," both psychologically and neurobiologically. Systematic research to determine efficacy of PFPP-XR to treat a variety of anxiety disorders is an important next step in the determination of this treatment's overall utility. We expect that this revised manual will further aid clinicians in refining their use of PFPP-XR for panic disorder, while also enabling them to adapt this versatile therapy to treat a greater range of anxiety disorders.

References

Alexander, P. C., & Anderson, C. (1994). An attachment approach to psychotherapy with the incest survivor. *Psychotherapy, 31*, 665–675.

Alighieri, D. (1472). *The divine comedy, I. Inferno* (C. S. Singleton, Trans.). Princeton, NJ: Princeton University Press, 1990.

Allen, L. A., McHugh, R. K, & Barlow, D. H. (2008). Emotional disorders: A unified protocol. In D. H. Barlow (Ed.), *Clinical handbook of psychological disorders* (4th ed., pp. 216–249). New York: Guilford.

American Psychiatric Association. (APA). (1994). *Diagnostic and statistical manual of mental disorders* (4th ed.). Washington, DC: American Psychiatric Press.

American Psychiatric Association. (APA). (1998). Practice guideline for the treatment of patients with panic disorder. *American Journal of Psychiatry, 155*(Suppl.), 1–34.

American Psychiatric Association. (APA). (2000a). *Diagnostic and statistical manual of mental disorders, text revision* (4th ed.). Washington, DC: American Psychiatric Press.

American Psychiatric Association. (APA). (2000b). *Diagnostic criteria from diagnostic and statistical manual of mental disorders, text revision* (4th ed.). Washington, DC: American Psychiatric Press.

American Psychiatric Association. (APA). (2000c). Practice guideline for the treatment of patients with major depressive disorder (revision). *American Journal of Psychiatry, 157*(Suppl.), 1–45.

American Psychiatric Association. (APA). (2009). Practice guideline for the treatment of patients with panic disorder (2nd ed.). *American Journal of Psychiatry, 166*(Suppl.).

Anderson, F. S., & Gold, J. (2003). Trauma, dissociation, and conflict: The space where neuroscience, cognitive science, and psychoanalysis overlap. *Psychoanalytic Psychology, 20*, 536–541.

Andrews, G., Pollock, C., & Stewart, G. (1989). The determination of defense style by questionnaire. *Archives of General Psychiatry, 46*, 455–460.

Arlow, J. A. (1963). Conflict, regression, and symptom formation. *International Journal of Psychoanalysis, 44*, 12–22.

Arntz, A. (2002). Cognitive therapy versus interoceptive exposure as treatment of panic disorder without agoraphobia. *Behaviour Research and Therapy, 40*, 325–341.

Arrindell, W., Emmelkamp, P. M. G., Monsma, A., & Brilman, E. (1983). The role of perceived parental rearing practices in the etiology of phobic disorders: A controlled study. *British Journal of Psychiatry, 143*, 183–187.

Bandelow, B., & Baldwing, D. S. (2010). Pharmacotherapy for panic disorder. In D. J. Stein, E. Hollander, & B. Rothbaum (Eds.), *Textbook of anxiety disorders* (pp. 399–416). Arlington, VA: American Psychiatric Press.

Barlow, D. H., Gorman, J. M., Shear, M. K., & Woods, S. W. (2000). Cognitive-behavioral therapy, imipramine, or their combination for panic disorder. *Journal of the American Medical Association, 283*, 2529–2536.

Bateman, A., & Fonagy, P. (2008). 8-year follow-up of patients treated for borderline personality disorder: Mentalization-based treatment versus treatment as usual. *American Journal of Psychiatry, 165*, 631–638.

Beck, J. G., Stanley, M. A., Baldwin, L. E., Deagle, E. A., III, & Averill, P. M. (1994). Comparison of cognitive therapy and relaxation training for panic disorder. *Journal of Consulting and Clinical Psychology, 62*, 818–826.

Bibring, E. (1954). Psychoanalysis and the dynamic psychotherapies. *Journal of the American Psychoanalytic Association, 2*, 745–770.

Biederman, J., Hirshfeld-Becker, D. R., Rosenbaum, J. F., Hérot, C., Friedman, D., Snidman, N., et al. (2001). Further evidence of association between behavioral inhibition and social anxiety in children. *American Journal of Psychiatry, 158*(10), 1673–1679.

Biederman, J., Rosenbaum, J. F., Bolduc-Murphy, E. A., Faraone, S. V., Chaloff, J., Hirshfeld, D. R., et al. (1993). A 3-year follow-up of children with and without behavioral inhibition. *Journal of the American Academy of Child and Adolescent Psychiatry, 32*(4), 814–821.

Biederman, J., Rosenbaum, J. F., Hirshfeld, D. R., Faraone, S. V., Bolduc, E. A., Gersten, M., et al. (1990). Psychiatric correlates of behavioral inhibition in young children of parents with and without psychiatric disorders. *Archives of General Psychiatry, 47*, 21–26.

Black, D. W., Wesner, R., Bowers, W., & Gabel, J. (1993). A comparison of fluvoxamine, cognitive therapy, and placebo in the treatment of panic disorder. *Archives of General Psychiatry, 50*, 44–50.

Blanco, C., Schneier, F. R., Vesga-Lopez, O., & Liebowitz, M. R. (2010). Pharmacotherapy for social anxiety disorder. In D. J. Stein, E. Hollander, & B. Rothbaum (Eds.), *Textbook of anxiety disorders* (pp. 471–499). Arlington, VA: American Psychiatric Press.

Bloom, H. (1973). *The anxiety of influence*. New York: Oxford University Press.

Borkovec, T. D., Alcaine, O., & Behar, E. (2004). Avoidance theory of worry and generalized anxiety disorder. In R. G. Heimberg, C. L. Turk, & D. S. Mennin (Eds.), *Generalized anxiety disorder: Advances in research and practice* (pp 77–108). New York: Guilford.

Bouchard, S., Gauthier, J., Laberge, B., French, D., Pelletier, M. H., & Godbout, C. (1996). Exposure versus cognitive restructuring in the treatment of panic disorder with agoraphobia. *Behaviour Research and Therapy, 34*(3), 213–224.

Boulanger, G. (2002). Wounded by reality: The collapse of the self in adult onset trauma. *Contemporary Psychoanalysis, 38*, 45–76.

Boulanger, G. (2007). *Wounded by reality: Understanding and treating adult onset trauma*. Mahwah, NJ: Analytic Press.

Breslau, N., Kessler, R. C., Chilcoat, H. D., Schultz, L. R., Davis, G. C., & Andreski, P. (1998). Trauma and posttraumatic stress disorder in the community: The 1996 Detroit Area Survey of Trauma. *Archives of General Psychiatry, 55*, 626–632.

Busch, F. N. (Ed.) (2008). *Mentalization: Theoretical considerations, research findings, and clinical implications*. New York: Analytic Press.

Busch, F. N., Cooper, A. M., Klerman, G. L., Shapiro, T., & Shear, M. K. (1991). Neurophysiological, cognitive-behavioral and psychoanalytic approaches to panic disorder: Toward an integration. *Psychoanalytic Inquiry, 11*, 316–332.

Busch, F. N., & Milrod, B. (2010). The ongoing struggle for psychoanalytic research: Some steps forward. *Psychoanalytic Psychotherapy, 24*, 306–314.

Busch, F. N., Milrod, B. L., Rudden, M., Shapiro, T., Roiphe, J., Singer, M., et al. (2001). How treating psychoanalysts respond to psychotherapy research constraints. *Journal of the American Psychoanalytic Association*, 49, 961–984.

Busch, F. N., Oquendo, M. A., Sullivan, G. M., & Sandberg, L. S. (2010). An integrated model of panic disorder. *Neuropsychoanalysis, 12*, 67–79.

Busch, F. N., Rudden, M. G., & Shapiro, T. (2004). *Psychodynamic treatment of depression*. Washington, DC: American Psychiatric Press.

Busch, F. N., Shear, M. K., Cooper, A. M., Shapiro, T., & Leon, A. (1995). An empirical study of defense mechanisms in panic disorder. *Journal of Nervous and Mental Disease, 183*, 299–303.

Caruth, C. (1996). *Unclaimed experience: Trauma, narrative and history*. Baltimore: Johns Hopkins University Press.

Cassidy, J., Lichtenstein-Phelps, J., Sibrava, N. J., Thomas, C. L., Jr., & Borkovec, T. D. (2009). Generalized anxiety disorder: Connections with self-reported attachment. *Behavior Therapy, 40*, 23–38.

Chambless, D. L., & Ollendick, T. H. (2001). Empirically supported psychological interventions: Controversies and evidence. *Annual Review of Psychology, 52*, 685–716.

Chambless, D. L., & Peterman, M. (2004). Evidence on cognitive-behavioral therapy for generalized anxiety disorder and panic disorder: The second decade. In R. L. Leahy (Ed.), *Contemporary cognitive therapy: Theory, research, and practice* (pp. 86–115). New York: Guilford.

Clarkin, J. F., Levy, K. N., Lenzenweger, M. F., & Kernberg, O. F. (2007). Evaluating three treatments for borderline personality disorder: A multiwave study. *American Journal of Psychiatry, 64*(6), 922–928.

Corradi, R. B. (2009). The repetition compulsion in psychodynamic psychotherapy. *Journal of the American Academy of Psychoanalysis, 37*, 477–500.

Cougle, J. R., Feldner, M. T., Keough, M. E., Hawkins, K. A., & Fitch, K. E. (2010). Comorbid panic attacks among individuals with posttraumatic stress disorder: Associations with traumatic event exposure history, symptoms, and impairment. *Journal of Anxiety Disorders, 24*, 183–188.

Cougle, J. R., Keough, M. E., Riccardi, C. J., & Sachs-Ericsson, N. (2009). Anxiety disorders and suicidality in the National Comorbidity Survey: Replication. *Journal of Psychiatric Research, 43*, 825–829.

Craske, M. G., Brown, T. A., & Barlow, D. H. (1991). Behavioral treatment of panic: A two-year follow-up. *Behavior Therapy, 22*, 289–304.

Craske, M. G., DeCola, J. P., Sachs, A. D., & Pontillo, D. C. (2003). Panic control treatment for agoraphobia. *Journal of Anxiety Disorders, 17*, 321–333.

Crits-Christoph, P., & Connolly Gibbons, M. B. (2003). Research developments on the therapeutic alliance in psychodynamic psychotherapy. *Psychoanalytic Inquiry*, *23*(2), 332–349.

Crits-Christoph, P., Connolly, M. B., Azarian, K., Crits-Christoph, K., & Shappell, S. (1996). An open trial of brief supportive-expressive psychotherapy in the treatment of generalized anxiety disorder. *Psychotherapy*, *33*, 418–430.

Crits-Christoph, P., Siqueland, L., Blaine, J., Frank, A., Luborsky, L., Onken, L. S., et al. (1999). Psychosocial treatments for cocaine dependence: National Institute on Psychiatry. Drug Abuse Collaborative Cocaine Treatment Study. *Archives of General Psychiatry*, *56*(6), 493–502.

Crits-Christoph, P., Wolf-Palacio, D., Ficher, M., & Rudick, D. (1995). Brief supportive-expressive psychodynamic therapy for generalized anxiety disorder. In J. P. Barber & P. Crits-Christoph (Eds.), *Dynamic therapies for psychiatric disorders (Axis I)* (pp. 43–83). New York: Basic Books.

Cross National Collaborative Panic Study, Second Phase Investigations (1992). Drug treatment of panic disorder. *British Journal of Psychiatry*, *160*, 191–202.

Deutsch, H. (1929). The genesis of agoraphobia. *International Journal of Psychoanalysis*, *10*, 51–69.

Dowling, S. (1995). The ontogeny and dynamics of anxiety in childhood. In S. Roose & R. A. Glick (Eds.), *Anxiety as symptom and signal* (pp. 75–86). Hillsdale, NJ: Analytic Press.

Faravelli, C. (1985). Life events preceding the onset of panic disorder. *Journal of Affective Disorders*, *9*, 103–105.

Fava, M., Anderson, K., & Rosenbaum, J. F. (1990). "Anger attacks": Possible variants of panic and major depressive disorders. *American Journal of Psychiatry*, *147*, 867–870.

Fenichel, O. (1945). *The psychoanalytic theory of neurosis*. New York: W. W. Norton.

Fonagy, P. (2008). The mentalization-focused approach to social development. In F. Busch (Ed.), *Mentalization: Theoretical considerations, research findings, and clinical implications* (pp. 3–56). New York: Analytic Press.

Fonagy, P., & Bateman, A. (2008). The development of borderline personality disorder: A mentalizing model. *Journal of Personality Disorders*, *22*, 4–21.

Fonagy, P., & Target, M. (1997). Attachment and reflective function: Their role in self-organization. *Development and Psychopathology*, *9*, 679–700.

Fraley, R. C., Fazzari D. A., Bonanno, G. A., & Dekel, S. (2006). Attachment and psychological adaptation in high exposure survivors of the September 11th attack on the World Trade Center. *Personality and Social Psychology Bulletin*, *32*, 538–551.

Frank, J. (1971). Therapeutic factors in psychotherapy. *American Journal of Psychotherapy*, *25*, 350–361.

Freud, A. (1946). *The ego and the mechanisms of defense*. New York: International Universities Press.

Freud, A. (1963). The concept of developmental lines. *Psychoanalytic Study of the Child*, *18*, 245–265.

Freud, S. (1893–1895). *Studies on hysteria*. In J. Strachey (Ed. & Trans.), *The standard edition of the complete psychological works of Sigmund Freud* (Vol. 2, pp. 1–181). London: Hogarth Press.

Freud, S. (1895). On the grounds for detaching a particular syndrome from neurasthenia under the description "anxiety neurosis." In J. Strachey (Ed. & Trans.),

The standard edition of the complete psychological works of Sigmund Freud (Vol. 3). London: Hogarth Press.

Freud, S. (1900). *The interpretation of dreams.* In J. Strachey (Ed. & Trans.), *The standard edition of the complete psychological works of Sigmund Freud* (Vol. 4/5). London: Hogarth Press.

Freud, S. (1905). Fragment of an analysis of a case of hysteria. In J. Strachey (Ed. & Trans.), *The standard edition of the complete psychological works of Sigmund Freud* (Vol. 7, pp. 3–122). London: Hogarth Press.

Freud, S. (1909). Analysis of a phobia in a five-year-old boy. In J. Strachey (Ed. & Trans.), *The standard edition of the complete psychological works of Sigmund Freud* (Vol. 10, pp. 5–147). London: Hogarth Press.

Freud, S. (1911). Formulations on the two principles of mental functioning. In J. Strachey (Ed. & Trans.), *The standard edition of the complete psychological works of Sigmund Freud* (Vol. 12, pp. 213–226). London: Hogarth Press.

Freud, S. (1914). Repeating, remembering, and working through. In J. Strachey (Ed. & Trans.), *The standard edition of the complete psychological works of Sigmund Freud* (Vol. 12, pp. 147–156). London: Hogarth Press.

Freud, S. (1917). Introductory lectures on psycho-analysis. In J. Strachey (Ed. & Trans.), *The standard edition of the complete psychological works of Sigmund Freud* (Vol. 16, pp. 241–463). London: Hogarth Press.

Freud, S. (1920). Beyond the pleasure principle. In J. Strachey (Ed. & Trans.), *The standard edition of the complete psychological works of Sigmund Freud* (Vol. 18, pp. 1–64). London: Hogarth Press.

Freud, S. (1926). Inhibitions, symptoms and anxiety. In J. Strachey (Ed. & Trans.), *The standard edition of the complete psychological works of Sigmund Freud* (Vol. 20, pp. 75–175). London: Hogarth Press.

Gabbard, G. O. (1992). Psychodynamics of panic disorder and social phobia. *Bulletin of the Menninger Clinic*, *56*(2, Suppl. A), A3–A13.

Gabbard, G. O. (1995). Countertransference: The emerging common ground. *International Journal of Psychoanalysis*, *76*, 475–485.

Gabbard, G. O. (2000). *Psychodynamic psychiatry in clinical practice* (3rd ed.). Washington, DC: American Psychiatric Press.

George, D. T., Anderson, P., Nutt, D. J., & Linnoila, M. (1989). Aggressive thoughts and behavior: Another symptom of panic disorder? *Acta Psychiatrica Scandinavica*, *79*, 500–502.

Gerber, A. J., Kocsis, J., Milrod, B., Roose, S. P., Barber, J. P., Thase, M. E., et al. (2011). A quality-based review of randomized controlled trials of psychodynamic psychotherapy. *American Journal of Psychiatry*, *168*, 19–28.

Gorman, J. M., Kent, J. M., Sullivan, G. M., & Coplan, J. D. (2000). Neuroanatomical hypothesis of panic disorder, revised. *American Journal of Psychiatry*, *157*, 193–505.

Greenson, R. R. (1967). *The technique and practice of psychoanalysis* (Vol. 1). Madison, CT: International Universities Press.

Griffin, D. W., & Bartholomew, K. (1994). The metaphysics of measurement: The case of adult attachment. In K. Bartholomew & D. Perlman (Eds.), *Advances in personal relationships:* Vol. 5. *Attachment processes in adulthood* (pp. 17–52). London, Jessica Kingsley.

Hofmann, S. G., Barlow, D. H., Papp, L. A., Detweiler, M. F., Ray, S. E., Shear, M. K., et al. (1998). Pretreatment attrition in a comparative treatment outcome study on panic disorder. *American Journal of Psychiatry, 155*, 43–47.

Hofmann, S. G., Rief, W., & Spiegel., D. A. (2010). Psychotherapy for panic disorder. In D. J. Stein, E. Hollander, & B. Rothbaum (Eds.), *Textbook of anxiety disorders* (pp. 417–433). Arlington, VA: American Psychiatric Press.

Hofmann, S. G., & Smits, J. A. (2008). Cognitive-behavioral therapy for adult anxiety disorders: A meta-analysis of randomized placebo-controlled trials. *Journal of Clinical Psychiatry, 69*(4), 621–632.

Huppert, J. D., & Sanderson, W. C. (2010). Psychotherapy for generalized anxiety disorder. In D. J. Stein, E. Hollander, & B. Rothbaum (Eds.), *Textbook of anxiety disorders* (pp. 219–238). Arlington, VA: American Psychiatric Press.

Jacobs, T. (1986). On countertransference enactments. *Journal of the American Psychoanalytic Association, 34*, 289–307.

Kagan, J., Reznick, J. S., Snidman, N., Johnson, M. O., Gibbons, J., Gersten, M., et al. (1990). Origins of panic disorder. In J. Ballenger (Ed.), *Neurobiology of panic disorder* (pp. 71–87). New York: Wiley.

Kaplan, D. M. (1972). On shyness. *International Journal of Psychoanalysis, 53*, 439–454.

Katon, W. (1996). Panic disorder: Relationship to high medical utilization, unexplained physical symptoms, and medical costs. *Journal of Clinical Psychiatry, 57*(Suppl. 10), 11–18.

Kernberg, O. F. (2006). The pressing need to increase research in and on psychoanalysis. *International Journal of Psychoanalysis, 87*, 919–926.

Kessler, R. C., Berglund, P., Demler, O., Jin, R., Merikangas, K. R., & Walters, E. E. (2005). Lifetime prevalence and age-of-onset distributions of *DSM-IV* disorders in the National Comorbidity Survey Replication. *Archives of General Psychiatry, 62*, 593–602.

Kessler, R. C., Sonnega, A., Bromet, E., Hughes, M., & Nelson, C. B. (1995). Posttraumatic stress disorder in the National Comorbidity Survey. *Archives of General Psychiatry, 52*, 1048–1060.

Klass, E. T., Milrod, B. L., Leon, A. C., Kay, S. J., Schwalberg, M., Li, C., et al. (2009). Does interpersonal loss preceding panic disorder onset moderate response to psychotherapy? An exploratory study. *Journal of Clinical Psychiatry, 70*, 406–411.

Klein, D. F., & Gorman, J. M. (1987). A model of panic and agoraphobic development. *Acta Psychiatrica Scandinavica, 335*(Suppl.), 87–95.

Klein, M. (1948). A contribution to the theory of anxiety and guilt. *International Journal of Psychoanalysis, 29*, 114–123.

Kocsis, J, Gerber, A., Milrod, B., Roose, S. P., Barber, J., Thase, M. E., et al. (2010). A new scale for assessing the quality of randomized clinical trials of psychotherapy. *Comprehensive Psychiatry, 51*, 319–324.

Koenen, K. C., Moffitt, T. E., Poulton, R., Martin, J., & Caspi, A. (2007). Early childhood factors associated with the development of post-traumatic stress disorder: Results from a longitudinal birth cohort. *Psychological Medicine, 37*, 181–192.

Krupnick, J. L., & Horowitz, M. J. (1981). Stress response syndromes: Recurrent themes. *Archives of General Psychiatry, 38*(4), 428–435.

Krystal, H. (1988). *Integration and self-healing: Affect, trauma, alexithymia*. Hillsdale, NJ: The Analytic Press.

Kudler, H. S., Blank, A. S., & Krupnick, J. L. (2004). Psychodynamic therapy. In E. B. Foa, T. M. Keane, & M. J. Friedman (Eds.), *Effective treatments for PTSD* (pp. 176–198). New York: Guilford.

LeDoux, J. (2002). *Synaptic self*. New York: Penguin Books.

Lee, S. (Director). (2006). *When the levees broke: A requiem in four acts* [Television series]. New York: HBO.

Leon, A. C. (2007). The revised warning for antidepressants and suicidality: Unveiling the black box of statistical analyses. *American Journal of Psychiatry, 164*, 1786–1789.

Leonard, H. L., & Rapoport, J. L. (1989). Anxiety disorders in childhood and adolescence. In A. Tasman, R. E. Hales, & A. J. Frances (Eds.), *Review of psychiatry* (Vol. 8). Washington, DC: American Psychiatric Press.

Lewin, B. D. (1952). Phobic symptoms and dream interpretation. *Psychoanalytic Quarterly, 21*(3), 295–322.

Lindy, J. (1996). Psychoanalytic psychotherapy of posttraumatic stress disorder: The nature of the therapeutic relationship. In B. van der Kolk, A. McFarlane, & L. Weisaeth (Eds.), *Traumatic stress: The effects of overwhelming experience on mind, body, and society* (pp. 525–536). New York: Guilford.

Lipsitz, J. D., & Marshall, R. D. (2001). Alternative psychotherapy approaches for social anxiety disorder. *Psychiatric Clinics of North America, 24*, 817–829.

Luyten, P., Blatt, S. J., & Corveleyn, J. (2006). Minding the gap between positivism and hermeneutics in psychoanalytic research. *Journal of the American Psychoanalytic Association, 54*, 571–610.

Malan, D. H. (1979). *Individual psychotherapy and the science of psychodynamics*. London: Butterworth.

Marks, I. M., Swinson, R. P., Basoglu, M., Kuch, K., Noshirvani, H., O'Sullivan, G., et al. (1993). Alprazolam and exposure alone and combined in panic disorder with agoraphobia. *British Journal of Psychiatry, 162*, 776–787.

McGrath, P. J., Robinson, D., & Stewart, J. W. (1985). Atypical panic attacks in major depression [Letter to the Editor]. *American Journal of Psychiatry, 142*, 1224.

Mennin, D. S., Heimberg, R. G., Turk, C. L., & Fresco, D. M. (2005). Preliminary evidence for an emotion dysregulation model of generalized anxiety disorder. *Behaviour Research and Therapy, 43*(10), 1281–1310.

Milrod, B. (1996). Anxiety as symptom and signal [Review.]. *International Journal of Psychoanalysis, 77*, 850–853.

Milrod, B. (2007). Emptiness in agoraphobia patients. *Journal of the American Psychoanalytic Association, 55*, 1007–1026.

Milrod, B. L., & Busch, F. N. (2003a). Epilogue to Psychoanalytic research: Current issues and controversies. *Psychoanalytic Inquiry, 23*, 405–408.

Milrod, B. L., & Busch, F. N. (2003b). Prologue to Psychoanalytic research: Current issues and controversies. *Psychoanalytic Inquiry, 23*, 211–217.

Milrod, B., Busch, F., Cooper, A. M., & Shapiro, T. (1997). *Manual of panic-focused psychodynamic psychotherapy*. Washington, DC: American Psychiatric Press.

Milrod, B., Leon, A. C., Barber, J. P., Markowitz, J. C., & Graf, E. (2007). Do comorbid personality disorders moderate panic-focused psychotherapy? An exploratory examination of the APA practice guideline. *Journal of Clinical Psychiatry, 68*, 885–891.

Milrod, B., Leon, A. C., Busch, F., Rudden, M., Schwalberg, M., Clarkin, J., et al. (2007). A randomized controlled clinical trial of psychoanalytic psychotherapy for panic disorder. *American Journal of Psychiatry, 164*, 265–272.

Milrod, B., Leon, A. C., & Shear, M. K. (2004). Can interpersonal loss events precipitate panic disorder? [Letter to Editor]. *American Journal of Psychiatry, 161*, 758–759.

North, C. S., Suris, A. M., Davis, M., & Smith, R. P. (2009). Toward validation of the diagnosis of posttraumatic stress disorder. *American Journal of Psychiatry, 166*, 34–41.

Otte, C., Neylan, T. C., Pole, N., Metzler, T., Best, S., Henn-Haase, C., et al. (2005). Association between childhood trauma and catecholamine response to psychological stress in police academy recruits. *Biological Psychiatry, 57*, 27–32.

Parker, G. (1979). Reported parental characteristics of agoraphobics and social phobics. *British Journal of Psychiatry, 135*, 555–560.

Pecknold, J. C., Swinson, R. P., Kuch, K., & Lewis, C. P. (1988). Alprazolam in panic disorder and agoraphobia: results from a multicenter trial. III: Discontinuation effects. *Archives of General Psychiatry, 45*, 429–436.

Perry, S., Cooper, A. M., & Michels, R. (1987). The psychodynamic formulation: Its purpose, structure, and clinical application. *American Journal of Psychiatry, 144*, 543–550.

Pollack, M. H., Smoller, J. W., Otto, M. W., Hoge, E., & Simon, E. (2010). Phenomenology of panic disorder. In D. J. Stein, E. Hollander, & B. Rothbaum (Eds.), *Textbook of anxiety disorders* (pp. 399–416). Arlington, VA: American Psychiatric Press.

Pollock, C., & Andrews, G. (1989). Defense styles associated with specific anxiety disorders. *American Journal of Psychiatry, 146*, 1500–1502.

Pontoski, K. E., Heimberg, R. G., Turk, C. L., & Coles, M. E. (2010). Psychotherapy for social anxiety disorder. In D. J. Stein, E. Hollander, & B. Rothbaum (Eds.), *Textbook of anxiety disorders* (pp. 501–521). Arlington, VA: American Psychiatric Press.

Resnick, H. S., Yehuda, R., Pitman, R. K., & Foy, D. W. (1995). Effect of previous trauma on acute plasma cortisol level following rape. *American Journal of Psychiatry, 152*, 1675–1677.

Rosenbaum, J. F., Biederman, J., Gersten, M., Hirshfeld, D. R., Meminger, S. R., Herman, J. B., et al. (1988). Behavioral inhibition in children of parents with panic disorder and agoraphobia. *Archives of General Psychiatry, 45*, 463–470.

Rosenbaum, J. F., Biederman, J., Hirshfeld, D. R., Bolduc, E. A., Faraone, S. J., Kagan, J., et al. (1991). Further evidence of an association between behavioral inhibition and anxiety disorders: Results from a family study of children from a non-clinical sample. *Journal of Psychiatric Research, 25*, 49–65.

Roy-Byrne, P. P., Geraci, M., & Uhde, T. W. (1986). Life events and the onset of panic disorder. *American Journal of Psychiatry, 143*, 1424–1427.

Rudden, M., Busch, F. N., Milrod, B., Singer, M., Aronson, A., Roiphe, J., et al. (2003). Panic disorder and depression: A psychodynamic exploration of comorbidity. *International Journal of Psychoanalysis, 84*, 997–1015.

Rudden, M., Milrod, B., Meehan, K. B., & Falkenstrom, F. (2009). Symptom-specific reflective functioning: Incorporating psychoanalytic measures into clinical trials. *Journal of the American Psychoanalytic Association, 57*, 1473–1478.

Rudden, M., Milrod, B., Target, M., Ackerman, S., & Graf, E. (2006). Reflective functioning in panic disorder patients: A pilot study. *Journal of the American Psychoanalytic Association, 54*, 1339–1343.

Sandler, J., Kennedy, H., & Tyson, R. L. (1980). *The technique of child psychoanalysis*. Cambridge, MA: Harvard University Press.

Sarles, R. (2004). *Letter from the Academy of Child and Adolescent Psychiatry to the FDA*. Retrieved from http://www.aacap.org/Announcements/antidepressents.htm

Shapiro, T. (1992). The concept of unconscious fantasy. *Journal of Clinical Psychoanalysis, 1*, 517–524.

Shear, M. K., Cooper, A. M., Klerman, G. L., Busch, F. N., & Shapiro, T. (1993). A psychodynamic model of panic disorder. *American Journal of Psychiatry, 150*, 859–866.

Shear, M. K., & Maser, J. D. (1994). Standardized assessment for panic disorder research: A conference report. *Archives of General Psychiatry, 51*, 346–354.

Sholomskas, D. E., Syracuse-Siewart, G., Rounsaville, B. J., Ball, S. A., Nuro, K. F., & Carroll, K. M. (2005). We don't train in vain: A dissemination trial of three strategies of training clinicians in cognitive-behavioral therapy. *Journal of Consulting and Clinical Psychology, 73*, 106–115.

Silove, D. (1986). Perceived parental characteristics and reports of early parental deprivation in agoraphobic patients. *Australian and New Zealand Journal Psychiatry, 20*(3), 365–369.

Subic-Wrana, C., Knebel, A., & Beutel, M. E. (2010). *The Mainz PFPP study: A RCT comparing a psychodynamic and a cognitive behavioral short term psychotherapy for panic disorder.* Panel presentation at Society for Psychotherapy Research, Asilomar, CA.

Twaite, J. A., & Rodriguez-Srednicki, O. (2004). Childhood sexual and physical abuse and adult vulnerability to PTSD: The mediating effects of attachment and dissociation. *Journal of Child Sexual Abuse, 13*, 17–38.

Tyson, P. (1996). Termination of psychoanalysis and psychotherapy. In E. Nersessian & R. G. Kopff, Jr. (Eds.), *Textbook of psychoanalysis* (pp. 501–524). Washington, DC: American Psychiatric Press.

Van Ameringen, M., Mancini, C., Patterson, B., Simpson, W., & Truong, C. (2010). Pharmacotherapy for generalized anxiety disorder. In D. J. Stein, E. Hollander, & B. Rothbaum (Eds.), *Textbook of anxiety disorders* (pp. 193–218). Arlington, VA: American Psychiatric Press.

Viederman, M., & Perry, S. W. (1980). Use of a psychodynamic life narrative in the treatment of depression in the physically ill. *General Hospital Psychiatry, 3*, 177–185.

Vinnars, B., Barber, J. P., Norén, K., Gallop, R., & Weinryb, R. M. (2005). Supportive-expressive psychotherapy in personality disorders: An outpatient randomized controlled trial. *American Journal of Psychiatry, 162*, 1933–1940.

Weiss, D. S., & Marmar, C. R. (1993). Teaching time-limited dynamic psychotherapy for post-traumatic stress disorder and pathological grief. *Psychotherapy Research, 30*, 587–591.

Weissman, M. M., Leckman, J. F., Merikangas, K. R., Gammon, G. D., & Prusoff, B. A. (1984). Depression and anxiety disorders in parents and children. *Archives of General Psychiatry, 41*, 845–852.

Wu, E. Q., Birnbaum, H. G., Shi, L., Ball, D. E., Kessler, R. C., Moulis, M., et al. (2005). The economic burden of schizophrenia in the United States in 2002. *Journal of Clinical Psychiatry*, *66*, 1122–1129.

Zerbe, K. J. (1994). Uncharted waters: Psychodynamic considerations in the diagnosis and treatment of social phobia. *Bulletin of the Menninger Clinic*, *58*(2, Suppl. A), A3–A20.

Zetzel, E. (1956). Current concepts of transference. *International Journal of Psychoanalysis*, *37*, 369–375.

Index

41432715R00130

Made in the USA
Middletown, DE
06 April 2019